THE HUNGARIAN MODEL: MARKETS AND PLANNING, IN A SOCIALIST ECONOMY

T0312085

Soviet and East European Studies: 64

Editorial Board

Soviet and East European Studies

Series list continues on page 206

THE HUNGARIAN MODEL: MARKETS AND PLANNING IN A SOCIALIST ECONOMY

XAVIER RICHET

Institute of Business Administration
Université Jean Moulin, Lyon

Translated by J. C. Whitehouse

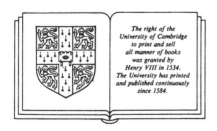

The right of the
University of Cambridge
to print and sell
all manner of books
was granted by
Henry VIII in 1534.
The University has printed
and published continuously
since 1584.

CAMBRIDGE UNIVERSITY PRESS

Cambridge
New York   Port Chester   Melbourne   Sydney

CAMBRIDGE UNIVERSITY PRESS
Cambridge, New York, Melbourne, Madrid, Cape Town, Singapore, São Paulo

Cambridge University Press
The Edinburgh Building, Cambridge CB2 8RU, UK

Published in the United States of America by Cambridge University Press, New York

www.cambridge.org
Information on this title: www.cambridge.org/9780521343145

Originally published in French as *Le Modèle hongrois: marché et plan en économie socialiste*
by Presses Universitaires de Lyon
and © Presses Universitaires de Lyon 1985
First published in English by Cambridge University Press 1989 as
The Hungarian Model: Markets and Planning in a Socialist Economy

English translation © Cambridge University Press 1989

This digitally printed version 2008

A catalogue record for this publication is available from the British Library

Library of Congress Cataloguing in Publication data

Richet, Xavier.
[Modèle hongrois. English]
The Hungarian model: markets and planning in a socialist
economy / Xavier Richet; translated by J. C. Whitehouse.
    p.   cm. – (Soviet and East European studies).
Translation of: Le modèle hongrois.
Bibliography.
Includes index.
ISBN 0 521 34314 3
1. Central planning – Hungary. 2. Hungary – Economic policy – 1968–
I. Title. II. Series.
HC300.28.R5313 1989.
338.9439–dc19   88–21414

ISBN 978-0-521-34314-5 hardback
ISBN 978-0-521-06064-6 paperback

Contents

Preface

My aim in this book is to examine the economic reforms introduced in Hungary over the last twenty years or so. More specifically, I wish to investigate decentralization procedures and the effects of decentralization on the Hungarian economy and the behaviour of agents. The mainly institutional approach adopted represents an attempt to describe the main features of the system which came into being as a result of the successive changes and modifications following the 1968 reform, and to reflect on the feasibility of a market socialism combining micro-economic efficiency, indirect regulation and socialist ethical principles. The situation-related and structural problems which the country is experiencing and the latest reforms, introduced during the first half of 1988, mean that the questions examined here are quite important.

For some years the Hungarian leaders have seemed to be embarked on a cycle of reforms to their system. Each successive one has led them to widen the area of decentralization and extend it to hitherto relatively unaffected fields, and we have seen such developments as a virtual capital market, a fiscal system now including income tax and value added tax, and a consideration of the possibility, however problematic it may be, of reforming political institutions as well as increasing the role played by indirect regulation in the form of a credit policy and a wider sphere of free prices and the like. Such reforms have been carried out in a fairly unfavourable economic environment reflected in the poor performance of the Hungarian economy. These latter questions have not been taken into account here, and little attention has been paid to foreign trade or agriculture. The mechanisms studied here, however, apply to both those sectors.

In my research, I have enjoyed the support of the CNRS (the French National Centre for Scientific Research) and the Hungarian Academy of Sciences, and have been able to spend several study periods in

Hungary as a guest of the Institute of Economic Sciences in Budapest. I
have also had the opportunity of visiting many institutions, research
centres and ministries, including the Finance Ministry, the National
Planning Office, the Hungarian National Bank, and several enterprises. During my investigations, I have always had considerable help
from my Hungarian colleagues and informants. My particular thanks
are due to Professor J. Kornai and the Messrs M. Tardos, J. M. Kovács
and T. Bauer, who regularly provided information. The constant help
and friendship of J. Koltay, A. Soós and L. Halpern must also be
mentioned. In addition, I should like to thank Professor M. Lavigne
and my colleagues A. Deszényi-Gueullette, P. Hare, M. Marrese and
H. Radice, who all in various ways had a beneficial effect on my
research.

Paris, April 1988   XAVIER RICHET

Foreword

Hungary is an exciting country to study, and this book could hardly have come forward (at least in its English version) at a better time. For Hungary's leader since 1957, János Kádár, was finally pushed aside (to the largely honorary position of Party president) at a special party conference held in May 1988. Many of the more conservative elements of the old leadership not only failed to retain their positions on the Political Committee, but they were not even re-elected to the Central Committee which changed over a third of its membership. Thus the new First Secretary of the Party, Károly Grosz, has many fresh faces to work with on the leading bodies of the Party and within the country there is now considerable optimism that reforms – both economic and in the country's social and political institutional structure – will be resumed with added vigour and commitment. This would contrast strongly with the closing years of the Kádár era, when the country seemed to drift from crisis to crisis, introducing partial and half-hearted reforms, but lacking clear direction.

Considered alongside the recent developments, Richet's book provides an exceptionally thorough treatment of the Hungarian economy and its important experience of economic reforms, leading up to a discussion on the limits on and limitations of the present Hungarian economic model. For students of Soviet-type economies (STEs), this is essential reading; some of the ideas might even be of benefit to Hungary's new leadership!

Alone among the European STEs, Hungary not only embarked on a programme of radical reforms in 1968 (known initially as the New Economic Mechanism), but unlike other radical reformers such as Czechoslovakia, never returned to the traditional, highly centralised model of an STE. There were, however, some twists and turns in the country's reform experience, including substantial recentralization in the early to mid-1970s and a renewal of reform momentum, from the late 1970s onwards. By now, it is evident that the major reforms undertaken so far have been insufficient to overcome the country's problems: in recent years, living standards have begun to fall, output has increased only very sluggishly, and hard currency trade and payments have been a major difficulty. Politically, the continuing difficulties have provided ammunition for those opposed to reforms, while the reformers have argued forcefully that reforms must go much further to be really effective.

At this point, it must be conceded that much early work on reforming STEs (including some of my own) was marked by what now appears as a striking degree of naivety. Reforms tended to focus on enterprise-level incentives, pricing and, in the Hungarian case, dismantling the apparatus of current planning. The latter, especially, sounded sufficiently radical to change the manner of the economy's functioning, not least because it was buttressed by exhortations to enterprises to study their markets and respond to market signals. To many observers, this was market socialism in the making.

How wrong we were! And one of the great strengths of Richet's book is that it explains what went wrong, and why. While traditional forms of planning were changed or abandoned and the market was permitted greater influence, the central institutions were not markedly reformed, and retained (*de facto*, at least) their formal and informal powers over the economy. As Richet puts it, 'the third type of mechanism – a particular method of allocating resources called social expectations. In STEs it is inseparable from planning, and it forms the natural complement to systems of injunction. It is all the more important because the other mechanisms – the plan and the market – have partially failed . . . and although it is typical of the administrative planning phase it has survived efforts to decentralize and introduce indirect regulation' (p.185).

Social expectations, the mainly informal 'guidance' that permeates the Hungarian economy and affects every enterprise, have continued to dominate the course of development partly because of the interpenetration of party and government that characterizes communist countries, ensuring that the political and economic spheres should not be separated; and partly because of Hungary's astonishingly high concentration of production, it is hard to see how markets and competition could have functioned within the limits of the domestic market alone. For the market to work well, Hungary must be a highly open economy whereas, ironically, its very failure to advance in that direction reinforces the conditions – low efficiency, poor innovative performance, over-protection of large domestic firms – that make such an advance so difficult to achieve.

In this respect, Hungary's development experience contrasts interestingly with that of the newly industrializing countries, the so-called NICs. Several of them (e.g. Taiwan, South Korea, Hong Kong, Singapore) have developed highly competitive, sophisticated industries on the basis of an extremely strong orientation of their economies towards participation in world markets.

In many of their speeches and articles, one can see this orientation proposed by Hungarian leaders; but it is one thing to say it, and another thing altogether to do it, especially in view of the persistence of the 'social expectations' approach to economic management noted above. In practice, Hungarian firms have been slow to modernize, and when they have done so it has often been with regard to the domestic or CMEA market requirements, rather than to the more demanding conditions of the Western world market. At the same time, import restrictions have sometimes inhibited the import of Western technology, and the prevailing protection of major enterprises by the State in any case makes change seem unnecessary. In this environment, it is not surprising to find that the most significant changes and the most dynamic developments are occurring in parts of the economy least under state influence, such as agriculture, small-scale private and co-operative businesses and much of the personal and business services sector.

Somehow, the same dynamism must be extended to the rest of the economy; and while Richet's book is not exactly a detailed blueprint for fundamental reform, it does at least set out a clear and full agenda for anyone with serious intentions to revive Hungary's lack-lustre economic performance.

PROFESSOR PAUL HARE

Heriot-Watt University
June 1988

1 A model of market socialism?

In many respects the planning system that has grown up in Hungary and is regularly modified by the government is unlike the classical model encountered in most Soviet-type economies. There is no apparent clash between planning and market forces, the economy is increasingly open to foreign trade (with market economies) and new forms of co-operation between enterprises are emerging. Individual initiative is encouraged, agricultural productivity is rising, and enterprises in the socialist sector are increasingly free to make their own decisions. At the same time, the function of macro-economic planning is merely to set guidelines, and a new decentralized financial system will, in principle, replace the old system of financing activities by means of the State budget.

It is of course true that the international economic climate is currently not very favourable and that adjusting the internal mechanisms of Comecon might, in the medium term, threaten the smooth running of a decentralized economy. Nevertheless, Hungary's economic performance after the stringent policy of adjustment adopted during the critical period of the 1980s has exceeded that of certain of its Comecon partners, despite a very considerable increase in productivity. Currently, it has one of the highest growth rates in Eastern Europe, along with a relatively high level of debt.

Despite problems and partial achievements of this kind, the Hungarian leadership is determined to pursue reforms and also plans to introduce new measures to increase decentralization. What is being attempted in Hungary is helping to give a more precise shape to the new model of market socialism to be described in this book. My task will be to present the striking features of that model, to analyse how it proved possible to introduce it into what had hitherto been a highly centralized economy, and to show clearly the constraints it is currently encountering.

The new features of Hungarian economic reforms

There are three immediately striking aspects of the reforms. In the face of periodic attempts to return to a centralized policy, they have been extensive, continual and progressive.

During the 1950s and 1960s, every Eastern European economy underwent more or less considerable reforms (Kaser, *et al.*, 1986). The aim was to smooth the passage from 'extensive' to 'intensive' growth, which meant using more sophisticated planning instruments whilst still retaining the principles of both micro- and macro-administrative planning. In other words, the introduction of market elements such as prices and profits was intended to help to bring about a more rational version of the centralized model rather than to replace it, which in general terms explains the secondary role allotted to the market. The age of reforms in Eastern Europe persisted for a few years before the centralized model once more became dominant. The only countries to reform their planning system were those (like Poland) which had no choice. The others preferred to return to the delights of 'perfecting the existing mechanism' (Richet, 1986a), thus avoiding the need for reform or limiting it to particular areas. The Hungarians alone continued to plough their furrow, extending the scope of their reforms from planning mechanisms to the institutional field.

Any thorough-going reform of planning takes a great deal of time, both to adapt mechanisms and to modify institutions and the behaviour of agents. In a highly centralized economy with a flourishing and ubiquitous bureaucracy, Schumpeter-type entrepreneurs do not emerge overnight. Moreover – and we can see in this another quality of the Hungarian reformers – there were a good number of economic and political constraints (external problems, recession, the leadership of the Communist party) affecting society that might on several occasions have cooled a vague desire to extend decentralization. Apart from one or two moves towards recentralization in the 1970s and early 1980s, however, the reforming spirit and determination remained paramount.

1. *The scope of the reforms*

In the typology of the models of various kinds of socialism, the two poles of the centralized and the decentralized (or market) models are generally taken as points of reference. Although the former, which is, roughly speaking, in operation in most socialist countries, is not hard to define, describing the latter is a more delicate task, given the degree of decentralization, the distribution of power, the organization of enterprises, the kind of tools used for control, and the roles allocated to planning and the market respectively. As we shall see later, the Hungarian reformers tried to introduce instruments compatible with the principles governing the way the socialist economy worked.

The aim of the reforms introduced in 1968, under the title of the New Economic Mechanism (NEM), was to adapt the Hungarian economy to the conditions of the international division of labour by attempting to guide investment towards those sectors offering sure economic advantages. This would mean opening it up and consequently giving it easier access to Western technology and the chance to modernize its productive apparatus and hence to pay for the acquisition of capital goods by means of exports bringing in convertible currencies.

An overall reform of the management system was initiated in order to achieve this. Indirect instruments of control – known as regulators – were introduced with regard to prices, taxation and incentives in the field of foreign trade. At the same time, the practice of a highly compartmentalized plan and the transmission of orders from the centre to enterprises was abolished, and as a consequence of market relationships the latter achieved a greater freedom to arrange their own supplies and organize their markets, importing raw materials and plant and fixing production levels freely. What happened in fact was that these indirect mechanisms were additional to the already existing direct ones. A number of the prerogatives of the plan were maintained, and a not inconsiderable proportion of investment was still determined centrally and financed by means of the State budget. The system of prices and taxation, as well as profits, were also highly controlled. The old bargaining practices, which had more to do with fixing rates of taxation or prices than levels of output or the provision of finance, were implicitly retained. Bargaining about planning objectives was replaced by bargaining about regulators (Antal, 1986). Until recently, foreign exchange regulators continued to reflect a preference for a protectionist system rather than an opening up and a dynamic approach oriented towards increased exports.

One of the factors partly accounting for the limited nature of the first wave of reforms is that it was restricted to the purely economic field. Indeed, there was no change in the institutional structure of planning (central power, a great deal of Party intervention in economic life, and so on) or the highly concentrated structure of industry. Two further factors also served to act as a brake on the effects of the reforms: Hungary's membership of and high level of trade with Comecon, and the end of the period of reform in most other Eastern-bloc countries.

Within the country itself, both the administrative apparatus and the trades unions also helped to slow down the process and led to an almost total recentralization in the early 1970s.

2. Ongoing cumulative reform and short-term recentralization

In the 1970s, both Hungary and the other socialist countries of Europe experienced a slow deterioration (and in the case of Poland a real collapse in growth) in their economic performance, a rising level of debt and the emergence of both internal and external imbalances. Recentralization seemed to offer the easiest immediate solution, particularly since the Hungarian leadership, like that of the other socialist countries, was slow to realize the seriousness of the crisis affecting growth in market economies and the reasons why its own was flagging. Reactions were tardy, particularly where putting defensive policies into operation was concerned.

Coupled with the brakes on reform, this delay in seeing problems and reacting to them accounts for several of the imbalances severely affecting growth, particularly with regard to foreign trade with Western markets and the Comecon zone. There was a very marked decline in the terms of trade, and both inflation and foreign-currency debts soared. There are a number of reasons for this decline.

On the one hand, there is a relative scarcity of energy and mineral resources. Hungary imports 45% of its energy, including 80% of the crude oil it consumes. Furthermore, since energy costs little domestically and modernization of the productive apparatus, which consumes more energy, has taken place, consumption has become highly elastic in relation to growth. On the other, given the structure of its foreign trade and changes in world prices, the country has experienced a decline of 20% in its terms of trade, which corresponds to a fall of 10% in national income. In the face of a high level of domestic demand and given the structural factors mentioned above, the government has been powerless to contain this trend.

In 1978, the new economic policy established two priorities that were to help slow the cycle down. These were that external balance should take precedence over growth and that maintaining the standard of living should be seen as more important than investment.

Achieving a moderate (3% on average) growth rate without increasing imports was deemed possible, and the considerable reduction in accumulated national income was expected to put the latter objective within reach. The expected results did not materialize. Not only did it take time to reorient growth, but maintaining the general standard of living also demanded a larger share of national income at the expense of investment.

Controlling and reducing domestic demand, stabilizing debt and getting back to external balance were achieved in the early 1980s by the introduction of a policy of depressing the economy, leading without doubt to balance, but at the cost of a long period of stagnant growth.

Given the background of stagnation, the effects of the second oil crisis increased the difficulties the Hungarian economy was facing. For a time, the fall in demand from abroad, and more particularly from countries with convertible currencies, made it harder to increase exports, and because of its many structural problems Comecon was no longer an enormous potential market capable of absorbing Hungarian surpluses. A lasting and vigorous policy of adjustment was therefore needed if the Hungarian leadership was to reduce imbalances and restore the relative position of their country's economy (Richet, 1985a). However, after implementing such policies and engaging in recentralization for brief periods (1974–9 and 1982–4) they came to the conclusion that administrative measures such as subsidies, reintroducing quotas, controlling investment and the like were not a suitable long-term answer and that only further reforms could provide the solution to Hungary's economic problems.

The second wave of reforms (1979–82) intensified decentralization and also came to grips with a hitherto exempt area, that of planning institutions. Two series of measures were introduced.

(a) *Adjusting the instruments of control*   The major reform concerned the price system. Prices, which had previously been more or less hybrid in the sense that they were half freely and half administratively determined, did not offer a satisfactory reflection of the relative scarcity of goods, particularly at a time when the prices of raw materials were increasing. The gap between producer and consumer prices was therefore reduced by lowering the level of subsidies. They were fixed by a competitive price system established to ensure that Hungarian enterprises exporting more than 5% of their production had to calculate domestic prices on the basis of the level of profitability achieved on exports. Enterprises were thus encouraged to make more rational use of their factors of production. The price of energy products other than for fuels burnt in the home was completely passed on at the domestic level, and products used within the country had to be closely linked, proportionally and depending on the extent to which they were used, to the level of world prices.

The exchange policy, which had hitherto been very protectionist, became much more active, with several successive devaluations of the forint. The tax system was also modified, enabling enterprises to keep a larger proportion of their income and thus increasing their capacity for self-financing. Similarly, investment credits are now for the greater part not provided from the budgets, and enterprises have to meet their own requirements from their own funds and bank loans.

(b) *Institutional reforms*   Three levels of decision are involved here.

(1) The centre, where planning is now purely macro-economic in nature and is based on information received from enterprises. Objectives are less strictly defined and can therefore be adjusted as planning progresses over time. At the same time, the functional ministries (Finance, Foreign Trade, the National Bank and the like) have become more important, reflecting the comparative weight of macro-economic constraint. At this level, Party organizations are less insistent on their prerogatives, more content to restrict themselves to supervise the way in which the plan is put into operation and to leave intervention of an administrative nature to lower echelons.

(2) At the meso-economic level, there have been two new measures. One is the final dismantling of the remaining branch ministries and the dissolution of the main socialist trusts, aimed at making enterprises more competitive and administratively more flexible. The second is the new role allotted to the Hungarian Chamber of Commerce (and its local branches) which is now, *inter alia*, the professional association replacing the former branch ministries.

(3) The most important reforms have been introduced at the micro-economic level. The following areas are involved:

(i) When the trusts were dismantled, new enterprises (300 new units) were established.

(ii) In the socialist sector, the direct election of heads of enterprises by the workforce was introduced. This followed what had already been the practice in agricultural co-operatives for some 20 years.

(iii) It became possible for socialist enterprises to set up subsidiaries and joint undertakings in Hungary or abroad with Hungarian or Western firms, or indeed with undertakings based in the socialist countries. The latter are allowed to be major shareholders and to send their profits back to their country of origin without difficulty. The aim of these important reforms is to facilitate the emergence of industrial sectors by breaking up the traditional type of branch-based organization, to create a significant sector of small- and medium-sized firms responsible for sub-contracting, and to encourage the transfer and acquisition of technology and the related skills by means of co-operation with Western firms.

(iv) The banking system was also involved in the new decentralization of industry. The move from the former single-bank system towards decentralization and devolution is aimed at widening the scope for financial mediation. To this end, new banks were set up and specialized institutions were changed into deposit and commercial ones for industry, agriculture, risk capital, small- and medium-sized firms and so on. 'Off-shore' and joint stock banks capable of operating in Hungarian forints and foreign currencies on markets at home and abroad were also created.

It proved possible to set up industrial, agricultural and service co-operatives, each of which could in its turn create subsidiaries.

There were a certain number of measures intended to legalize and create various types of small firms, including those in the transport, food, service and data-processing sectors with payment by results, and work collectives belonging to socialist or independent enterprises. The latter represent a subtle form of organization enabling a group of between 2 and 30 people to enter into a contract with their employers (or in the case of independent collectives, to offer their services to any enterprise) to do work that would normally be impossible because of the labour shortage. This new system is in fact an attempt to increase productivity by getting round current social legislation, since it makes it possible to hide wage differentials and avoid creating an excessively open labour market by retaining the fidelity of a labour force that would otherwise be tempted to offer its services to small private concerns (and this is particularly true of the most highly qualified workers). There are already several tens of thousands of such associations. In addition, the State loans back many small concerns, chiefly in the service sector, and to private operators on a tenant-manager basis.

By giving enterprises greater freedom in decision-making, integrating the second economy and developing private initiative on the fringes of the socialist sector and extending the system of indirect control, it is hoped to create a routine mechanism limiting the functions of the centre to those of control by achieving the greatest possible efficiency in decentralized units.

There is a fair distance between such measures and those currently being advocated in other socialist countries. We need to see exactly why this particular model has been able to take shape within the framework of a Soviet-type economy.

An attempt to account for the originality of the Hungarian reforms

A conjunction of political, economic and historical factors offers an explanation for the actions Hungary has taken since 1968. Most important were the failure of hyper-centralization and the shock of the dramatic events of 1956, the quality and richness of economic ideas, the feeling for compromise that marked Kádár and his team, the rapid success of agricultural reforms after 1956, and serious and constant external constraints coupled with an exigent and growing domestic demand.

It might seem paradoxical to see a connection between the present-day liberalization of the Hungarian economy and the 1956 crisis, which swept away in a few weeks the structure that Rákosi, the local emulator of Stalin, had steadily built up in the early 1950s (Berend and Ránki, 1985). The tragic outcome of those events, however, was the starting-point of future reforms that were not to see the light of day for another 12 years. By distributing national income between branches in a different way, the planners gave the overall pattern of industrialization a new shape as a result of the development of those branches closest to the stage of final consumption by households.

The scope and quality of the investigations and reflections undertaken by the Hungarian economists were very important. Strangely enough, only a few months before the 1956 uprising they had analysed the system and put forward solutions to the contradictions that were to lead to its collapse (Szamuely, 1986a and 1986b). For the first time in a socialist economy, the causes of dysfunction were not assumed to be 'subjective' or to lie outside the system, but to be attributable to the planned economy itself, given the nature of the decision-making process, the distribution of powers, and the lack of ways of guiding and stimulating the economy. A few years later, the idea was given formal expression in the term 'the economies of shortage' (Kornai, 1986). From then on, the solution proposed by the economic reformers was to reduce shortages and make the system work in a more regular way. The underlying idea was that of a model of market socialism in which the market at first plays a subsidiary part and then gradually extends its sphere of influence. The high level of economic thinking is in some measure attributable to the fact that at an early stage the discipline was brought down to the level of everyday reality, which explains why there was none of the theoretical *aggiornamento* with regard to the role of profit, prices and the like which was (and still is) a feature of the other socialist countries.

Nor was the willingness to listen evinced by the members of leadership a negligible factor. Although they did not necessarily carry out all the recommendations and proposals put before them, they managed to adopt those solutions that were compatible with the prevailing social and political constraints. Their role in the post-1956 period deserves mention. They attempted to create a consensus around a certain number of values (cost of living, individual autonomy, social peace) by seeking to steer a path between interests that did not always coincide. This 'Kadarism' was certainly the factor largely accounting for the direction the desire for reform took in Hungary (Kende, 1983; Comisso and Marer, 1986). Despite all the intentional and unintentional changes in the economic and political situation over the years, it has managed to stay on course throughout the last three decades.

This spirit of compromise was first evident in agriculture, where the post-1956 reforms helped to create a new type of model combining private initiative and collectivization responsible for the marked expansion in this sector, the most efficient in Eastern Europe (Swain, 1985). The initial successes in this area meant that greater attention could be paid to industrial and planning problems, and it was at this time that specialists and the leadership looked critically at the shortcomings of partial adjustment and the idea of an overall reform began to take shape.

Last but not least, the ongoing importance of external constraints must be mentioned. Hungary is a small country with few natural resources or comparative advantages. The temptation to recentralize that is detectable from time to time generally tends to be fairly short-lived, even if at first sight recentralization and falling back on administrative instruments seem to offer the easiest solution. The fact of the matter is that such periods of recentralization have not provided any way of solving the serious problems of foreign debt (either a liquidity crisis or stimulating growth between 1982 and 1984) or of getting growth under way again after the rigorous policy of adjustment during the same period. At the end of the day, the reformers always opt for extending the scope of the mechanisms of indirect guidance.

If we consider a certain number of limits this liberal option has currently come up against, we can reflect on what the future might hold in store for it.

The limits of the reforms

A difficult mid-point in the implementation of these reforms has now been reached. It is hard to turn back, for doing so could wipe out all that has been achieved with such difficulty by the pragmatic approach they have adopted. At the same time, widening the reform movement, however desirable it may be, raises a number of technical, social and political problems we can usefully examine at this point.

A new series of reforms is proposed for the period up to 1990 (Csaba, 1986; Marer, 1986) addressing three outstanding problems: the extent to which enterprises may be autonomous, the weakness of the price, taxation and wage-fixing systems, and the creation of a mechanism making it possible to resolve the economic conflicts between interest groups (employers and employees, the distribution of income between social groups, sectors and regions).

1. The limit of the instruments of control and competition

The instruments of indirect control are not fully performing their function, in some cases because they are more or less hybrid creations, in others because of the limits imposed on them.

Although they have become more flexible, prices are not really determined by scarcity, and even when they are left to find their own level, they are closely watched by the centre, in the form of the Prices and Materials Office. The centre has to decide the relative importance of increased openness in the process of price formation and protecting and maintaining purchasing power (by means of subsidies), and enterprises – particularly those most sensitive to variations in world prices – negotiate adjustments of their own prices.

Profits, too, are partly an administrative matter, since price control and taxation help to maintain their normative nature, and wage levels are also determined by the same principle despite the modifications that have taken place. There is a greater attempt to bypass the principle of equality rather than to question it directly. This means that at the level of the firm the link between productivity and rates of pay is not always very obvious.

The regrouping of industries at the sectorial level arising from the dissolution of the branch ministries is still at the blueprint stage. There are those who would like to see a movement towards the creation of powerful industrial groups and hence faster progress towards the new industrial structure of the country.

Similarly, competition between enterprises is still relatively limited for several reasons. First, Hungary has restricted itself to simulating a market economy (of the price system) rather than introducing true competition on the basis of enterprises which fail, are absorbed, and the like. Secondly, although the monopolistic structure of the industrial system has been modified, it is still of considerable importance and benefits from what Kornai calls state paternalism. This is also true of the banking and intermediary financial sector. Thirdly, the retention of protectionist measures and the difficulty of increasing the market share of Hungarian products abroad in a very competitive situation have also helped in limiting the part played by competition.

2. Obligations to Comecon

These raise problems of two kinds. In the first place, the risk represented by a dualistic structure within enterprises or the Hungarian economy must be stressed. The fact of the matter is that organizing trade, fixing prices and deciding on the volume of goods flowing from or to Comecon increasingly takes place outside the logic of decentralized control in which firms themselves decide their level of production and organize their own markets. Enterprises linked to the Comecon market (which accounts for over 50% of Hungary's trade) are not subjected to the same degree of competitive pressure as those exporting to the West. Convertible currency limitations and obligations within Comecon can also lead those enterprises most committed to Western markets to fall back on less competitive technologies.

The recent reorientation of Comecon objectives might play a part in modifying and slowing down reform in Hungary. Here, three factors need to be taken into consideration:

1. The Soviet Union's insistence that the deficits in the clearing system be made good.
2. The Comecon scientific and technical development and integration programme adopted in December 1985.

3. The collapse of energy prices and the consequent fall in Soviet receipts.

Despite the equilibrium in bilateral trade envisaged in the clearing system, the Eastern countries have accumulated deficits as a result of the financial crisis of the early 1980s, increases in the cost of raw materials and a worsening of their terms of trade with the Soviet Union. Given the nature of the transferable rouble (the unit of account) these deficits were originally credits (Lavigne, 1984). The Soviet Union now insists that its partners increase delivery of finished goods and plant, some of which could be sold to the West for convertible currency. This change in the pattern of trading has also been accompanied by a reduction in Hungary's trade within Comecon payable in US dollars, which has worked to the country's particular disadvantage, since it had previously benefited from such non-quota exchanges.

At the same time, the scientific and technical integration plan, presented as the socialist counterpart to the European Community's Eureka programme, provides for increased co-operation based on specialization in certain leading industries (data-processing, auto-mation, the electro-nuclear industry, new materials, bio-technology) as a result of the restructuring of the internal economies of member states. This new flow of trade – and in particular a considerable increase in Hungary's exports to the Soviet Union – is already being reflected statistically.

The third factor, the fall in energy prices, and particularly in that of petroleum, may have negative effects on Eastern European countries in general and Hungary in particular. Hydrocarbons and gas account for almost 80% of the Soviet Union's convertible-currency exports, and a fall of a dollar per barrel represents a loss of 500 million dollars. The Soviets may well therefore be led to adjust their exports by adjusting the volume of their deliveries to the Eastern countries in accordance with the fall in prices and insisting that those countries play a larger part in developing infrastructures in the Soviet Union, or that they should deliver more capital goods.

There is a final factor, that of the reforms currently taking place in the other Eastern countries and the USSR. With the exception of Poland, the socialist countries have opted for modifications to the centralized system, even though attempts at rationalization may reduce the importance of intermediate planning authorities, where bureaucracy is active and thrives. The GDR and Czechoslovakia are both fairly openly hostile to any idea of a market socialism. As for the

'Gorbachev effect', it is still too soon to risk any serious prognosis with regard to his projected reforms.

3. Social and political constraints

Although the reforms attract a great deal of support from the most immediately concerned social strata (top civil servants, small entrepreneurs, workers' collectives, intellectuals etc.) they do not unite Hungarian society in its entirety, and indeed opening up the system presents certain social risks and has many political consequences.

Developing the market mechanism is producing a double-edged effect as far as the distribution of incomes is concerned. A not inconsiderable section of the population is seeing its income stagnate and sometimes decline as a result of price rises and the difficulty it experiences in moving into sectors of activity where rewards are higher, as is the case with retired people and civil servants. A large proportion of the population was, of course, already affected by the deficiencies of the centralized system. It is estimated that 75% of Hungarians made use of the second economy before it was legalized (Gábor, 1986). By spelling out more clearly the degree of difference between incomes and admitting that there was a certain inequality, partly made up for by the introduction of graduated income tax, the reformers and the political leadership have seriously undermined one of the basic principles of socialism. The latent discontent that has surfaced might well be fed by certain sections of the bureaucracy who see a certain loss of status as a result of decentralization.

Extending market mechanisms in a socialist economy raises a further problem concerning the type of control that the Communist Party – a vertical structure – can develop over an increasingly decentralized and fragmented horizontal structure. It is true that over the last few years it has modified its *modus operandi* by withdrawing from the day-to-day running of affairs and has managed to adapt the organs of control to its new task and to make its function – that of guiding and encouraging – quite clear. Nevertheless within a single-party framework it must, as the consensus obliges it, express and synthesize the very varied aspirations of social strata whose values are not entirely those of the classical pattern hitherto expressed by official ideology. This can be seen, for instance, in timid attempts to reintroduce a certain pluralism at the political level (a choice between two candidates for parliamentary elections, with one being nominated by the voters; the restoration of certain tasks of control to parliament; and the like).

The assumption of power by new leaders who have known neither the Stalinist period nor centralized planning can also be seen as a factor likely to ensure renewal, but it also means that there will be great uncertainty about medium-term political orientation in Hungary. Will Kadarism survive Kádár, whom absolutely anyone could succeed? A long period of stagnant growth and the development of the negative effects mentioned above could help to usher in a hard-liner from the potential candidates for the leadership of the Hungarian Communist Party.

The Hungarian reformers have gradually traced the outline of an original economic system far from the classical Soviet type but retaining certain of its features. Within the framework of a system of collective ownership of the means of production, they have developed market mechanisms and modified the institutional structure of planning by separating the functions of ownership and management. The economy may be more flexible and more efficient as a result of their efforts, but it is not yet out of the wood. An ongoing instability of the environment and a stronger movement towards integration within Comecon on the one hand and the inherent risks in the development of a dual system within the country with all its attendant social and political consequences on the other, may well once again put a brake on the most recent round of reforms. Recent history, however, shows us the danger of judgements that are too clear-cut. So far, the Hungarian reformers have managed to keep on the road to market socialism.

2 The centralization and decentralization of the socialist economy

It is impossible to analyse the model of decentralized planning without referring explicitly to the experiments carried out in the economies in which this way of allocating resources and organizing economic activities is already in operation.

The partial reforms taking place over the past 20 years and more in the systems of managing enterprises in the planned economies of Eastern Europe are a particularly interesting field of study, and an analysis of them helps to add a new dimension to a question that had already attracted the attention of economists in the first half of the present century.

It might seem strange to offer as a model an experiment conducted in the smallest European member state of Comecon at a time when there are specialists telling us that there are absolutely no reforms now taking place in any Eastern European country (Brus, 1979) or that the economies in question currently constitute an increasingly homogeneous system (Lavigne, 1975: 5).

Although it is true that since the introduction of the New Economic Mechanism in 1968 Hungary has been directed towards a model of market socialism, it is nevertheless still firmly rooted in Comecon and has an excessively centralized management system as an ongoing feature of its planning system. From many points of view, however, the unique economic reforms the country has experienced are still quite novel in their scope and consequences.

One of the reasons why so much attention has been paid to economic reforms in a centrally planned economy is that planning cannot be reduced to a mere theoretical model. The opposite is the case, for it must be analysed as a complex process establishing relationships between agents and authorities via a multiplicity of activities and objectives. This means that if we are to try to provide a pertinent description of the features of the decentralized model we have to take into account the various factors influencing the way the system works.[1] An approach of that kind also makes it possible to understand more exactly how structures and agents behave, to what extent the regulatory system is capable of modifying them or unable to modify their importance.

Any system is made up of a certain number of elements and behaviour patterns. The system arising as a result of applying the principles of the NEM brings with it a behaviour pattern of the agents and various authorities engaged in the planning process arising from both the way the old planning system worked and the introduction of indirect regulation. Such a system is rational not because of the hypotheses in force when the new decentralized model was set up, but because of the juxtaposition within a particular system of elements from both modes of organization. At both the theoretical and practical levels a number of characteristic behaviour patterns of agents and the appearance of dysfunctions therefore arise in a system thought up specifically to remedy the deficiencies in the centralized model.

Regulating economic systems

The concept of regulation referred to here, and defined later, conflicts both with the kinds of spontaneous adjustment arising from market relationships and the overall organization of activities imposed from the outset by means of planning. In the first of those two cases, the way the economy works is the result of the continuous and simultaneous adjustment of the supply and demand of products, money and labour. The price system it furnishes provides the necessary information to co-ordinate the actions of the various agents operating in a decentralized economy (Boissieu, 1978: 88) and, by the same mechanism, the price system produces at the lowest possible cost the information agents need to make their decisions. As Nove points out, no action can be taken in a system unless three elements – information, motivation and means – are present (Nove, 1980: 40, and 1983a). In contrast, in a centrally planned economy decisions as to which aims to pursue and the co-ordination of activities are both carried out by purely administrative means by the transmission of information and injunctions through a vertical hierarchical structure.

Decentralized planning, however, borrows elements from both modes of allocating and managing. In it, regulation is thus seen as a way of co-ordinating activities with the help of rules, norms and principles taken from each of them.

In addition, the notion of regulation recognizes the complex nature, the multidecisional aspect and the multiplicity of the objectives aimed at in any system. Its goal is therefore to control both the various activities and levels of the hierarchical system in order to persuade the latter to move in the direction desired by central authority.

Regulation from the centre ensures that on the one hand the various tasks carried out by sub-systems and on the other the different objectives the system sets itself (a higher GNP, full employment, a balance of payments surplus and the like) are co-ordinated in the best possible way. In addition, the 'aim' function as defined by the society under consideration combines several variables, which may be *quantitative* (disposable income, redistribution, GNP) or *structural* (both technical and institutional) in order to draw up an optimal programme in the terms of such constraints. In carrying it out, the system of decision-making also refers to a range of instruments – taxation, currency, institutions – which can be used to varying degrees in seeking to attain those objectives.

With central planning, reference to such instruments of economic policy is implicit only, since making economic policy an integral part of planning means that such variables lose the whole of their autonomy. The opposite happens when the centralized model is opened up. The instruments are explicitly used, even if a form of regulation akin to control is also maintained.

If we are to appreciate how complex regulation is, we also need to consider the heterogeneous character of the forms it takes in a given system and the need to isolate a dominant one, as the theorists of monopolistic regulation suggest.

> Taking a mode of functioning as a starting point presupposes that a dominant form of regulation can be separated from the rest. This form is generally combined with one or more elements of a different one. And a historical approach suggests that moving from one to another kind of dominant regulation is a slow process. In particular, there may be significant time lags between the appearance of structures containing the seeds of a new form of regulation and achievement of dominance. (Benassy, Boyer and Gelpi, 1979: 400)

Contemporary economic systems share an essential feature. They are all marked by the presence of various types of regulation. Those subject to central planning, in which there is overt control, are also simultaneously regulated by various other modes of allocation.

Frey's typology (Frey, 1978: 13) distinguishes four main ways in which decisions are taken and allocations made, namely the *market or price system, democracy, hierarchy* and *bargaining*. In any given system, they all co-exist, with their importance varying according to the basic features of the system in question. Our sole concern here will be to pinpoint their working in a socialist economy.

The *market* may be explicitly recognized as a secondary means of regulation (free purchase of consumer goods by households, a free market for agricultural and artisanal co-operatives) or hidden in the hierarchical system in the form of a 'black' or what is nowadays called a 'parallel' or 'second' market (Duchêne, 1980 and 1984).

Democracy (or suffrage) also exists, but in a quite atrophied form as a result of the power structure, in which economic choices are directly imposed.

Hierarchy is the dominant mode of allocation, particularly through a centralized planning system featuring a pyramid structure in which production units and the system of information and control are incorporated vertically.

Bargaining also operates in socialist economies, where it forms a particular mode of allocation aimed above all at achieving objectives that cannot be achieved in any other way. It is used horizontally to allocate investment to the different branches and vertically to share it out amongst the various units within a given branch.

The growth of these different mechanisms alongside the dominant mode (hierarchy or planning) ultimately reflects its failure to allocate resources optimally in terms of a single rationale. The fact that they coexist within a single system helps, however, to encourage external effects and bring about totally unintended forms of allocation. If, moreover, we refer to the typology, we note that moving from the centralized to the decentralized model involves taking one in particular of these different types of allocation and concentrating on it on account of its presumed efficacy *whilst at the same time explicitly or implicitly maintaining recourse to other regulators*.

It follows then that we cannot evaluate how rational a decentralized system is merely in terms of hypotheses and features ascribed to market socialism. What any assessment has to take into consideration is indeed both the part played by the other regulators and the reactions observable in the structures in which the new form of regulation is active.

Frey's typology needs to be compared to that proposed by Kornai (1984) which is very similar as far as planning (bureaucracy) and the market are concerned.

The starting point of the analysis is the concept of the co-ordination of complex systems. Without such co-ordination, no society can survive, for it includes not only the regulation of production and the distribution of goods produced by an economic activity, but also every activity leading to transformation or affecting social transactions. The author is therefore led to distinguish four types of co-ordination, each with its own mechanisms. These are co-ordination by means of the *bureaucracy*, by means of the *market* and by *ethical* or *aggressive* means.

In the first and last cases, individuals and organizations do not receive parity of treatment. Bureaucracy involves the growth of vertical relationships and hence a hierarchical structure of functions. As Weber has pointed out, the pressures and constraints codified in legislation recognizing rights and duties ensure that the instructions emanating from the co-ordinator will be carried out. The fact that all those involved accept the rules institutionalizes the vertical relationship. With an 'aggressive' form of co-ordination on the other hand, the domination/dependency relationship is a temporary phenomenon that is never fully accepted. Generally speaking, it does not last for any length of time.

The situation is different in the second and third cases. Those involved are equal and emancipated and establish horizontal relationships. Where the market is concerned, exchanges are expressed in monetary terms, and the price of the transaction reflects the agreement between buyers and sellers. In the case of ethical co-ordination, there is reference to moral values. It may be based on reciprocity, mutual aid or take the form of a unilateral gift.

It is only in the case of co-ordination by means of the market that relationships are *necessarily* expressed in monetary terms. They may be expressed in such terms *incidentally* in those of 'bureaucratic' or 'aggressive' co-ordination (administrative price fixing or theft) but not as far as 'ethical' co-ordination is concerned, except where monetary gifts are involved.

These differing kinds of co-ordination are not mutually exclusive. In history or daily life, they have combined or developed simultaneously to varying degrees, with some predominating at one point and falling back at another. If, for example, we apply the typology to the history of socialist economies, the following sequence becomes apparent: an 'aggressive' form of co-ordination (a dictatorship) followed by a dictatorship and bureaucratization, then a combination of bureaucracy and socialist ethics with some element of a market system (legal transactions and a market economy) with episodic returns to aggressive co-ordination and finally (as is particularly the case with Hungary) bureaucratic and market co-ordination with other types much less in evidence.

Planning and degrees of decentralization

The model of centralized planning is rational not so much in terms of the logic of its chosen ends and the means at its disposal as in terms of the way in which it formulates the aims it can achieve, both through economic means and by making use of extra-economic factors, which may, for example, be political, ideological or coercive in nature.

The way in which centralized planning is organized, on the other hand, is two-fold. In the view of many socialist theoreticians, centralization is the way of countering any mercantile relationship and hence of organizing the economy on non-market principles.

A market economy, which is based on horizontal links between various units, works on a principle – that of the profit motive – which to their mind does not take social needs into account. Since such a market leads to a social division of labour which reflects relationships of domination and exploitation, centralization and planning are seen as an antidote to it, and structuring economic and social activities in a vertical and hierarchical way is seen as a means of breaking with the principles of the system of horizontal relationships characterizing a market economy.

Planners also feel that what is called for is a system of production in kind taking directly into account the needs of the population as a whole by weighing them against the means society has of satisfying them. To some extent, demand is 'interiorized', producing a paradox that has played a large part in the development of what in socialist terms is known as the supplier's market. A system of that kind seems to provide a means of both controlling all economic processes and thus managing the whole economy as if it were a single large enterprise. The principle of what Katzenelboigen calls 'the visible hand' is brought into operation.[2]

One of the factors involved in the process of centralization is rather more dependent on circumstances. The latter is seen as by far the most suitable method of distributing resources and organizing the economy when there is a chronic shortage of capital, skilled labour, raw materials and the like, and attempts to go beyond the social division of labour by eliminating market relationships have led to a combination of a marked functional division of society and a powerful bureaucracy at the various hierarchical levels within it.[3] Once the aims a planned economy sets itself increase in number and the system becomes more complex, it becomes ubiquitous.

In the early stages, the aims inherent in extensive industrialization do not impose the use of any very sophisticated instruments of control on planners. Their very simple nature creates no problems, and at such a point the economic nature of socialism is in fact assessed in terms of more than purely economic criteria. The political, ideological, administrative and coercive methods used make economic calculations even less important.[4]

Planning has many functions in a centralized system. In the first place, it is an expression in quantitative terms of the economic choices made administratively by the central authority. Secondly, it is a way of co-ordinating all economic activities, both as regards establishing the various objectives involved and determining the relationships between the different sectors. To some extent, it reflects both ends and means. It determines the volume of output and hence expresses the aim of production, and is a means of integrating economic policy, which is never independent, and its function is epitomized in the time scale adopted for planning. The system of control remains purely administrative and contains no feedback function. As the productive system becomes increasingly complex as a result of industrialization, however, an administrative management system gives rise to a greater number of negative external effects such as waste, a stagnant growth rate, inefficiency, and a worsening of the terms of trade and bureaucratization. The information it provides is also either partly wrong or to some degree insufficient to make it possible to pursue a higher growth rate or to justify the choices made by planners. In other words, if there is an unsatisfactory relationship between growth and the system of management, the latter will have to be substantially modified and a certain number of objectives identified.

In Hungary, the recognition of the inconsistencies resulting from the centralized model and the desire to remedy them led those responsible for economic policy to establish through the New Economic Mechanism a number of major objectives. These were: provisions for a more rational allocation of capital to branches, to be achieved in particular by developing the most productive ones; participation in the international division of labour; the transformation of the structure of the seller's market to enable it to take developments in demand into consideration; an increase in the productivity of the factors of production; and the establishing of a link between personal and enterprise income and economic results.

A number of measures were taken to achieve these aims. The decision-making process was decentralized and greater autonomy given to micro-economic units; the price system was changed and a new policy of including scarcity to some degree was introduced; the activity of enterprises was indirectly regulated by means of financial regulators and wages; and an active exchange policy (foreign trade multipliers) was put into practice.

Opening up the model was an explicit recognition of the fact that planning could no longer claim to cover the whole range of economic processes and that certain areas of economic activity are directly regulated by market forces. At the same time, certain functions of economic policy were associated with carrying out the plan. There was also a certain amount of rationalization with regard to the choices made by planners, aimed at providing them with more efficient instruments and ways of reaching decisions than those available in an administrative system of management. These included a reduction in the number of ratios and the substitution of value ratios for the centrally imposed physical ratios, a reassessment of the part played by currencies in calculating them, and the introduction of indicators measuring the effectiveness of capital and investments. As regards prices, for example, the desire for greater efficiency meant that the archaic system of value prices was replaced by a parametric equivalent. Direct regulation by means of physical ratios was replaced by an indirect system based on the introduction of a complex fiscal structure in production, making it possible to regulate profits and wages at the micro-economic level.

With regard to agents and institutions, opening up the centralized model brought a new pattern of the various authorities making up the planned economy system. In particular, a centralized system sees the enterprise merely as a lowly link in a hierarchical system, and the decisions affecting it (provision of factors, required volume and distribution of output and so on) are taken at branch level.

As against this, the notion of decentralization questions the vertical nature of the structure to some extent and adds market features to it. In such a system, the function of the enterprise is changed, since it tends to become the area where maximization takes place. Upgrading this function entails a parallel decline in some of those of the meso-economic authorities (branch ministries). There is an attempt to replace the old three-level hierarchical structure (centre, ministries, enterprises) with a binary relationship operating through indirect regulation. In addition, the new stress on the efficiency of productive units means that the income of agents is partly determined by the results enterprises achieve.

In opening up the centralized model, however, the reformers deliberately set themselves certain limits. There was to be a controlled degree of decentralization with a certain number of the structures and functions of the model remaining intact. This applied in particular to the structure of the productive system and the size of enterprises, for example. In addition, the behaviour of agents in the decentralization model was still determined on the basis of what had become normal practice in administrative planning, with enterprises preferring to receive funding rather than seek increased profits on the market, workers not increasing their productivity, the centre still being directly involved in the affairs of enterprises, and so on.

The combined effect of these various factors led to a paradoxical situation, with the dysfunction of the old centralized model (declining efficiency, waste, etc.) being followed by a dysfunction of its new decentralized counterpart as a result of the coexistence of several modes of regulation in the recently introduced system of planning. Imposing a decentralized model on two distinct foreign markets – capitalist and socialist – also meant that growth was even more erratic and that the system could not work properly. This led to measures aimed at a partial recentralization and policies intended to produce greater stability. There were successive partial reforms of the instruments of regulation, and the various endogenous and exogenous constraints had to be built into the new decentralization model. In addition, the fact that various forms of regulation were visibly combined in centralized planning both perpetuated some of the features of the old system of allocation and considerably modified planning functions and objectives. Rather than expressing the will of the centre imposed on the whole range of subordinate activities, it increasingly became a structure for co-ordinating group interests.

The rationality of the plan and the market in a socialist economy

From the earliest days economists were interested in the rationality of the two ways of allocating resources represented by the plan and the market. It is not appropriate to go into the various aspects of the question here, but it is important to look at the part played by each category and the way they were incorporated into a socialist economy. This will enable us to see clearly the real difference between them and to provide a sketch of both the centralized and the decentralized model, each of which to varying degrees combines both plan and market elements.

The former has been more or less equally dominant in all socialist countries, with the latter, described as market socialism, most often appearing in the guise of a remedy for it and seen as having all the virtues centralized planning lacked. At times, market socialism has served as a foil for the defenders of the true faith, for whom using the word 'market' quite simply means abandoning socialist objectives. At others, it has been an obligatory point of reference for reformers in search of a more rational and efficient model.[5]

It is difficult to say just how rational market socialism is without first describing the specific features of each of the two alternatives – the centralized and decentralized forms – that socialism has at its disposal. Nevertheless, the difficulty of defining the real degree of decentralization in an economy and thus pinpointing the features arising from each of these possible forms of organization is quite obvious. Adam Smith or Stalin? The invisible hand or the iron fist? The truth of the matter is probably that a socialist economy runs somewhere along the spectrum bounded by the two extremes and combines elements proper to each system. This means a shift in emphasis, since the rationality of the system we are considering is not to be established by simply adding up the rational features ascribed to the plan and the market respectively. It is rather the case that rationality in operation is more the consequence of the blending of the features specific to each of the systems into a new and particular one. When describing the way the latter works, we shall try to bring out those aspects most characteristic of it.

It may well be objected that the rationality of both systems has already been demonstrated at the theoretical level, in particular in the contributions to the debate made by the Italian economist E. Barone and his Polish colleague O. Lange and the work of the liberal school on economic calculation in socialism led by von Hayek and von Mises. In both these examples, the mathematical formulation tends to prove that rational economic calculation and the optimal allocation of resources are possible in both cases. Nowadays, however, the debate no longer seems fully relevant, since the criteria on which economic decisions are based are grounded in both market relationships and social and macro-economic considerations.

This means that questions about the relevance of the theoretical models are raised by comparing them with the reality they are supposed to represent. Mathematical economics has established two types of model. The first is that of a completely centralized economy as described by Barone, the second is the fruit of Walras' system of equations and the advances made by Arrow and Debreu.

As Kornai (1975) suggests, subjecting the models to the test of reality shows that neither the completely centralized nor the completely decentralized one has ever effectively been applied. With the latter, there have always been many and varied interventions by the public authorities, and with the former a socialist economy in the real world partly escapes absolute control by central bodies.

It is however important to analyse the features of the centralized model and deduce, by comparison, those prevailing in its decentralized counterpart. It must however be stressed that the latter is being considered in the framework of an economy in which the collective ownership of the means of production has been achieved.

1. The origin of the centralized model

The centralized model is the product of a number of historical, political and ideological circumstances. Introducing it has also given rise to a particular type of division and hierarchical structuring of society in general and of the apparatus of production in particular.

The vertical nature of the structure of the economy is two-fold in origin, with both doctrine and socio-economic and political contingencies playing a part. The doctrinal element has its roots in Marx's analysis of the movement of capital. There is a contradiction in the dynamics of accumulation that sets it in motion, since in Marx's view the logic of the system is towards a constant increase in the mass of capital per worker, with the consequence that it goes through a process of concentration and centralization. As is well known, of course, he saw socialism as both a continuation and a negation of capitalism. A negative image of it produces a positive way of seeing socialism. In this sense, the enterprise is seen in two lights, on the one hand as a relatively autonomous unit in a network of market relationships, with its production and its social nature ratified *post factum*, and on the other, if the image is reversed, as a place where the whole range of the social relationships of production is dominated by a single centre. Within the enterprise, too, different jobs are carried in different workshops, products circulate, and so on, without, however, ever achieving the status of merchandise; hence the idea of a prior adjustment of production that removes any reference to ratification by value. It follows, therefore, that the idea of a plan is the antidote to the market, since the utility the latter affords is no longer necessary as a means of evaluating the social nature of production. The opacity of the market, Marx maintained, must yield to the transparency of the various social activities. In addition, the dynamics of capitalism leads to some degree to the socialization of productive forces and a ready solution of the problem of moving from capitalism to socialism (Richet, 1978a).

So what seemed to be an irreversible trend towards an ever-increasing number of trusts and monopolies in the branches of the economy becomes in fact a means of ensuring a new kind of production in a socialist economy. Here, the way in which socialism directly descends from capitalism is obvious, as the latter has throughout its development socialized productive forces by developing technology, a process which leads both to a reduction in the costs of production and, as a result of the effects of size, an increase in its volume.

This particular theoretical approach has been examined in the real world. Socio-economic contingencies seemed obvious to the leaders of Soviet Russia, as can be seen in particular in Lenin's famous call in 1918 for a combination of State capitalism and Soviets. The particular type of State capitalism he had in mind was that to be found in Germany during the First World War, specifically characterized by a very high level of concentration and centralization. The only way of achieving such a level of industrialization seemed to be through a process of concentration. Developing a major socialist enterprise was the implicit consequence of a determination to model the structure and organization of industry on those characteristics of the Party, which were of a military type. The symbiosis of a war-economy model (German State capitalism) and the military principles underlying the way in which political matters were organized was to leave a lasting and indelible mark on Soviet institutions and even more on the Soviet-type economies taking shape after the Second World War. In answer to the observation that along with the concept of State capitalism the bolshevik leaders talked of *Soviets*, that is, of what they saw as the possibility of control of the apparatus of production by the workers, it can be said that by 1919 the re-establishment of the unity of command at the level of the enterprise removed the idea of worker control, that embryonic form of co- or self-management predating the invention of the terms.

In a certain sense, the greater or lesser degree of centralization may seem quite fortuitous in so far as decisions concerning enterprises were not taken at that particular level but by higher bodies that subsequently became branch ministries, which themselves represent an intermediate level between enterprises and the central organs of management.

This pattern, developing in the USSR in the 1920s and 1930s was repeated in the various socialist countries in the 1940s and 1950s, with the absolute centralization of the means of production giving rise to the idea of a collective appropriation of them. At the same time, the 'central will' held sway over an economic space and structure akin to a single large enterprise.

There is also a dimension to the centralization of the economy that plays an important part in the mobilization of men and resources: totalitarian ideology, which leads to an almost total takeover of society by the State.[6] Planning thus makes it possible to see the national economy as a single large enterprise, and through the collective appropriation of the means of production, centralization offers a way of organizing and controlling the whole process of production. The economy can be organized around a centrally defined plan on a macro-economic scale which is reduced in stages to the level of the enterprise.

The rationality of planning is not based on optimal achievement at that level by maximizing profit, but on centrally determined priority aims. The rationality of the aims' function lies in the way in which the available means are organized and used in order to achieve the desired end, which accounts for the macro-economic dimension in economic calculations. The conscious control of the productive process also makes it possible to ensure balanced and regular growth by the allocation of the surplus released to the various branches. This way of looking at things lies behind the idea of a completely harmonized society working towards specific ends.

We still need, however, to link such a concept of a society based on rational redistribution to a general model of civilization and earlier social and economic patterns in Eastern Europe. As Konrad and Szelenyi (1979) stress, Western liberal evaluative models on their own cannot fully take into account the reality that too often tends to be presented as the mating of a totalitarian political system and an economy ridden with costly dysfunctions.

2. The features of the centralized planning model

Planning performs various functions. Primarily it is the institutional framework for the management of the productive system, the means of putting into practice the objectives prescribed, the way of measuring production in terms of both quantitative and qualitative indexes, of allocating resources, of operating intersectorial links, and of balancing out resources and jobs at both branch and economy level.

Its task is therefore to ensure that choices are consistent and to seek the greatest possible efficiency. It is also a model, since it structures the field of the economy, affects the behaviour of agents, and works hand in hand with all the different institutions whose joint effort is directed towards establishing, starting and running the plan.

Using a highly hierarchical structure, centralized planning brings together the various authorities playing a part in the working and reproduction of the system. This structure entails a management system based on a pyramid of decision-making procedures. Its main features (Brus, 1968: 85) can be seen as: the central concentration of all economic decisions (except those involving individual choices about consumption and employment); the hierarchical nature of plans and the vertical relationships between the different links in the economic apparatus; the 'command' form in which decisions are transmitted downwards; and the predominance of economic calculations and planning in terms of natural scales.

Despite its declared intention to dominate and control the whole productive process, however, the centralist model cannot reach every corner. In a general way, there are limits to absolute centralization, and certain aspects of economic activity cannot be controlled by orders emanating from the centre. There are many reasons for this and primarily they are connected with the pyramid-shaped structure of the system of transmitting orders, which to some extent shields subordinate units from central control. A further explanation is the difficulty of the move from macro- to micro-economic scales.

In contrast, it is much more problematic to try to define the decentralized model, since the term brings together two apparently conflicting ideas. The fact is that a feature of it is the coexistence of a horizontal market and a vertical institutional (planning) structure. The model, in which ownership relations remain the same, has a centre that still keeps a great many of its macro-economic prerogatives, since that centre draws up the plan in accordance with its own system of preferences by defining the main aggregates, such as the growth rate, accumulation rate, distribution of investment among branches, increase in the productivity of factors, growth in income and the aggregate remuneration of employees, foreign debt level, the total amount of money in circulation, and the like. Elements of economic policy are linked to these macro-economic functions with a view to achieving macro-economic aims by means of indirect indicators. The chief devices to this end are prices, incomes, taxation and budgetary policies.

With regard to day-to-day decisions at branch and enterprise level, central decisions expressed in terms of physical indexes are replaced by those expressed in terms of value and by indirect regulation, which make it possible at this level to take autonomous decisions about such matters as the range and volume of production and the choice of supplies and outlets.

There is a dividing line between centralization and decentralization, particularly if we take into account the three levels of decision-making. These are decisions concerning the major macro-economic questions, taken at the *centre*; those concerning the volume and distribution of production, taken at the *sectorial level*; and individual decisions made by *households*. It runs through the second group, since in both models it is the centre that ensures the pre-eminence of its own choices by means of an evaluation of an administrative nature. The third group is not affected, as in the centralized model households are free, within the limits of the range of consumer goods available, to spend their income as they like. Given that it is in the second group that the mechanisms of direct and indirect regulation are applied, it is there that considerable changes take place.

The degree of real decentralization a socialist planner can hope to achieve comes up against the predetermined limits set by the very nature of the Soviet-type model. Market mechanisms can in fact never be the major way of regulating the system unless the whole primacy of the plan is called into question. Indeed, limits are set for them from the outset (Richet, 1978b: 127; Nyers and Tardos, 1978, for example) and how far decentralization goes is really a reflection of the appropriate compromise achieved, given the various constraints involved, between plan and market. Brus notes this when describing the function of the market in the plan:

> The market mechanism in a decentralized model is endowed with at least two important features: (1) the market magnitudes must always preserve their parametric character in relation to the subject of choice

and (2) the market magnitudes must be determined or at least
effectively influenced in an indirect way by the central planner
according to the public scale of preference. Hence, it is useful to call
the market mechanism in this model a 'regulated market mechanism'
in order to emphasize its role as an instrument of the plan and not as a
spontaneous factor, independent of or even contradictory to planning. (Brus, 1973: 10)

3. The paradoxical and specific nature of the decentralized model

A paradox is the juxtaposition of two apparently contradictory
ideas. The concept of socialism implies a form of central regulation,
whereas a market is self-regulating. The question that arises is that of
the relative importance of planning and the market in decentralized
planning. A further question has to do with whether there can indeed
be such a thing as market socialism or, more exactly, with whether two
such very different logical approaches can exist side by side in one and
the same economic structure without explicitly criticizing the domi-
nance of one of the two forms of regulation. A third has to do with
comparing a theoretical scheme based in the one case on an analysis in
terms of a model and in the other on the heterogeneous nature of
markets and productive structures.

A socialist economy is the result of a political will, and the form of
regulation it gives rise to is organically linked to it and has the task of
operating and ensuring aims provided by the centre. Such a system is
based, for its fulfilment, on a centralized management going against
the autonomy of subordinate authorities and agents. Yet market
socialism necessarily implies that subordinate authorities will enjoy a
certain degree of autonomy, not only with regard to day-to-day
management choices but also in connection with certain investments,
price fixing and similar matters. As we have seen, however, the
planners restrict the range of problems it can tackle to certain areas
clearly defined in advance. In such a situation, it is not clear whether
one can properly speak of market socialism. It is perhaps rather a
question of a partial reorganization of the central system. When we
talk about a degree of decentralization of socialist economies, we see
the process as taking place along a spectrum running between State
socialism and self-management. That spectrum, however, is vertically
divided by a barrier, since we cannot conceive of a surreptitious and
regular movement from one of the limit situations to the other, even if
there is a liberalization of economic policy in specific circumstances at
a particular juncture. At some point, the need to reject the main

features of one of the systems is bound to arise. Self-management in Yugoslavia, for example, could only develop as a result of the break with the Soviet Union in 1948.[7] It was only after freedom had been achieved again that the country's leaders could adopt the system empirically. It must be borne in mind that its principal feature was the dismantling of the structures of central planning, what was in effect the dissolution of the branch ministries, a newly reactivated economic and monetary policy, a more dynamic role for enterprises, and a complete opening-up of the economy.

Consequently, if the market socialism model is applied, the notion of an all-powerful centre must necessarily be abandoned, and some recognition of the autonomy of agents, particularly at the level of subsidiary authorities and above all enterprises, is inevitable. If, on the other hand, the plan is still seen as playing the crucial part, introducing market elements will have little effect on the features of the centralized model.

It should also be noted that developing reforms of a decentralizing nature can never be a straightforward matter. With the plan-or-market alternative, both factors and structures helping to shape the socialist economy have to be taken into account. For a number of reasons, this means that a direct shift from a centralized to a market socialism model with all its attendant virtues is a complicated undertaking.

In the first place, not only is the information system inadequate, but the productive structure produced by administrative planning has given rise to an imbalance between the levels of supply and demand. The characteristic feature of the socialist market is its supply structure – a seller's market – brought about by the type of industrial development and created by central planning decisions which also shape demand. This is also accentuated by the mode of regulation, and particularly by the price system, currently obtaining. What happens is that the 'value price' system increases the part played by supply and consequently reduces that played by demand. A 'non-market' organization of the economy for the allocation of resources amongst branches removes from competition the suppliers, whose objectives are centrally planned. In the field of consumer goods on the other hand, the opposite happens. There is competition amongst buyers, and it is increased by the chronic shortage characteristic of a vertical organization of economic activity. But what typifies the market-economy model is a high level of competition amongst suppliers who, as Kornai puts it, exert pressure on demand, whereas it is really demand that creates expectations (Kornai, 1971). Given that particular structure, market socialism must, if it is ever to come fully into being, switch the imbalance towards a situation in which demand plays a decisive part.

The second reason, although in this case the inadequacy is only relative, has to do with the monopolistic structure of the productive apparatus in socialist economies. As Lavigne notes, if we want to provide a theoretical account of market socialism or analyse the trading relationships observable in socialist economies, we need to picture not perfect competition, but rather imperfectly competitive markets or in particular *strategy* markets, i.e. oligopolies (Lavigne, 1977: 994).

It can readily be seen from these observations that it is difficult to define a model of market socialism in a way other than negatively in relation to centralization, when the various structural, institutional and system-related constraints that affect it are applied. This view will be confirmed if we also consider not the types but the chronological sequence – and occasionally the simultaneous presence – of the various forms of allocation and management that develop within the framework of socialist planning.

4. Socialist planning and the organization of activities

Three systems of control existing consecutively or sometimes simultaneously within socialist planning can be noted.

The first is that in which administrative management targets for enterprises and the instruments and inputs necessary to achieve them are expressed in *kind*, that is in physical quantities, and recourse to currency or any kind of economic calculation is limited. Here, the allocation of inputs is based on criteria established by central authority on the basis of its preferences.

This was – and at least in spirit still is – the dominant system from the beginning of Stalinist planning. It made it possible to launch major industrialization projects without the burden of the constraints of economic calculation that circumstances would in any case have made meaningless. This enabled political will to give consistency to the idea of a physical or natural kind of planning even if it turned out in fact to be ineffective with plans simply following the trend of things and being adjusted *post factum* (Zaleski, 1984).

The second is that of 'khozraschet', or accountable autonomy, which saw, at enterprise level, an increasing use of value rather than material indicators. It was at this level that costs and resources were to be balanced. Although it was an attempt to rationalize the centralized model, this system did not manage to put an end to the pre-eminence of the centre or get rid of the inconsistencies in macro-economic planning or the conflicting strategies adopted by subsidiary units and the centre.

The third, that of the 'socialist enterprise' (Hegedüs, 1976) paid particular attention to the behaviour of subsidiary institutions whose role, along with that of regulation by means of prices, taxation and currency, was increasing in importance. Such regulation remained parametric, however, in so far as the indicators in question and the instruments of encouragement achieved their purpose only in part, given the intervention and manipulation practiced by the centre.

The three types of systems developed partly or fully in the socialist countries, especially in Hungary. There was no rigorously chronological pattern in the way they succeeded each other, and there were relatively long periods when, to varying degrees, they might exist simultaneously, a fact which shaped a specific form of control system that tended to incorporate an amalgam of the three forms of organization.

Thus, instead of a dichotomy between a plan and a market, each with its own distinct logic, what we tend rather to note in the Hungarian reforms is the two kinds of logic working in collusion. The question then arising is that of whether the reforms were bound to lead to that outcome and of how the synthesis between the two was initially understood. What makes it hard to describe that synthesis is the inconsistency in a dialectic that makes the enterprise part of a uniform system of appropriating the means of production, a system in which state enterprise is seen as an inalienable part of state property but also and at the same time as an economically separate unit of production. In such a situation, the function of the ability to compete is greatly reduced, since it cannot be viewed as an activity integrated into macro-economic choices.

The definition of the decentralized model is not at all clear-cut, and it is just as difficult to offer a relevant definition of market socialism as it is possible to give a sufficiently precise one of the essential features of the centralized model, particularly by means of a norm.

Writers like Andreff (1976) may suggest measuring how far an economy has been decentralized by considering several alternatives, but there are many difficulties and constraints – some of them not easily overcome – in the way of putting such a model into operation. As we shall see, therefore, introducing reforms with a view to decentralizing such a type of economy is akin to a long process of trial and error.

3   Opening up the centralized model

In this chapter I propose to examine both the way in which the centralized model was opened up and the consequences for Hungarian industrial organization and planning institutions.

When the model based on Stalinist planning was opened up on the adoption of the New Economic Mechanism (NEM) in 1968, there had already been partial modifications to the system both in the fields of planning and guideline instruments and that of organization. Following the dramatic events of 1956 (for which hyper-centralization was partly responsible) the Kádár government had also embarked on a radical and successful reform of agriculture, modifying its structure and making it more dynamic. This meant that later reformers could concentrate on industry.

Nevertheless, the industrial structure and mode of organization that had grown up prior to 1968 and the Hungarian leadership's ideas for reforming them created in-built limits as to what and how much could be done. Although it was originally seen as a means of adapting the planning system by creating incentives, and was restricted purely to the economic field, the introduction of the NEM very soon had an impact in political areas, which gave rise to a fear that it might spread too widely, and so led to a consequent narrowing down of its field of application. However, such self-imposed limitations had negative counter-effects, which periodically led the Hungarian leaders to widen the scope again.

The centralization and concentration of the productive apparatus

It is usually impossible to separate centralization and concentration in Soviet-type economies. They form a two-fold process attributable, as we have seen, to several factors. In line with what

Table 3.1. *Main indicators of economic development (average annual %
increase)*

	1951–5	1956–60	1961–5	1966–70
Net national production (from product viewpoint)[a]	5.7	5.9	4.1	6.8
Industrial production[a]	13.2	7.5	7.8	6.3
Industrial productivity[a]	3.7	4.1	5.4	6.0
Construction	3.4	3.0	4.7	2.1
Agricultural production	3.4	0.4	1.2	2.8
Investments[b]	1.2	13.1	5.1	11.6
Real wages	1.0	8.0	1.8	3.5
Retail trade	8.7	13.7	7.0	12.2
Exports[b]	12.8	7.8	11.6	8.9
Imports[b]	11.9	12.0	9.3	10.5

[a] in comparable prices
[b] in current prices
Source: *Hungarian Statistical Yearbook*, 1975.

happened in the USSR and the other people's democracies, the
Hungarian economy underwent a profound restructuring of its productive apparatus, with a number of economic, institutional and
political objectives.

These were a speeding up of the rate at which an economy with a
low rate of industrialization, predominantly agricultural and largely
unspecialized, was being transformed (see Table 3.1); the setting up of
an autarkical accumulation system similar to that tested in the USSR in
the 1930s (from an institutional point of view this had the double
advantage of matching the form of economic organization and that of
political power, in the administrative management of branches, and,
for the USSR, of providing a better way of controlling each country by
favouring bilateral relations and avoiding attempts to form regional
alliances, such as the Yugoslav and Bulgarian project before Tito was
excluded from the Cominform in 1948); a further factor was the fear of
a new conflict, which helped speed up the development of the new
industrial structure and thus made it possible to turn civilian industry
into military industry rapidly (Berend and Ránki, 1985).

Concentration is also of symbolic significance, providing as it does a
way of expressing the new social order in real and concrete terms. This
means that it is made possible through property. Logically it seems

simpler to combine a single proprietor's holdings into one or two units. This legal argument is not alien to the economist's way of thinking, since concentration is a way of achieving economies of scale by bringing together, reducing the cost of and hence increasing the means of production. Once it has been set up by the central authority, such a form of concentration may make it possible to achieve directly the size required for the frequently excessive objectives set for society in the initial plans. The effect of size, however, is not necessarily synonymous with the optimum, and it may take a few years for the idea of *viable* units of production to take hold.

In the specific case of Hungary, industrial concentration can also be explained in terms of the political choices of the leaders of the Rákosi era (1947–56), which were of similar scale and intensity to those made in the USSR. In addition, industry was completely reorganized in 1963, further increasing the degree of concentration of the apparatus of production and in fact turning it into a sort of cartel run by the branch ministries.

This situation affected the way in which the reforms proceeded. A new system of control had been planned without any change in industrial structure, which indicated one of the ambiguities implicit in the changes being introduced: the introduction of market mechanisms in an oligopolistic framework.

In a very short period of historical time, Hungary went through a rapid and intense phase of industrial development. Alongside it, a process of centralizing and concentrating the productive apparatus went hand in hand with a declared desire to move rapidly through the stages of a growth that were to lead to a developed socialist society. All this was part of the 'great transformation' described by Polányi (1983) aimed at replacing, by means of State control of the means of production, the deficiencies of the market economy, which in the view of those initiating the projects was incapable of ensuring a more rapid economic development.

In addition, Hungary at the end of the Second World War was in the Soviet sphere of influence and, like those neighbouring countries with which she formed what was to become the people's democracies, received what one economist has called 'revolution as a gift' (Janossy, 1970). That gift – the Soviet-type economic and social system – was created in circumstances we are aware of over almost three decades and various stages until its final features emerged. The model of one particular experience achieved a universal status once it was applied to each of the people's democracies.

Its universality, however, was confronted with a different reality from that in which it had been created. It was usual to get round the contradiction by means of recourse to various practices all aimed at helping to achieve objectives of an economic nature (industrialization) or with a social purpose (the classless society). Thus political and ideological methods (dictatorship, the exclusive use of one explanatory social theory) were used as invaluable aids to economic instruments.

The usual pattern of events when the Soviet model was applied was for East European economies to be destructured and rebuilt in the Soviet likeness. That is why, in particular, priority was given to heavy industry, which was seen as a means of both ensuring autarkic development and creating a working class, hitherto very small in number. The pursuit of this pattern of industrialization often entailed risky choices leading to a great deal of waste. For example, Hungary invested heavily, and at great cost, in the iron and steel industry in a country importing 80% of its iron ore and 90% of its coke with no possibility of exporting to pay for its imports. Such decisions, even though they clearly illustrated an ignorance of the idea of technological complementarity and comparative advantage (Brown and Licari, 1976: 272) were very much in accordance with the political and ideological aims of the government.

This policy was followed in the various people's democracies, and for some of them, particularly those already industrialized, it brought in its wake a restructuring of industry on the soviet model which partly wiped out the level of development already achieved. Czechoslovakia and East Germany are examples.

In the case of Hungary, the degree of post-war industrialization matched the extent to which the country had earlier fallen behind in this area. Before the communists came to power, there had been a certain dualism in the social structure, which both had features of a semi-feudal economy as a result of its agrarian system and had also seen development in certain downstream industrial sectors often dependent on external demand.

In Hungary, the experience of enforced industrialization occurred at the interface of two requirements. The first, which was political and ethical, was a direct consequence of applying socialist principles. The second arose from the need for the means of carrying out the policy. In other words, enforced industrialization was a response to the country's chronic under-industrialization and the means used in association with it were also a result of the double requirement.

Centralization in Hungary during the 1940s and 1950s occurred for more contingent reasons. Well before the Communist Party came to power, raw materials and industrial materials were in short supply, and certain departments (the Office of Prices and Materials, for example) were set up to deal with shortages and allocate resources in limited quantities. The rapid and widespread nationalization of the whole industrial and banking system after 1947–8 speeded up the process of centralization.

Although concentration and centralization are inherent consequences of the introduction and development of a Soviet-type economy, it must however be pointed out that certain prerequisites, which are not necessarily always present, are essential if enforced industrialization supported by the concentration and centralization of the apparatus of production is to achieve its aims. Jánossy lists these in the case of the Soviet Union as being a population with an extremely low level of demand and, after the First World War and the Civil War, capable of making great sacrifices; an agriculture providing a labour force for industry and at the same time capable of supplying the population, albeit for the moment at a very low level; sufficient natural resources to meet industry's raw materials and energy needs; and, as a result of these resources, the ability to pay for imports of machinery and plant by exporting raw materials (Jánossy, 1970: 364).

He points out that despite serious problems economic equilibrium was preserved in the long term even when industrial development peaked, reducing the supply of goods to the population to its lowest level. Industry, energy, the production of coal and iron ore and transport were a closed circle for several years, their sole purpose being to supply factories in those sectors. Although the industrial sector was capable of supplying the Soviet Union's war industry, it could barely provide the population and agriculture with essentials. This can be compared with the situation later obtaining in Hungary. There, general living standards before the Second World War were higher than those in the Russian Empire before the First. The needs of the population were higher and increasing more rapidly. Agriculture was able to supply the market. There was a great disparity between available natural resources and industry's needs for raw materials. Imports of the latter increased as industry developed. Although a certain proportion of the imports needed to develop modern technology was temporarily paid for by exporting agricultural produce, this by no means covered all the needs, and it later became less easy to use this device.

The prerequisites for autarkic and enforced development were thus present in the Soviet Union, but not in Hungary. In the latter country, for industry to develop at such a rate required Hungary to pay for imports of raw materials and machinery by exporting manufactured goods, which correspondingly reduced the proportion of the national income that could be accumulated in industry.

Before the development of this process, the prime function of Hungary's first three-year plan (1947–50) had been to reconstruct the economy, in particular the productive apparatus and transport, since between 80% and 90% of both had been destroyed. The very high demand at that time for both agricultural and industrial products explains why pre-war production levels were very rapidly achieved. In industry, for example, the level of production in 1950 was 50% higher than that in 1938.

The change of ownership of the means of production became more marked. In agriculture, the redistribution of land was speeded up, with the particular aim of counteracting the semi-feudal structure characterizing the sector. In industry, most branches were nationalized at an increasing speed during the first three-year plan. Coal mines, electricity undertakings and the four main banks were included. This was extended in 1949 to every firm employing over 100 workers. By that date, the State sector controlled 99% of mines, industry and transport in terms of jobs, and economic management moved from enterprise to branch level.

It was during this period that the organs of State management, both functional (the Planning Office, the State Bank and the like) and sectorial (the branch ministries) were set up. Thus controlling the economy on the principles of the management of a large firm was introduced. Subordinate units were stripped of their former prerogatives and only allowed to act within the framework of a purely administrative system.

The first five-year plan (1950–4) saw enforced industrialization really take off. The plan's two priorities were heavy industry and the accumulation rate. The investment rate, which during the reconstruction period had already doubled in comparison with the pre-war period, was chiefly aimed at heavy industry to the detriment of such other sectors as light industry, agriculture and the income of households.

Once the first aims of the plan had been successfully achieved, there began the process of a permanent upward revision of planning objectives. The result of this was a further increase in growth, investment and production rates, even though generally speaking there was no economic justification for doing so. The effect of such a policy was consequently to create serious imbalances in growth, principally by producing wide discrepancies between the major sectors of activity. The structure of the working population was also considerably modified, with a large proportion of the agricultural labour force moving into industry. Before this trend peaked, that is, in the workers' and people's revolt of October 1956, it had been modified to some extent when the first of the reformers, Imre Nagy, took over from the 'local Stalin' during 1954. It is true that the reforms of the first Nagy government were aimed at restoring equilibrium between sectors, reducing the investment rate and encouraging the development of light industry and agriculture, but the methods of drawing up the plan and managing enterprises were not really changed. In addition, the reforming period came to a sudden end in 1955, when the advocates of centralization and enforced development returned in force and once again fixed inordinately high growth rates for both production and investment. The effects of this were disastrous, and last-minute partial reforms were tried. These were, however, insufficient to prevent the wave of explosive popular discontent that in the space of a few days swept away the social and economic system. It was finally only saved by Soviet intervention, which crushed that first anti-totalitarian revolution, which is still the most radical and profound and perhaps the most fertile of the subsequent movements in unsettled countries before the major Polish strikes of summer 1980.

It was to take almost a year for the economy to get moving again, an achievement largely due to the massive aid provided by the countries of the Warsaw pact. From 1957, partial modifications to the planning and management systems gradually leading to an overall reform of regulation were envisaged. At this stage, the desire for a partial decentralization of the economy was confronted with the continued existence of a still totally centralized decision structure that minimized the timid attempts at modifying the management system. Alongside this, however, the growth rate was starting to stagnate now that development was more balanced, and this situation ultimately reawakened the desire to reform all, not just parts of, the management system.

We have seen that the Soviet model was applied during the early years of industrialization in Hungary. For the planners, this had its good points, for it meant that they were introducing a system that had been tried out elsewhere over a longer period, even if that did not guarantee that it would be completely successful in Hungary. We have looked briefly at some of the consequences of grafting such a model onto the Hungarian economy.

The Soviet model has four basic features: socialist, State and co-operative forms of enterprise; enterprises directed by a central instructions system aimed at increasing the volume of production; the allocation of plant and investment and the establishment of major objectives in physical terms; and the fixing of prices by the centre, with no account taken of supply and demand. These make possible a quantitative development of production which is purely intrinsic and takes no account of either efficiency or quality. However, the system does provide – along with extra-economic vectors such as political and ideological constraints – a powerful spur to rapid industrialization.

Applying the Soviet model to a specific socio-economic structure in a semi-industrialized country was bound to lead to some dysfunction. This dysfunction was, in fact, not analysed and corrected but increased by administrative and political measures going completely against the real needs of society.

Until the 1956 rising, therefore, Hungary underwent a pattern of industrialization that gave priority to a very high rate of investment at the expense of consumption. To the same degree, if not for as long, the country lived through what the USSR had experienced with all its constraints, violence and unpredictability before the war. That, however, was the price to be paid, according to Rákosi, the local dictator, for turning Hungary into 'a land of iron and steel'.

The violent challenge to the centralized model and this pattern of accumulation brought the reforms into being. Only after 1956 was there to be any thought of modifying the management system, and only a dozen years later, in 1968, did it assume concrete form with the introduction of the NEM.

The logic of the plan and adjustment procedures

The determination to use the plan to reinforce government from the centre ran into problems arising from both the choice of instruments and the system of decision-making. The planners tended to deal with these by continual modification. As they did so, it became less and less of an overall scheme for the future and more and more of an instrument of management diverging considerably from its initial objectives.

There are numerous studies of such dysfunctions in socialist economies (Kornai, 1959; Balassa, 1959; Nove, 1983). Using Zaleski's work (1984) as a basis, we can trace the outline of the way plans were applied and how planners subsequently modified them.

Contrary to a view widely held among Western authorities on planning, the function of Stalinist planning was not to co-ordinate plans but primarily to impose a view of the future on the country. The first stage in the planning process was to establish a summary central plan that the central authority used to allocate tasks arising from the aims imposed on subsidiary units via the organizational hierarchy. As these mini-plans moved down the ladder towards the basic units, they increasingly became real plans. Co-ordination was therefore achieved *post factum*, once they had been put into operation. Planning was thus rather like a continuous process in which tasks were imposed on and resources allocated to the basic units through the hierarchical structure.

It would be interesting to examine the chief features of the model. The central plan was heterogeneous in nature. It was the result of an amalgam of projections starting from different bases, with aims that were often very general, and judgements about the behaviour of economic units that relied on very imperfect instruments of guidance. Estimating the part played by both exogenous and endogenous factors (climate, harvests, demography, technical progress and the like) was often a rather hit-or-miss affair. Planning was therefore the result of a cluster of the expected outcome of actions decided upon by the government on the basis of more or less reliable forecasts.

In such circumstances a coherent and perfect central plan extending to and carried out at every level is no more than a myth. Reality consists rather of a multitude of constantly developing plans that are not finally co-ordinated until they have been put into operation. Hence the emergence of the single concrete reality of a power of management embodied in an administration rigidly hierarchical, from the level of branch ministries to that of enterprises, and subject to strict discipline. Zaleski maintains that it is therefore more appropriate to speak of a centrally controlled economy, in which excessive centralization is not incompatible with a plethora of individual economic decisions and manages, in fact, to make whole areas of autonomy available to intermediate and subordinate authorities. A bargaining procedure emerges as negotiations between the various authorities proceed, with each subordinate authority enjoying a small area of power escaping the control of its superior. The fact that such a situation can exist arises from the sheer number of frequently contradictory objectives and the way authority is shared.

Can such disequilibrium be compensated for by imperative plans achieving an overall consistency at the macro-economic level? It would appear that the large-scale use of the system of balances can in fact produce an equilibrium between resources and jobs, to a large extent in the case of homogeneous products and much less so with diversified ones. The existence of an arbitrary price system, however, reduces the role and importance of such values and brings in its wake disequilibrium situations that the centre remedies by means of rationing. Rigid planning also imposes progressive norms in the fields of productivity at work and the use of plant. Working out the details of the plan becomes a matter of filling in an increasing number of forms rather than a search for the optimum. The point of balance achieved by the final plan – that is, the one that is in fact put into operation – is the point where the influences of the various pressure groups intersect.

Apart from being to some extent incoherent, the plans had a rather limited effectiveness in practical terms, with the government being obliged to concentrate on some objectives rather than others. This was particularly so with regard to provision in the material and technical fields, where a list of priorities had to be drawn up. In this context, Kornai was to speak of shortages as a determinant of allocation, a situation which had a number of consequences, including less effective orders, a reduced scope and field of action for the central plan, and a greater area in the planned economy in which the plans of enterprises fell outside overall control.

It is easy to see how the centre would react in the face of such imbalances. The number of indexes in its plan was increased and in the following one an attempt was made to extend the area of imperative administrative planning in order to control the affected sector.

Zaleski puts forward the idea that inconsistent imperative administrative plans proved pointless solely because in the Soviet economy there were other spheres than those of the planned economy and the market economy (the latter being very limited) which replaced each other and softened the harsh effects of plans with in-built contradictions, often made more severe by the fact that plans operating over different time scales (five-year, annual, quarterly, 'sliding') would run side by side. Planning was of course a continuous process, a matter not of separate plans but of the same plan established for different periods. Interlocking sub-divisions aimed at limiting the sphere of political economy were the order of the day. Although annual plans, for instance, were parts of the five-year plan, they were essentially operational in nature, designed to meet the needs of the moment by facing up to a wide range of constraints, and they also contained their own inconsistencies. They were launched piecemeal and at different times, and would collapse before they were fully implemented.

In the face of such conflicting choices and inadequate instruments, adjustment policies were needed. These were put into operation either by means of rationing, with non-priority demand being eliminated, or by adjusting the plans of branches, sectors, activity groups or those of the national plan itself. What this meant was the introduction of an implicit national plan resulting from the combination of the overall effects of authorized micro-economic plans and the establishment of priorities. The unavoidable apportionment of shortages led to a situation in which one kind of planning was ousted by another.

The fact that political rationality – or the determination to control, manifest in absolute power over human beings – was the primary factor and economic rationality only secondary accounts for the combination of authoritarian and spontaneous elements in planning. On the one hand, plans were marked by authoritarianism and political will; on the other, economic activity, the heterogeneous nature of the decision-making system, the inevitable adjustments, were all characterized by a certain degree of spontaneity. Stalinist planning can therefore be seen as a combination of impulses and constant pressures with unexpected results. And yet, as the tool of a strategy of power paying little attention to the means it used or the people it dominated, it achieved its aims.

From partial adaptations of the centralized model to the idea of reform

The years between 1957 and 1968 were a turning-point for economic management and growth in Hungary. They were also critical for the political and theoretical reflection that was to lead to the preparation and ultimately the introduction of the 1968 reforms.

In addition to favourable political circumstances, several other phenomena came into play in a non-linear fashion. The most important of these were reforms to the system of inducement, particularly with regard to prices; an increase in *per capita* income; reforms in enterprises increasing industrial concentration; and more reflection on the type of planning that should replace that of an administrative nature. Two factors were important here: the need to change the model of growth by taking into account factors hitherto seen as being of secondary importance, such as consumer goods and agriculture; and Hungary's relative indebtedness and the increasing imbalances in her trade.

1. Adapting the system of planning and guidance

As early as 1957, the planners took several measures to make up for the shortcomings of the administrative planning system. Amongst them was price reform. The old, purely artificial system was abandoned, to be replaced by prices taking into account the relative scarcity of inputs (capital and labour). Since the new system both maintained central price control (fixed prices) and broke the link between production and consumption, however, it soon became ineffective. Demand and the (foreign) market could not change the way in which prices were formed at enterprise level.

In addition, the number of directives in the plan was reduced. Each ministry was allowed to determine how many obligatory directives there should be, and in certain industries the number of compulsory indexes fell from several dozen to a mere five. This did nothing to increase the efficiency of enterprises, however, and some of them called for more central control.

Nor did increased inducement by means of State/enterprise profit sharing or the opportunity for direct export afforded to certain mechanical construction enterprises have any effect on enterprise behaviour. The export price mechanisms did not make it possible to calculate the advantages of trading.

2. The radical reform of agriculture

The 1957 reforms in the agricultural sector were, however, very successful. Indeed, the Hungarian leadership is now trying in its industrial reforms to make use of some of the methods that made agriculture so dynamic. These include elected factory managers, co-operation between socialist and private sectors, and the like.

The aim of the agricultural reforms was two-fold. In the first place, there was an attempt to create a consensus by seeking to encourage peasants to join voluntarily in a more flexible and workable type of co-operation. Second, agriculture was to be made more efficient, with

Table 3.2. *Contribution of social sectors to total agricultural output* (% *distribution*)

	1966	1975	1980	1984
State-owned farms	16.4	18	16.8	15.3
Co-operatives	48.4	50.5	50.4	51.1
Household farming	23.7	19	18.5	18.4
Auxiliary production and private farms	11.5	12.5	14.3	15.2

Source: *Statisztikai Evkönyv*, various years.

the particular aim of producing a lasting reduction of shortages and an increase in the offer of products to the population.

The means used, which were non-coercive and unorthodox in comparison with those used in the past (Richet, 1985b) were intended to create a symbiotic relationship between the co-operative and private state sectors by both encouraging specialization and co-operation and transferring a great deal to the peasants. The liberalization and subsequent suppression of compulsory deliveries, the free sale of produce from individual plots, the choice of production at co-operative level and the introduction of a more effective and democratic decision-making system (with elected managers) were a significant contribution to the success of the experiment.

This combination of an agricultural policy stimulating demand and an income redistribution policy aimed at producing a regular increase in the purchasing power of the population very soon had a positive effect. Between 1957 and 1967 household consumption increased constantly and regular and ample supplies soon eliminated the shortages and queues that had hitherto been features of distribution in the sector.

3. *Reshaping the industrial structure*

Things went quite differently with regard to the policy concerning industrial structures followed during the 1960s, when the centre and the branch ministries increased their power. The effect of this functional recentralization was to increase significantly the degree of concentration in industry and consequently to encourage the meso- and macro-economic authorities to intervene in day-to-day decision-

Table 3.3. *Enterprise concentration in the socialist sector*

	below 50	51–100	Total numbers 101–500	501–1000	over 1000	total
1950	34.9	14.7	33.3	10.0	7.1	100
1960	8.1	10.4	48.1	18.7	14.7	100
1965	5.5	10.3	40.8	13.2	30.2	100
1970	5.0	5.7	35.6	18.3	35.4	100
1975	5.6	3.5	34.4	19.9	36.6	100
1980	4.6	2.0	27.3	22.6	43.5	100
1984	5.5	2.4	25.8	24.0	42.3	100

Source: Statisztikai Evkönyv.

making. This also meant a reduced management role at firm level and the possibility of using guidance instruments like the new prices system effectively.

As Table 3.3 suggests, the trend towards concentration in industry was not limited to the pre-1968 period alone. Subsequently, indeed until the recent reforms of the 1980s, the temptation to amalgamate enterprises was to remain constant. Industrial co-operatives, which generally perform better, were also affected. Láki (1982) has shown not only that there was frequent recourse to combining enterprises but also that it was not necessarily done for purely economic reasons. Indeed, that kind of attitude was typical of central planners, who naturally tend to restructure the productive apparatus when they are faced with unexpected problems or when the alternative mechanism (indirect guidance) fails to produce the desired result of a regular flow of production and supplies.

As we shall see, the behaviour of the authorities was to help limit the impact of indirect regulation when the NEM was put into operation. This was the result of a prior reduction of the sphere of indirect regulation by the maintenance of an oligopolitical structure and either partial recentralization or the temporary suspension of the NEM.

One of the explanations for such behaviour is provided by the aims of planners at the time. Although there was stress on the need to rebalance growth by developing in particular those branches producing consumer goods and consequently by reducing accumulation, the country's energy needs and the development within Comecon of a programme for industry in the chemical sector made serious inroads into resources allocated to the aim of achieving self-sufficiency. The policy also had adverse effects on the development of more highly skilled mechanical engineering. Despite its declared aims, and in particular the rejection of the import substitution policy, the reform of the objectives of political economy was never more than partially achieved. It was inconsistent, and on balance a failure (Berend and Ránki, 1985).

It is obvious that economic thinking played a major part during the period in question, with regard to both the observations and the proposals put forward by professionals.

As has been pointed out in a number of studies, especially those of Szamuely (1982, 1984, 1986) it is paradoxical that although prior to 1956 the planned Hungarian economy was heading for a resounding crash, the country's economists had already provided a severe diagnosis of it and had analysed the causes of its principal dysfunctions. There were some naive solutions put forward, when we consider the ground since covered by the reformers. At the time Kornai[1] published the first systematic analysis of the failure of administrative planning, attributing it to the hyper-centralized control system and the over-concentration of the apparatus of production rather than to the non-economic factors ('subjective' factors, 'sabotage' and the like) that had hitherto been the usual explanation.

After 1956, the path taken by economic thought was less certain. It gradually moved away from analysis in terms of organizational efficiency, assuming the superiority of administrative management, towards a study conducted in terms of the mechanisms of encouragement such as the role of economic stimuli and profit. At the time, of course, expressions like 'profit' and 'market socialism' were unacceptable and could not be used explicitly, and those who talked of such concepts were often attacked. It is, however, interesting to note the conceptual shift in the thinking of Marxist theoreticians like Péter (1956), who is now seen as the pioneer of the decentralized mechanism at the theoretical level. Another point that needs stressing is that economic thinking of this kind and its lasting effects – such as the separation of the profession from orthodox dogma – took place in Hungary long before the Libermann debate and that from the point of view of political economy its consequences were far more important and permanent.

Planning theory was also enriched by other contributions of a more technical nature, in two important fields in particular. The first of these was planning methodology. Research in mathematical economics led to the construction of a two-tier planning model based on the exchange of information between the centre and decentralized units. In this model, the breaking down of the plan was no longer a consequence of the procedure of splitting up macro-economic objectives carried by the centre, but was rather seen as following an iterative process (Kornai and Liptak, 1965).

Since it introduces several levels of decision-making, their model explicitly raises the problem of decentralization. Making use of the breakdown of the overall planning programme into sub-programmes corresponding to the activities of the various branches introduces an economic as well as a purely technical problem. The iterative process between centre and branches has to make it possible to return to the original programme once prices have been equalized.

In outline, the two-level model of planning can be described as follows. The centre first decides how production objectives are to be allocated and how quantitative limits are to be ascribed to the various sectors. Bearing in mind the indications and constraints determined by the centre, branches are then obliged to decide on their own sub-programmes and provide the centre with information in the form of imaginary prices, indicating what modifications they would like to see in the plans for allocating production and the production plans themselves. The centre then amends the programme and sends instructions to the branches.

The second area of investigation was the analysis of price models. Here, they established a link between the Marxist theory of reproduction and growth and modern mathematical economics as developed by linear algebra in order to use the latter as an instrument of analysis and forecasting and a means of planning and controlling a planned economy (Brody, 1970). An interesting contribution to the investigation was the construction of a multi-channel price model regularly used by planners when the NEM was introduced.

The combination of these various factors – agricultural reform, new analyses of the causes of dysfunction, the persistence of certain problems, the desire to change the rate of growth and the priorities of the plan, and the search by the leadership for practical solutions – had a two-fold effect. There was a perception that successive and piecemeal reforms to the system of management were in the end ineffective, and a conviction that only an overall reform could bring in a new type of growth and establish on a lasting basis new decentralized guidance mechanisms that would make it possible both to achieve a more efficient management of resources and to induce units of production to increase their productivity.

During the three years leading up to the introduction of the NEM there was wide-ranging discussion, under the auspices of the central committee of the Hungarian Socialist Workers' Party, involving political leaders, representatives of the ministries, heads of enterprises, trades unionists and economists. They were to provide the decision-makers with new ideas and lead to the adoption of the principle of reforms and subsequently to the introduction of the NEM on 1 January 1968.

Adopting and implementing an overall programme

Before the project was approved, there was a great deal of discussion of the first proposals put forward by the leadership, where there had been evidence of apparently contradictory opinions and ideas.[2] These ranged from advocating keeping the status quo to resorting quite simply to the Yugoslav model of self-management, as though by premonition. Certain proposals even went as far as recommending adopting the level of world prices at the domestic level to ensure a more effective allocation of limited resources.[3] Despite the wide range of opinions voiced, however, the field for extending the scope of the reforms was limited by several constraints, even though they were, on the whole, accepted.

As at different periods in other socialist countries, adopting overall reforms raises the question of the need for reform and the ability of the leadership to carry it out (Brus, 1986). In other words, the problem is reconciling technical and political imperatives: how can instruments of guidance and economic mechanisms be modified without diminishing the political prerogatives of the centre? It is present in the idea of planning in a socialist system. Technically, such planning is a medium-term projection of logical choices making it possible to achieve objectives harmoniously. On the other hand, it is the *modus operandi* of the bureaucracy and enables it to exert its control over economic activities at the various echelons of the hierarchy. To some extent, reforming the planning system means trying to resolve that dichotomy and reducing control at the expense of the technical function.

Despite such limitations, a number of factors meant that agreement about the projected reforms was reached without too much difficulty. Other socialist countries had adopted the same solution of reforms of a similar nature. Given the current high level of concentration and centralization, there were relatively few competing groups (top civil servants, managers and the like) with workers being excluded. This meant that contrary to what had happened in other countries, notably Poland,[4] the redistribution of powers or certain functions amongst the groups involved was effected fairly easily. In view of the rather blurred distinction between economic function and bureaucratic control within the planning sphere, however, the absence of clear-cut distinctions was to be the cause of future demarcation disputes.

1. The new instruments of indirect control

The main objectives of the reforms were: to provide a more rational allocation of capital to branches, chiefly in order to develop the most productive of them; to enable Hungary to share in the international division of labour; to change the seller's market structure (the result of sectorial imbalance) and make it capable of taking changes in demand into account; and to increase the productivity of the factors of production, particularly by linking growth in personal and enterprise income to economic results.

A number of measures were introduced to achieve these results. Decision-making was decentralized and the part played in it by enterprises was increased. Under the NEM the old planning system based on quantitative indexes and instructions to subordinate authorities was discontinued. Enterprises now arranged their own inputs and were responsible for using the market to sell their products. The old branch ministries were formally abolished, with the few remaining simply acting as advisory bodies to enterprises, particularly with regard to investment projects. Although they no longer issued orders, they continued to appoint and dismiss the main heads of enterprises and to award subsidies, thus maintaining considerable powers of persuasion as far as enterprise management was concerned.

Alongside these developments, the functional ministries (Finance, the National Bank, the Planning Office, Foreign Trade) assumed an important role as vehicles of macro-economic regulation. This also made political economy more independent of planning. Annual plans were now the immediate controlling factors, with the five-year plan playing a more strategic role. Economic policy thus assumed greater importance as a means of adaptation.

At the micro-economic level, inducement was achieved by means of indirect regulation, including financial, wages and foreign trade regulators and a prices policy.

They were means of indirectly controlling economic activity and provided norms for combining state preferences and the results of enterprises and for allocating surpluses between the two areas. Within the enterprise itself, any surplus was divided between wages and investment funds, which enabled the state to regulate the mass and rate of wages and tax profits to control allocation to the various levels of economic activity and to combine its preferences (particularly in the field of social policy) with micro-economic efficiency. This meant that the centre could modify the various capital tax rates according to current circumstances and regulate the flow of income of enterprises.

The keystone of the reforms was the price system. Without it, a logical pattern of decision-making at enterprise level or a way of regulating prices and profits would be impossible to imagine. The guiding principle adopted was that of the so-called multi-channel producer price system. In such a system, prices must simultaneously reflect the proportion of capital and labour expenditure in the costs of production. In addition, profits provided a proportionate remuneration for the factors of production used.

Under the NEM, prices also had to fulfil a three-fold function, since they were expected to reflect state preferences, the costs of production and the level of demand. In concrete terms, this requirement could only be met by the introduction of a system in which prices were allowed to fluctuate within certain limits. Several categories of prices were therefore established: fixed, free, and those allowed to vary between fixed minima and maxima.

There were valid reasons for such controls. In the first place, there was a determination to keep inflation down and to avoid any mishaps that might lead to it. Second, they were to ensure that the objectives of the incomes policy were achieved. Under the NEM, certain areas were still under direct state control. As the incomes policy was still determined centrally, the prices of current consumer goods were also maintained administratively, and considerable controls of industrial products were also retained. A further function of the reforms was to rationalize the price system, more specifically by unifying producer and consumer price levels. In an administrative system, the authorities have discretionary powers and can use subsidy policies to break the link between producer and consumer prices where State preferences call for it. This leads to an unclear and heterogeneous taxation system. The system in force in Hungary found room for over 2,000 different rates, which were reduced to a few dozen after 1968.

It can be seen how difficult it was to introduce a rational price system. Numerous exceptions were retained, and during the decade the State did not hesitate to resort to direct intervention. This did not, however, wipe out inflationary phenomena.

Opening up the economy to foreign markets was both an aim and a necessity. The planners sought to benefit from the advantages of international trade and specialization. Since Hungary had few raw materials of its own, it was in fact obliged to specialize. By introducing commercial exchange rates, the planners attempted to increase the average value in forints of the inputs needed to obtain a unit of foreign currency from exports, with regard both to countries with convertible currencies and to those in the rouble zone.

2. The institutional dimension of the reforms

Economic reform was seen as a modification of the management system in an unchanged social and political framework. This meants that right from the start there were both internal and external limits as to how far it could go, and it was torn between two structures that seem difficult to reconcile in a single homogeneous system.

The aim of reforming the management system was to develop a horizontal pattern of relationships between units of production, the task of which was to maximize output and minimize costs and the use of inputs. In such circumstances, the horizontal links were the means of achieving those aims, particularly by getting rid of the vertical authorities that functioned as so many screens between units of production.

The new horizontal structure was developed within a vertical social and economic structure, where power was based on a hierarchical system within which subordinate and intermediate authorities were subject to instructions from the centre. In concrete terms, social and economic planning institutions were a reflection of the structure of political power, namely a single-centred hierarchical party.

In the centralized model the branch ministries were a sectorial division of the economy, with the responsibility of expressing in quantitative terms (in the form of indexes) the objectives to be achieved at the level of each branch. To this end, they allocated the means of production and inputs and directed the activities of enterprises by means of detailed instructions. The latter were seen as natural extensions of the ministries rather than as autonomous productive units. In this scheme of things, each ministry developed its own rationale with regard to other ministries and the State with, as its aim, a quantitative increase in both the volume of its production and its productive capacity.

Although the number and importance of the ministries were reduced, the political structure remained unchanged and was to prove very effective in reactivating the old forms of organization. The persistence of centralizing structures is explained by the prime objective of the reforms as described by those introducing them, namely ensuring macro-economic choices at the level of the plan and having recourse to the market only in the case of micro-economic decisions. It was made quite clear that it was still the task of the plan to establish macro-economic choices and that enterprises were to fit into the new structure.

In addition, however, those authorities inevitably brought into being by the old system showed a certain reluctance to disappear. A certain kind of bureaucratic mechanism facilitated and encouraged by the vertical structure of the pre-reform political system could not of course be expected to fade away overnight.

A further point arises from Hungary's position in Comecon. It was not easy to set up a system of market socialism that could co-exist with the economic relationships pertaining within that organization, which functioned on the basis of bilateral trade between administered economies. The 1968 reforms, however, coincided with a more general reform movement within the socialist countries and the assumption was that this wider trend towards decentralization would make it possible to co-ordinate planning on another basis. Yet only Hungary turned towards a different system, and the other countries either reformed their management systems without any attempt to decentralize decison-making (e.g. the GDR) or saw their attempts to do so brutally halted (Czechoslovakia).

In such a situation, Hungary was rather out of step with the other socialist countries. In 1968, economic necessities and political reasons largely, albeit briefly, coincided to further economic reform, the aim of which was to replace the vertical relationships produced by the old system with new functional ones. The system of vertical relationships was to be suppressed and, at the same time, functional institutions were to be strengthened to enable them to carry out their task fully, in particular by means of the introduction of a series of indirect regulators.

The branch ministries lost their former tasks, particularly that of providing subordinate authorities with detailed instructions and allocating resources. The jobs they kept were much reduced, and they now acted more as an advisory body for enterprises. One of the functions they did keep, however, was not unimportant, as will be seen. They continued to appoint and pay the three main directors (managing, financial and technical) of enterprises.

A number of central bodies now had a more important role. These were the National Planning Office, the National Bank, the Ministry of Finance, the National Prices and Materials Office, the Ministry of Foreign Trade, and the Ministry of Labour.

Ministries no longer acted as a filter, which meant that horizontal relationships between enterprises and vertical ones between them and the centre were now possible.

Clearly, this process of readjusting institutional structures was carried out through a power shift. Powers originally belonging to some of the civil servants in the branch ministries were handed over either to the functional ministries or to enterprises. It was at the institutional level – the most important – that the first contradictions in the new management system were to appear.

The recentralizing process: the ministries strike back

Reform was more the result of the need for a dynamic adaptation of the apparatus of production than a voluntary choice. In such a situation, the ministries about to be abolished instinctively produced their own antibodies in an attempt to preserve their own existence, retain a few of their prerogatives and regain some of their former powers. The reform passed through various cycles of alternating progress and hold-ups in the political, economic and even cultural fields. The following phases can be distinguished.

The period from 1964 to 1968 was one of preparation. Following a resolution passed by the central committee of the Hungarian Socialist Workers' Party, *ad hoc* committees of specialists in different disciplines met to discuss ways and means of reform and the areas appropriate for it.[5] This was an important time, as setting up the commissions and the consequent discussions produced a ferment of ideas. These bodies were stages along the way and forums producing very different ideas, ranging from those of the supporters of the status quo and centralization to those of the partisans of self-management urging a major upheaval in the economic and social structure arising from the central planning model. One of the real achievements of the political leadership was the way in which it managed to bring together and highlight the radically differing opinions expressed in the commis-

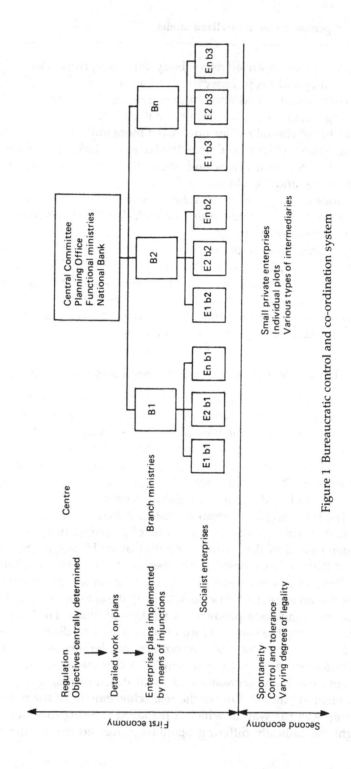

Figure 1 Bureaucratic control and co-ordination system

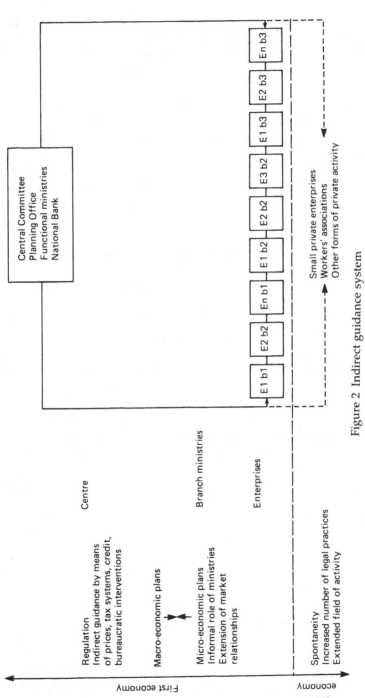

Figure 2 Indirect guidance system

sions, thus creating an opportunity for dialogue that won it the support of a large part of the intelligentsia.

Between 1968 and 1970, there was a great deal of anti-reform discussion within the party. It was fed by heavy industry, which was not affected by the NEM. The unions were also opposed to any extension of the NEM, the implementation of which had produced certain repercussions, and in particular the policy of over-investment by enterprises was sufficient to produce obstructive measures.

November 1972 saw the victory of those opposed to the reforms, and recentralization measures were introduced. This trend continued from 1972 to 1975. A measure to put the fifty leading enterprises of the country under direct surveillance was passed by the central committee and implemented. Officially, it was a matter of observing how they worked in concrete terms, but in reality there was direct interference in the way they were run. Other areas, such as investment, were also affected. It was during this period that the branch ministries regained their power by opposing the functional ministries, which lost some of theirs.

There was a period of decentralization from 1975 to 1978, with the market playing a much greater part. In 1976, the regulators were modified. Paradoxically, they seemed to increase the power of the central organs, but in fact introduced greater flexibility into centre/enterprises relationships. The new trend towards decentralization did not, however, put an end to the equivocal situation in which there was a desire to make enterprises more efficient and at the same time to maintain institutions cramping growth in their activities.

Between 1979 and 1982 important reforms were put into operation (see Chapter 7). At the institutional level, the branch ministries were finally abolished, certain industrial trusts began to be broken up, the activities of the 'second economy' were legalized and the sphere of the private sector was extended. In the field of indirect regulation, the price system was reactivated, fixing them at the level of world prices.

In the reform project, the powers of the sectorial ministries were, to say the least, greatly reduced, as it was intended that the old system of mediation between meso-economic bodies should be replaced by a binary relationship between the centre and enterprises by means of indirect regulation. However, there was still a considerable gap between a concept of reform and the more complex reality of the decentralized model shaped by many factors such as the productive structure and the earlier form of regulation. The persistence of the productive and institutional structure produced by a combination of the centralized model and the way things were developing was to play a large part in restoring the functions of the intermediate authorities, which had been greatly reduced in 1968.

As soon as indirect regulation was introduced, the reformers built in a number of checks to enable them to verify more easily how the new mechanism was working. The bases of social policy and full employment also had to be maintained and the distribution of incomes scrutinized. In addition, certain of the functions of the branch ministries were maintained to enable the State to keep an eye on enterprises more easily. It cannot be gainsaid that measures of this kind immediately provided ways of intervening directly in economic activity.

The other main factors accounting for the fact that one or two of the more important prerogatives of the branch ministries were retained were both political and international. The balance between reforming and conservative elements was unstable, and reorganizing the whole of the State bureaucracy would have involved certain risks the leadership was not prepared to take. In addition, as the institutional structure was similar in the various Comecon countries, the complete disappearance of the ministries would have changed bilateral relations between them. The functions they relinquished were divided between the functional ministries and enterprises.

While the functional ministries were being restructured, however, the branch ministries reorganized themselves and gradually built up their old power again, even though their staffing and funding were reduced and they were no longer the channel through which funds passed between the centre and enterprises.

It was matters of economic policy that gave them the chance to regain certain of their former functions, and in addition to the prerogatives they still enjoyed in the new institutional framework (such as appointing and dismissing the heads of enterprises) they still had an advisory role to play with regard to enterprises and central bodies. Their advice was occasionally sought, particularly during the argument about the distribution of incomes arising shortly after reforms had been implemented. They were also called in to study the problem of over-investment by enterprises.

Initially their work here was of a purely administrative nature and they were no more than links between macro- and micro-economic bodies. As the agents of the functional ministries, they had no executive power. Gradually, however, they used their old and new powers as intermediaries to re-establish their authority and control over enterprises by intervening more frequently in various areas such as investment allocation, reviewing investment projects, price increase agreements and ministry approval for the manufacture of new products. In the second half of the 1970s, and particularly during the 1976–80 five-year plan, the branch ministries became more important as informal go-betweens, systematically reviewing planning provisions, giving their opinion and taking part in bargaining aimed at influencing the heads of enterprises. The most effective kind of bargaining between the ministries and enterprises was to negotiate by imposing production targets on enterprises in exchange for the supply of materials, or by assuring them that if they manufactured a particular product the branch ministries would organize their market for them . . . and so on. Although informal, this kind of bargaining was akin to what had gone on under the old system.

This situation was the result of a complex cluster of factors not primarily explicable in terms of political pressure brought to bear by the party. What in fact happened was that a process of institutionally encouraged self-reconstruction began to take place almost of its own accord. If an attempt is made to set up a market for goods without a capital and labour market – which is what the reformers envisaged – the system can easily seize up.

Another explanatory factor has to do with the very nature of the single-party machine and its place in the economy, which becomes a particular system with many functions.[6] The Party machine has a multi-dimensional function, it is personalized, and it has an informal role. It has an economic, political and a union line; it acts informally through the branch ministries, the central bodies, bargaining and, in the sector outside the planned economy, also through the second economy; the various functions are personalized in real people who have had the same training or followed the same career pathway in the Party apparatus or the ministries.

In this kind of situation there is no single right way of implementing the main economic decisions, which arise from the participation of different economic and social organizations. A political leader, for example, sees economic decisions as the responsibility of State institutions, whereas the Planning Office sees the Party as primarily responsible for them, and so on. In reality, however, decisions are taken multi-dimensionally, most frequently by *ad hoc* organizations. There are a certain number of inter-branch sub-committees set up for specific purposes which nevertheless perpetuate themselves and try to acquire wider powers as institutions are bureaucratized.

In institutions, conflict relationships of balance and imbalance are a great burden on the mechanism receiving orders that go against the rationality sought in horizontal relationships. How rational the orders transmitted by the central bodies will be is determined by the balance of power within the political and economic caucus governing society.

The influence of the ministries became so great that it made itself felt even in functional management bodies, some of which lost some of their power, with others being absorbed by the ministries. A characteristic example – to which we shall return later – was the position of the Planning Office, which was both a functional and a branch structure.

The emergence of group interests in decentralized planning

Within centralized planning there emerged several forms of power which did not however contest the system of control in operation. One of the more paradoxical aspects of the reform movement had to do with the two-fold nature of forms of control and centres of decision-making in the decentralized model. In addition to a functionalist approach aimed at linking macro- and micro-economic bodies, there came into being centres of decision-making that, although they could not be described as alternative, were nevertheless relatively autonomous.

Parallel to the unified system of party, branch ministries and enterprises, certain micro-economic units (in particular industrial co-operatives and the large enterprises on which the range of extra-plan activities making up the second economy were centred) assumed their own right to make decisions, notably with regard to the centre. The group of industrial co-operatives was not a major factor as far as size was concerned, but from the point of view of its production and operation it could not be controlled by the meso-economic bodies. Until the 1980–2 reforms, co-operative enterprises received no credit, and when they made a loss they disappeared from the market. To use Kornai's phrase, they were directly subject to a 'hard budget constraint', whereas state enterprises were affected only by a 'soft budget constraint' (Kornai, 1980).

The membership of co-operative enterprises was often composed of highly skilled workers, led by men who before the war or during the liberation had been small-scale capitalists. They worked fully on the principle of a market economy, which meant quality products and wages higher than those paid in State firms. Very often engineers preferred to work in this sector, as they had greater opportunities to use new techniques. They were better organized and consequently produced goods more rapidly than in the State sector, where innovation took place very slowly.

The industrial co-operatives accounted for over 10% of production and employment, and their growth was more rapid than in the State sector. They numbered between 800 and 900 in Hungary and produced, for example, 20% of exports abroad. They were also more profitable, as their profit ratio was higher and profit was the only source of finance for them. The consequence was that until the 1981 reforms they were working in precarious circumstances and found it hard to accumulate and use sufficient quantities of capital goods.

The second group mentioned – large industrial enterprises and the big State farms – was managed by people often in direct contact with political power and consequently often succeeded in avoiding excessively close ties to the hierarchical system. Their high level of concentration was largely a result of their efficiency rather than merely a consequence of the process of concentration taking place in the 1950s and 1960s. They were strategically placed, particularly with regard to foreign markets, where they dominated their sectors. Their ability to innovate and the level of modernization they achieved enabled them to absorb the most advanced techniques, to pass on their effects to the domestic or Comecon markets and to win a place for themselves in trading with the West. They were also instrumental in integrating the Hungarian economy horizontally by specializing in standardized products that could be sold both at home and abroad. In both industry (Rába) and agriculture (the Babolna State farm) examples of such enterprises could be found. They were the jewels of socialist industry, and their initiative often put them outside the control of the meso-economic bodies, since they were more oriented towards a market strategy.

The characteristic feature of such quasi-international undertakings (some of them had branches in Western Europe, and Rába owned companies in the Federal Republic of Germany) was that their achievements were the result not of a monopoly position but of a market policy based on a determination to win a place in the international division of labour, a situation which put them in a better position to receive the necessary credits. Those directing them were also part of the technocratic elite whose power was mainly based on their professional competence.

Between the two groups there was the classical hierarchical division and the specific system of control implying the subjection of the directors of enterprises to the branch ministries. The *modus operandi* of the body of functionaries directing and running the apparatus of production under the old system remained in place and reproduced the same behaviour in the new.

That subjection did not, however, necessarily mean that the directors of enterprises were subordinate to the branch ministries. The undertakings in question in fact had enough influence to negotiate with branch ministries or other bodies. In reality, however, the relative autonomy they enjoyed was very much limited by the fact that they were linked to the particular career profile of their director, who had come from the branch ministries.

Typically, they had familiarized themselves with the workings and problems of a particular industry within a ministry and had subsequently been appointed to a headship of department there dealing with the industry in question. At a later stage, they were appointed to head a factory and ultimately – usually after eight to ten years at most – returned to the ministry. Information circulated with men. It was important for a factory director to be able to return to the central bureaucracy, and a member of that bureaucracy knew that one day he might be running an enterprise.

This mixture of jobs helped to modify the attitude of the director of an enterprise who had been a civil servant. His behaviour in the enterprise was quite different from that he would have as a bureaucrat. Since he had to buy plant and sell what he produced, negotiate with representatives of the Party and the unions and bargain with workers, the kind of administrative demeanour he might adopt in the ministry would be totally out of place in the enterprise. In other words, when face to face with the way the enterprise really worked, he had to act in a micro-economic context, since he perceived the real world at the level of this context and was subject to its constraints. In the ministry, on the other hand, his attitude and demeanour were of a more meso- (or even macro-) economic nature.

The head of an enterprise needs a variety of skills, and has to speak both the language of the market (in connection with the enterprise) and that of the bureaucracy. In Hungary, that very specific kind of bilingualism was a result of the incomplete nature of the reforms and a situation in which features of the old system and market elements were both present. A bad bureaucrat made a bad head of an enterprise. There was a good side to this rather schizophrenic situation however. Someone running an undertaking which was going through a difficult period on the market had the opportunity to call on the help of people he knew in the administration, just as later on, when back in his ministry, he would be able to turn to those he knew in the market. It can thus be seen that such a situation could be quite advantageous if things worked out satisfactorily.

Here we are touching on an important problem that concerns the stratification of the managerial class. Without entering into a detailed sociological analysis, we could say that the way reform was progressing was inevitably reflected in a considerable change in the behaviour of directors. Some theorists have seen the Hungarian reform as a kind of recasting of the elite with the parts played by the lower classes of society remaining the same. To a certain extent, those in positions of political power did yield up some of their authority, particularly in the economic field. In the old system, however, that authority was assumed by the central bureaucratic bodies (ministries and planning institutions). The introduction of increased economic rationality appealed of course to actors other than those running such bodies and the associated sub-systems (enterprises). It is important to note that the system was rationalized not only by reorganizing the management system, but also by the intervention of those responsible for the new rationality, namely the class of engineers and technicians whose job was to produce it by means of an optimal use of the factors of production. There was an unavoidable clash between their actions and those of the representatives of the earlier system.

There was thus a double side to the productive and institutional structures. The former combined those large-scale enterprises, the behaviour of which, given their oligopolistic position, remained the same as it had been before the reform. Other units of production were able, with the advent of the NEM, to fit in with micro-economic developments and changed their range of products and their relationships with the central authorities.

4   The instruments of indirect guidance

The planners replaced the old system of commands typical of centralized planning with a series of indirect regulators ensuring a flow of information between macro- and micro-economic bodies. The main regulators were concerned with profits, wages and foreign trade. Seen both as the key to income distribution and as ways of providing economic indicators, the planners assumed that in decentralized planning there was a homogeneous price system capable of functioning, as the reformers required, as a way of reflecting the wishes of the centre, costs and the level of demand. The price system and regulators were a rough and ready means of assessment and have been adjusted many times over the past 15 years, which reflects the latent conflict between plan and market.

The price system in the NEM

The 1968 price reform was preceded by an important theoretical debate and led to the introduction of a so-called producer price model combining capital and labour expenditure and a proportional profit. In it, the notion of profit retained a *normative* aspect. Prices did not only reflect an equilibrium and scarcity situation, but were still partly administered according to the preferences expressed by the centre.

Within the framework of centralized planning, prices are normative in nature and have a parametric function. They are centrally administered and more akin to indexes than an expression in monetary terms of some expenditure or cost, and are not autonomous forces deciding production but are manipulated by the central authorities in pursuit of their objectives. In fact, price fixation reflects the interests of the planned economy as expressed in production plans. As the productive system becomes more complex as socialist accumulation progresses, however, certain negative effects become obvious and highlight, amongst other things, the inconsistencies of the price system. Thus, in pre-1968 Hungary, the old planning model no longer afforded a uniform measure of value applicable to the whole economy and, as has been shown (Horchler, 1974: 129), the major categories (industrial, wholesale, consumer, agricultural and foreign trade prices) evolved independently of and frequently hindered each other, and were more a consequence of political exigencies than of the economic environment.

This resulted in a distortion of the price system in relation to values and hence the inclusion of the difference in the budget by means of State subsidies. Divergences were allowed for by the planning principle behind such rigid compartmentalization, but were also justified by economic and social imperatives. The former arose from the need for industrialization and meant that planners had to control the formation of prices at all levels, in particular by avoiding the cumulative effects of price rises. The latter meant keeping the prices of public or private consumer goods relatively low to keep them in line with incomes as distributed, which were also centrally planned.

Although such a procedure had the advantage of keeping prices at the level desired by the centre, it also had the drawback of entailing adjustment at the macro-economic level if equilibrium was to be achieved during periods of excessive distortion.

The price system implemented in the late 1950s was based on cost prices. Production expenditure – i.e. capital and wages costs – were recorded, but net income was recovered by the State at the level of consumer prices by means of a turnover tax. The price system was kept until the 1959 reforms, when one based on 'value' was introduced.

The justification for a price system based on the notion of cost price was that the State fixes prices, which do not govern production but do, to a certain extent, control demand. In it, the 'law of value' was held in check by decisions from the centre. By setting up a two-tier price level – that is, by deliberately maintaining a gap between producer and consumer prices – the State imposed a completely controlled structure of supply, which made it possible both to have stable prices and to engage in long-term planning. A further argument for such a system was that marketed consumer goods represented only a small proportion (about a quarter) of production and that demand therefore came almost entirely from the planned sector. In such circumstances, adjusting supply and demand took place in advance. The system also had the further advantage that within the planned sector prices were neutral in themselves and akin to accounting systems, making it possible to evaluate the extent to which planning aims had been achieved and to compare the performance of enterprises within the same branch.

It had its drawbacks, however, even though it provided great price stability and enabled the planner to achieve long-term projections.

Maintaining a gap between values and prices therefore presupposes that there will be no change in the conditions of production (technical progress, productivity and so on) which might affect planning projections. Such practices, which generalized lower costs of raw materials and provided subsidies for industrial branches, made it all the harder to see how the system really worked and meant that any effective economic calculation was increasingly a hit-or-miss affair.

The same was true of cost price. Establishing it was a very arbitrary process, as it was not based on an assessment of expenditure at enterprise level but fixed centrally by the planning bodies on the basis of two types of calculation, either the average expenditure of a branch or the cost price of the most viable enterprise. Despite this rigidity, however, this price model sometimes made it possible to play a part in the allocation of resources, particularly in bargaining between the central authorities and the heads of enterprises.

In 1959 there was a general reform of production prices, the aims of which were to recoup the cost of socially necessary work and to stimulate technological development. It meant that producer and consumer prices could now be brought to more or less the same level, even though the feature of centrally determined prices was maintained. The new system did not, however, adequately reflect either changes in value in the relationship between domestic and foreign prices or differences in the conditions for technical progress. Foreign and domestic prices were separate from each other, and the difference was made up by a system of foreign trade multipliers. Prices did not reflect the continuous changes in relationships of value. The introduction of a new system was hampered both by the considerable delay in bringing about a change in official prices and the need to recalculate planned prices and to establish correct relationships.

Nevertheless, there was a more positive side to the price system within the framework of administrative planning, particularly if it is considered from the point of view of what was expected of it. Its prime function was to be an accounting device, its second to provide criteria for decisions about production. What made its inadequacy clear, however, was that it afforded no satisfactory way of overcoming the problems of managing fixed capital. All this was reflected in the 1959 and 1964 reforms, in particular in the gradual introduction of the idea of scarcity.

Price models

During the 1960s the debate on prices took place in two stages. In the first, the debate's main concern was to use a conceptual apparatus based on matrix algebra to find an appropriate price model that could be used in current planning to make up for the deficiencies of the old system still in use. The arguments for and against 'value'-type and producer-type prices were aimed at creating a climate of opinion in favour of a concrete method of establishing prices that would make it possible to avoid dismembering a system constantly reflecting proportional values. In the second stage it went beyond merely creating models to a reflection on the new form of regulation to replace that based on central planning. The object of all these theoretical investigations was to work out a system that would perform three tasks – analysis, calculating normative change(s) in both the level and the relative structure of the price system, and forecasting its future development (Laurencin, 1976: 264).

Another aspect of the debate was also important, however, since it marked a shift from a dogmatic approach based on Marxian economics to a pragmatic or praxis-based one, making use of the ideas of contemporary economic science. Its theoretical interest lay in its attempt to combine the analyses and ideas of Marx (social reproduction, value category, quantities of labour, and so on) with the logical structure of Leontief's model. Theoretical reference to the latter can be justified by stressing its relative neutrality with regard to both theory and ideology, a feature absent from any use of linear programming:

> From a theoretical point of view, it is less suspect than the programming model inevitably is. It puts into operation interdependence relationships which are free only in the choice of the standard of measurement. It offers a single and non-extreme solution, since technological alternatives and possible substitutions are not covered by it. Since it can be seen as a generalization both of the equations in Marx's *Capital* and the 'logical' structure of Leontief's model, its theoretical relevance can be taken for granted. (Laurencin, 1976: 225)

As the writer in question correctly points out, the latter model still raises the most crucial theoretical questions, particularly that of the measurement of value. That explains why the planners had already used these models of calculation even before the debates of the 1960s. The 1959 price reform was already a result of calculations based on inverting the matrices in the input–output table for 1957, which immediately showed how greatly prices were distorted.

Any price reform, even a partial one, implies a modification of all relative prices. Input–output tables make it possible to engage in such calculations, particularly those used to work out the effects of price changes in one sector on the whole structure of prices and costs in the economy. A major problem arises when price changes brought about by calculations using different price systems are being compared with real prices. In particular, using such a method means that all the price changes involved have to be calculated simultaneously, which necessitates reconstructing the weightings in the input–output tables. In addition, since it is not possible to take into account developments and changes in several thousand prices, the calculations were based on average prices in the various branches, which meant that a certain form of aggregation was necessary. Despite the simplification this entailed, however, the method made it possible to produce fruitful comparisons of the various price systems. In the course of the 1959 modification, it was noted that the prices of manufactured goods had been widely over-valued and agricultural prices systematically under-valued.

1. The features of the various price models

As the debate opened, the theoreticians had very concrete concerns. The main point of discussion was the way in which net income (profit) is determined and how it can be ascribed to the factors of production combining to create productive activity.

1 *Prices based on value.* Here, profit in each of the branches of the economy is proportional to wage costs. This particular system, a reflection of Marx's labour theory of value, was initiated by the Soviet economist Strumilin and long used as a point of reference in price planning in socialist economies. It involves adding to the costs of production a net income proportional to the expenditure on wages they have entailed. In practice, however, as we have seen, there are many exceptions to the rule in systems of prices based on value.

2 *Prices based on average costs or average value.* In a system of this type, profit is proportional to 'prime costs' (material costs and wages). To

calculate the appropriate selling price, there is added to the *monetary cost price* of each product a 'net income' obtained by multiplying it by a certain 'profitability norm'. This system too developed in socialist planning. It does, however, have a certain arbitrary quality in so far as the cost price, or prime cost, is not necessarily the real cost but is in fact often the average cost price estimated at the level of a branch or a *limit* cost price, such as the cost price of an enterprise in the branch functioning at the highest or lowest cost in terms of planning decisions. Its chief virtue, however, is the great ease with which it can be put into operation, since at any given time the real or normalized cost price of production can be calculated on the basis of real money expenditure without any real need to reflect on the value of the productive funds.

3 *Prices based on 'producer' prices.* In this case, net income is allocated to branches and products in proportion to the fixed and circulating capital utilized in production. The profit level in each sector becomes proportional to the stock of capital in it. There is nothing fortuitous about the shift occurring between this and the first of the systems described here. Where prices were based on value, the connection between the two was wrongly broken, with the result that capital expenditure and what it produced were both neglected. The 'producer-prices' systems *did* take capital expenditure into account, although it meant that the profit rate had to be defined in advance. Despite all this, it was not towards a 'pure' system of producer prices that things were moving, but simply towards one in which capital expenditure and wage costs were taken into account.

4 *'Two-channel' prices.* Here, the profit of each sector is divided into two. In each branch, part of the profit is proportional to the stock of capital and the rest to wage costs. There is both an interest rate on capital and a mark-up on wages. This is a compromise between the system of prices based on value and that involving producer prices. In theory, it is based on the fact that all the costs associated with expenditure on labour (direct and indirect, including training costs and the like) are taken into account. In practice, it was applied when capital and labour (5% and 35% respectively) were being taxed. In neither case, however, did it provide an ideal way of sharing out profits between capital and labour.

5 *Income-type prices.* This is a system in which wage costs are not included in a definition of costs, and the added value in each sector becomes a multiple of the stock of capital. Relative prices are determined solely on the basis of material inputs and the structure

of capital in the economy, and the model follows from the planning procedure based on linear programming.

6 *Prices based on the world market* The proponents of this system advocated fixing domestic prices, even those for domestic consumption, on the basis of world prices. The reason for this was the important part played by trade in the Hungarian economy. It did, however, raise certain problems. One of these was the problem of knowing exactly what world prices were, but the chief one was that introducing such a system would mean redirecting the whole structure of national production towards profit-making sections. It would also entail incorporating international price movements, a situation in which the country had found itself and still found itself periodically when it adjusted prices radically as a result of bouts of world inflation impinging on the Hungarian economy. It must however be stressed that if national conditions of production are taken as the major reference base for a price system, they must not be allowed to diverge to any great extent from international norms for, say, production levels and trends of relative prices, which would mean opening up the Hungarian economy if this solution were adopted. Despite vigorous opposition, it was ultimately adopted and almost universally applied during the reforms of 1980–1 (see Chapter 7).

Calculations were in fact carried out using models 1, 2 3 and 4, which, as a result of their common origin, incorporate the same hypotheses and limits as those in the input–output analysis they are based on, namely constant and average production weightings reflecting a certain level of technology, etc. (see Ganczer, 1966 and Bródy, 1970).

2. Price distortion

The economists and mathematicians involved in these debates did not merely operate a certain number of formal mathematical structures, but also worked out afresh all the price indexes in the various systems, thus making it possible to compare the differences between them. In order to do this they had to make certain modifications to the input–output tables and provide extra data. It was particularly important to include both foreign trade and amortization as productive activities in the technical weightings. Exports and imports had to be expressed in convertible forints and the value of fixed and circulating capital calculated.[1] This meant that there were

Table 4.1. *Price indices of the major sectors of the economy in various price systems*

Sector	At actual prices	At value-type prices	At averaged value-type prices	At producer-type prices	
				Var. a	Var. b
Industry	100	85.90	95.43	84.46	84.49
Construction	100	107.65	107.10	99.00	102.00
Agriculture	100	146.02	125.28	139.83	141.91
Transport and communications	100	115.34	110.98	144.92	135.28
Home trade	100	97.50	82.13	109.97	105.69
Foreign trade	100	95.81	107.09	123.46	114.28
Other productive activities	100	83.99	70.09	60.69	68.44

Source: Ganczer, 1966: 62.

nine headings in the shortest form of the table of economic activities, namely those shown in Table 4.1 above, plus exports–imports and reconstruction (amortization), the latter two being in fact imaginary productive sectors for which no data are available.

Their chief findings for 1961, arrived at with reference to tables for incoming and outgoing products, can be expressed as in Table 4.1. A comparison of the various price systems calculated on initial prices shows that the greatest differences are between value-based and producer-type prices. In certain cases, there is a wide range between the two systems in relation to the reference model. At the opposite end of the spectrum, the price system diverging least from the reference system (excluding 'other productive activities') is the own-costs system.

It can be seen that with the existing price system, net income was, generally speaking, proportionally greater (in industry as a whole) than capital expenditure or expenditure on wages. On the other hand, if net income (s in Marx's formula, $c + v + s$, it should be remembered) were distributed to branches in proportion to wages, as it was to capital expenditure, the amount of it achieved in industry would be much lower than in the reference system. It would tend to thrust the industrial price index and the value of industrial production downwards.

In other branches, however, it was relatively low in relation to capital or wage expenditure and immobilized capital. In the case of the building industry, for example, changing the price system showed a slight modification in the systems based on value and average value, which did not occur in the other two systems.

In agriculture, price indexes tended to rise in the various price systems by fairly large percentages (25% in the average value and 46% in the trade value systems). There are various reasons for this. In the first place, some of the prices in the sector had been fixed while the structure of the industry was still underdeveloped and it was largely State subsidized. Agricultural production was also used as an input into the other branches and a change in its value had an automatic effect on their prices. Third, there is an explanation concerning the very nature of the socialist system, which lays great emphasis on the industrialization of the economy and on industry as the vital moving force in economic development. The effect of this is to increase the value of industrial production in relation to that of other branches, and of agriculture in particular, the role and importance of which are often underestimated.

The various stages of the debate on prices can be summarized as follows. At first, discussions took place in the context of a command economy in which the volume of production and prices were both centrally decided. Within this framework, prices were more of an accounting device than a means of allocation, and an attempt was made to use Marx's idea of value in a more coherent way. The debate then moved more towards questions of value, use, utility, competitive prices and so on, compatible with market relationships in a planned framework. It is somewhat paradoxical that discussions of this kind should have induced wider reflection on the economic mechanism as a whole.

The introduction of the new price system

An overall reform of the machinery of planning was indeed the much vaster topic to which those involved addressed themselves. Once that stage was reached, the rationality of the price system was no longer a matter of its proper place within administrative planning, but rather of how it could be coherently fitted into the central plan. In such a system, prices acquire a parametric function; to a certain extent the market is manipulated and its automatic working used as a means of achieving the price trend seen as appropriate. Operating within these constraints, the price system must, in the process of regulation, meet several demands. It has to reflect the social costs of production and evaluate both the market and government preferences. To do so, it must gradually introduce producer prices, increase the proportion of net income in prices (above all by encouragement, using the profit motive) and harmonize the price structure by means of a prices policy.

1. Producer prices

The first task assigned to the new price system was that it should take production costs into account. Here, the aim was two-fold. The first objective was to apply the two-channel system and extend the principle of producer prices by taxing each of the factors involved in production. Once this had been achieved, it would mean that the second objective, the reorientation of the regulatory mechanisms to allow expenditure on socially necessary work, could be attained. The trend was therefore to use the introduction of the new price mechanism to enlarge the function of prices at enterprise level. It was not merely a case of setting up a means of directly evaluating production costs but also of providing the basis for real autonomy for enterprises.

The structure of production costs in the formation of industrial prices

1 *Direct costs*
   Direct material cost
   Wages
   Taxes on wages
   Production
2 *Production costs*
   Fixed costs
   Amortization
   Taxes on assets
   Other production costs (technical development, repairs, etc.)
3 *Profit*
4 *Taxes*
5 *Subsidies*
6 *Prices* (1 + 2 + 3 + 4 − 5)

The structure was normative and provided enterprises with a frame-work for calculating their prices. It expressed in concrete form the choice of the two-channel price system − more especially so since it took into account the real cost of the inputs enterprises used. The rules were drawn up and transmitted to enterprises by the branch ministries.

This provides a way of measuring the change in the draining off of net income, essentially by reference to the resources of an enterprise, and a way of noting the types of links that grew up between enterprises and central bodies. Turnover tax now had a function which, if not purely residual, was much more relative than it had been under the old tax system, whereas taxes on assets and increased amortization became widespread. Another new feature was that enterprises now kept a large proportion of profits. These were, however, divided amongst various funds which in turn attracted taxes, such as bonus funds (bonuses, socio-cultural expenditure, subject to progressive taxation), development funds (subject to 60% tax) and reserve funds (accounting for 10% of bonus funds).

The norm for fixing prices varied according to whether it was a case of determining free prices or those that were fixed or subject to a ceiling. With regard to fixed prices, market effects were taken into account by enterprises which were thus able to establish how their prices were made up on an annual basis. For others, information compiled by the ministries was a factor in determining how costs were to be allocated and prices calculated.

In some branches, there were substantial changes in the amortization rate (see Table 4.2); others introduced amortization. Sectors like agriculture, for example, paid no taxes on capital or land, and the state used subsidies to ensure that capital used was replaced.

The thinking behind this reorganization of the price system was based on the increasingly major role assumed by the factors of production in the productive process. The measures introduced in the areas of taxation, fixed assets and labour[2] were the minimum necessary to ensure the efficient, if not the optimal, use of those factors and to release a sufficient amount of profit at enterprise level.

There were to be one or two exceptions, however. In particular, the agricultural sector was exempted from all charges on capital and labour, which were covered by the State budget, which meant that it had to be able to restructure its margins and, in the medium term, ensure that it was self-financing. Agricultural prices were also lower than industrial prices, often by the percentage of tax that should have been paid. However, the same kind of thing also happened in

Table 4.2. *Changes in amortization rates*

| Branch | % of gross value of fixed assets | | % of production costs |
	Old rate	New rate	New rate
Heavy industry	3.9	5.2	9.0
Light industry	2.7	4.2	2.7
Food industry	2.0	4.0	3.6
Construction	5.2	7.8	2.1
Agriculture and forestry	3.0	4.1	8.0
Transport and communication	3.1	4.4	1.7
Total for the economy	4.3	5.0	5.0

Source: Csikós-Nagy, 1971: 142; and Hare, 1976: 372.

industry in sectors where considerable immobilization of capital and/or a large labour force were required, or where, because of international competition, capital and labour taxes would push up costs and hence prices, leading perhaps to a situation in which imports might replace domestic products.

Such exceptions, which tended to become the rule, were reflected in increased budget expenditure. They also had some undesired side effects. Instead of the hoped for unified and homogeneous price system which would provide a means of assessing the real costs of production, these anomalies led either to watertight divisions between sectors or to the opposite situation, in which prices in some sectors were brought into line with those in others where they were subsidized.

Although dysfunctions of this kind persisted, there were profound changes in the structure of costs, which was now more directly based on those at branch level. It is true that it was still not homogeneous and still contained certain disparities attributable, it must be admitted, to the varying degrees to which different sectors had adopted capitalistic practices. The object of the exercise – the inclusion of 'socially necessary inputs' – was, however, more nearly achieved and it was possible to define both how profit was formed and the part it played in the new mechanism.

2. The reform of consumer prices

We have seen that in the old system producer and consumer prices were kept rigidly separate, a decision made for many reasons. The first was the belief that prices could be manipulated in isolation from value and that it was therefore possible to redistribute and adjust without taking market factors into consideration. There is also the fact that in the planners' view only a small proportion (about a quarter) of production was destined for household consumption. In addition, there was fiscal pressure from the State, which imposed taxation at enterprise level. The final reason is the link between the level of retail prices and that of distributed incomes. The hybrid nature of the consumer price system was attributable to all these factors (and constraints). The lack of any connection between producer and consumer prices in particular was responsible for the growth of a two-tier price system, and the chief task of the reformers was to unify the system by reducing the gap between the tiers.

The new system was expected to produce a degree of homogeneity and, more particularly, to link price levels, to make them move in the same direction at the same rate, and finally to combine them in a single-level system. However, the above-mentioned constraints were factors operating against this aim. A political decision was the dominant factor in maintaining a consumer price structure in harmony with income distribution.

There followed a divergence, or a deliberately maintained distance, between consumer prices and those of the inputs needed to produce goods for either private or public consumption by households. The need for such inputs, which arose from the government's economic policy, entailed in its turn maintaining and even extending the policy of subsidies.

The structure of consumer prices can be represented schematically as follows:

Consumer prices = industrial wholesale prices, plus wholesale trading margin, plus retail trading margin, plus turnover tax, minus subsidies.

3. The mixed-price system

The basic principles of the reform were a reaffirmation of the prime importance of economic development based on rational economic planning and the need to refer to market mechanisms to

Table 4.3. *Types of producer prices relating to domestically produced raw materials and typical intermediary products*

Group of products	Fixed	Maximum prices	Prices moving between official limits	Free prices
	% of production affected			
Sources of energy	75	10	—	15
Other minerals and raw materials for heavy industry	10	25	—	65
Metallurgical products	—	85	5	10
Textile thread	—	75	—	25
Leather	—	60	—	40
Building materials made from silicates	—	40	—	60
Wood and paper materials	10	30	—	60
Total	30	40	2	28

Source: Csikós-Nagy, 1971: 142.

achieve harmonious development. The structural constraints, which were largely the result of the structure of economic planning, did not disappear as soon as the NEM was introduced. The heterogeneous nature of the economy was reflected, particularly in the area we are concerned with here, in the measures adopted to build bridges between the rather inefficient sectors mentioned above and those where productivity was higher and to create a boundary between producer and consumer prices. In short, there was no chance of homogeneous prices if the productive sphere itself had no unity and, as Hungarian writers on the topic have frequently stressed, it was difficult to ignore the constraints and move immediately, with no transitional period, from one type of control to another.

Indeed, abandoning administrative constraints at such a time would inevitably have led to a price explosion, with newly autonomous enterprises triggering off an inflationary process that would have called the whole incomes policy into question. That risk was avoided by a compromise, that of mixed prices, a system including prices that

Table 4.4. *Types of prices in the processing industries*

Group of finished products	Fixed	Maximum	Prices moving between official limits	Free prices
		prices		
	% of production affected			
Chemical products	10	35	5	55
Engineering products	—	30	5	65
Textiles and clothing	—	10	—	90
Finished wood and paper	—	—	—	100
Building structures	—	—	—	100
Food products	5	5	5	85
Total	3	16	3	78

Source: Csikós-Nagy, 1971: 149.

were fixed, free, or subject to an upper and lower limit or a ceiling. Prices of this type were applied to various products, including some within the same branch. The reformers expected the new system to introduce greater flexibility, whilst at the same time making it still possible for the centre to control the movement of prices. The primary task was therefore to include both administered and free prices determined by market forces in a single system.

A functional ministry, the Prices and Materials Office, was responsible for determining categories and types of products, as a result of the constraints discussed above. The pattern shown in Table 4.3 for basic and intermediate industries was later to change considerably.

Except in the case of certain goods, 70% of prices were either fixed or subject to a ceiling. It must be stressed that at this level of the production process price stability made it possible to keep prices down and thus avoid a chain reaction. The situation in the transformation industries however was quite different, with the prices of a large number of products being established freely, as is shown in Table 4.4.

These figures should not, however, be allowed to hide a certain ambiguity. At prior stages in the production process, the products from which they emerged were largely subject to price controls or fixing (70%), and later the corresponding consumer prices were also to

Table 4.5. *Types of prices of agricultural products purchased by the State agencies (in % of total production)*

Production branches	Fixed prices	Prices moving between official limits		Free prices	Total
		closely	loosely		
		regulated			
Plant production	44	21	20	15	100
Animal husbandry	73	—	21	6	100
Agriculture, average	60	10	20	10	100

Source: Csikós-Nagy, 1971: 150.

a great extent either fixed or subject to a ceiling. This meant that an enterprise having to produce such goods and ensure that its free prices reflected the real costs of production was not in a position to pass the latter on to the customer at the retail stage. The combination of high production costs and lower profits meant that subsidies from the central budget were allocated to ensure that the firm's income and expenditure balanced. This procedure seems quite satisfactory in terms of macro-economic price control, but is quite unsuitable as a means of making sure that the latter carries out its task of allocating profit.

In planning, the trend was to be towards favouring stable prices rather than encouraging them to play an active part. In the case of consumer prices, the aim was to preserve the balance between their level and that of real pruchasing power.

The same was true of agriculture, in so far as prices were largely fixed. There was no obligation to set up an amortization fund, which was covered by the State budget, and a lower profit (net income) rate was applied than in the industrial sector. The latter was a consequence of the desire of those responsible for economic policy to maintain relatively low price levels and avoid a clash between prices and distributed purchasing power.

Of the total agricultural production 70% was covered by fixed or highly controlled prices. Vegetables and fresh fruit from individual plots or agricultural co-operatives, for which there was a free market in the towns, were the main exceptions.

With regard to consumer prices, the same desire for stability was evident. Of the planned turnover of consumer goods, 50% came from fixed prices or those subject to a ceiling, compared with only 23% from free prices.

4. The effect of foreign trade on domestic prices

In a different area, the economic reforms reflected the desire to open up the Hungarian economy and give it a satisfactory place in the international division of labour whilst at the same time maintaining its favoured position in regard to the other members of Comecon.

The reform of producer prices was extended to include export prices. A particular aim had been to introduce greater sensitivity and to make the apparatus of production more efficient. Against this was the fact that the monopoly of foreign trade and administratively fixed export prices cut domestic production off from the movement of world prices, a policy which also made the productive apparatus even less competitive and production costs and domestic prices high and this was damaging to the economy of a small country whose foreign trade brought in 50% of national income.

With the NEM, the national plan no longer stipulated either how much was to be produced or how enterprises were to obtain the necessary inputs, which were now to be acquired freely on either the domestic or foreign market according to what they needed and what they could afford. Production too could be sold either at home or abroad.

The country's effective co-operation in the international division of labour would, it was hoped, provide a supply of hard foreign currency which would make it possible to acquire the technology needed to modernize the apparatus of production. An export strategy influencing both the quality and the variety of Hungarian products was seen as essential. Enterprises were allowed to look after their own foreign sales. In most cases, however, they used central import–export agencies as experienced intermediaries.

Exports were priced in foreign currencies, imports in forints converted using foreign trade multipliers, a weighting reflecting their relationship to a (weighted) basket of currencies used in commercial transactions. Since 1978, the forint rate has been officially based on the various convertible currencies. Firms exporting were credited with the forint equivalent of their profits after deduction of the various costs incurred, such as customs dues and the agency's fees. Importers of goods or raw materials without the necessary funds received subsidies equivalent to the difference between their purchase price and their domestic production cost, if production occurred in Hungary.

Strategically, it might be advantageous for an enterprise to be export-oriented, but the State introduced a progressive profits tax affecting in particular those whose profits were or might be too high. The aim was to avoid too great a differentiation between such firms and those not chiefly engaged in exporting.

Holding back foreign currencies and the progressive profits tax were certainly a result of a desire for equity, but they also reflected a very definite view of centre–periphery relationships. In the first place, it was an attempt to avoid centrifugal movements – like those in Yugoslavia in the early 1970s – arising from the distribution of foreign currency amongst enterprises or, within the Federation, between rich and poor republics. It was also a case of checking any autonomous expansion of enterprises which might be tempted, if they had large incomes, to acquire interests either within their own branch or in others. Any grouping or combining was centrally decided. The result of this policy was that go-ahead enterprises sometimes felt that they were in the same boat as those still conducting their affairs in the old way. Thirdly, there was a need to keep an eye on exports and to make sure that an increase in them did not bring in its wake a fall in domestic supply, which would have meant importing that proportion of national production sold abroad.

The reform of export prices only affected the prices of goods exported to Western countries. Those going to the Comecon area were planned as the result of bilateral and multilateral agreements between member states.

By means of these changes in export prices, the planners tried to bring domestic prices in line with world prices whilst seeking to avoid the effects of price variations on the (capitalist) world market in order to prevent the appearance of excessive differences and to reduce inflationary pressure. In this field, price policy was one of relative inaction with regard to foreign exchange, but it went hand in hand with a permissive policy as regards the possibility of importing machinery for Hungarian firms.

These actions were counter-productive, and were one of the factors contributing to the difficulties the country's economy experienced in foreign trading. These were an exchange rate that did not reflect cost conditions, the subsidizing of certain exports to pass on the difference between high domestic costs and world prices, and the lack of inducement to modernize the productive apparatus.

The reforms, which were seen as the keystone of the national regulatory system, had not achieved all that they set out to do, largely because of the parametric nature of the new price system. Through the Prices and Materials Office, the centre kept its hold on enterprises by manipulating prices, adapting them to branches and enterprises according to their needs. This had several consequences, namely the introduction of a hybrid price system with room for various ways of establishing prices and hence no overall unity, a lack of inducement for competition at home and abroad, and a limited role for the market.

Putting this admittedly incomplete system into operation did however introduce a degree of rationality that had previously been lacking, particularly at enterprise level.

Regulating profits and wages

In the view of the reformers, regulating prices and wages should, once a coherent price system was achieved, replace the earlier methods of transmitting instructions and exercise functions that could broadly be described as *guidance* and *distribution*. The former entailed bringing the behaviour of enterprises into line with macro-economic planning decisions and providing an inducement for them to reach autonomous decisions. The latter meant making it possible to distribute the value added created by enterprises. At the micro-economic level, the value added was to be divided between accumulation and the remuneration of wage-earners (salary funds), and at the macro-economic level some of the resources of enterprises were to be transferred to the State budget.

1. *Regulating profits*

In theory the division of profit is determined by the degree to which branches are capitalistic or by 'the organic composition of capital', the ratio of constant capital in total capital (K/L). Marxism holds that value is transformed into profit according to the organic composition of capital, that is because of the degree to which it is concentrated.

In order to establish standards of comparison and take wages into consideration, the centre established wage multipliers. The aim was to increase L in relation to K in highly capitalistic branches so as to provide a wages fund largely equal to the average distribution of capital and labour amongst branches. Capital-intensive enterprises in particular were thus enabled to re-establish proportionality between K and L in relation to the average organic composition. In 1968 the multiplier was 2, but it subsequently rose to 3 in 1971 to take labour-saving investments into account. In certain cases, however, it could vary from 0.5 for enterprises engaged in foreign trade to 8 for those engaged in transport, with a figure of 4 for other industries (fertilizers, bauxite, aluminium, paper) and 6 for the extractive industries.

1 *Determining profits*

Under the new methods of determining prices, profits were calculated by adding net social income (the surplus) to the average cost for the branch. Part of the former was paid directly to the State, with the remainder making up taxable profits, properly speaking.

2 *Taxing and distributing profits*

Profits were taxed for two main reasons, namely *to provide the State with resources* and *to ensure a balanced distribution between investment and wages.*

Of the profits 55% were centrally channelled by the State, and other taxes at production and distribution levels also helped to provide State finance. These were fixed-asset charges, expenditure connected with wages and social security contributions, land tax, customs duties and import taxes, production taxes and taxes on the use of sites.

In the profits tax system introduced in 1968, pre-tax profits had to be divided in the ratio of fixed assets to wage costs, the denominator being known as the wage multiplier. In applying the ratio, two funds were recognized: a development fund, or that part of the enterprise's resources used for its investments, and a participation fund, or sums used to increase wages or pay bonuses. They were taxed differently, the former attracting a linear 60% rate and the latter a progressive rate depending on the division into bonuses and wage increases.

Tax rates for development funds were fixed by the central authorities on the basis of estimated central expenditure during the five-year period, covering running and equipment costs (replacements and central development plans). For participation funds, the method chosen had to provide for factor payments at the micro–economic level. It subsequently attracted some criticism because of its rigidity. It was indeed by no means flexible enough, particularly as it was disadvantageous for those enterprises which increased fixed assets as a result of labour-saving investments. These observations led to the introduction of the idea of a wage multiplier into the method of calculating the profit rate:

$$Profit\ indicator\ = \frac{P}{aW + A}$$

where P = annual profit
      a = wage multiplier
      W = annual value of wages
      A = value of committed fixed and circulating capital

3 *Differentiating profit rates*

As was the case when the amortization rate was calculated, the profit rate was different from branch to branch. The same criteria were usually kept for justifying the decision (namely, that it was intended to protect branches such as those exposed to foreign competition, where prices had to be in line with those on the world market). The differences in rates were also justified on grounds of output and the efficiency of capital committed in the various branches. They were also reduced when there were connections between branches or products to avoid such dangers as chain reactions.

Granick gives the following examples:

> Low profit rates in mining, electricity, and steel reflected the belief that investments in these sectors must be so large that they could be financed only by the state, and thus that enterprises here need no substantial profits for investment purposes. The low profit rate for the food processing industry was partially a response to the desire to hold down consumer food prices. The result was an amalgam which departed seriously both from the notion that the profit rate on capital should be at the same average level in all sectors, with higher realized enterprise profits thus indicating greater enterprise efficiency, and from the alternative concept that higher profit rates should be reserved for those sectors which must expand particularly rapidly in order to equilibrate or keep up with demand. (Granick, 1976: 259)

Implicit in the reference to an average branch profit rate is a diversity of rates for products or groups of products arising from the task allocated to prices in the NEM. This is even clearer if we examine the system of mixed prices put into operation as a result of the reforms, where profit will mean different things according to whether the price system in the branch in question is imposed by the relevant ministry or by market forces. In the former case, the industry ministries either establish the level of profit to be included in fixed prices or establish norms in terms of which enterprises can decide the matter for themselves. In a market situation, however, profit is largely determined by a quasi-spontaneous adjustment of supply and demand.

Profit nevertheless played a fairly active part in so far as it enabled enterprises to break free of the straitjacket of the old regulations. This also accounts for the importance of regulation as a means of stabilizing the various processes when there was a considerable differentiation between certain branches in the early 1970s.

One reason for using different profit rates was connected with the different output of branches. Another was the fact that different production processes had an effect on each other, or, in other words, the relationship between sectors of differing productivity all engaged in manufacturing the same product or group of products. The NEM contained no provision for moving capital between branches as a way of bringing profit rates closer together in a competitive situation.[3] Consequently any change in the costs of production of a given branch brought about either by the introduction of taxes (if production costs fell) or subsidies (if they rose) was contained. Several objectives were achieved in this way, and the desired level of profitability in the branch in question was maintained without the need for a change in prices. Between 1968 and 1975 there was very little price movement, and it seemed administratively simpler to change a few taxes or subsidies than to allow an adjustment of prices as technology developed.

2. Distributing profits

Having established the way profits were made up, we can now, following Marrese (1981), examine the various stages of their distribution. Profit was divided into four parts by means of a regulatory tax system. These were *profit taxes*, which secured revenue for the State budget; a *sharing fund* to be used to augment base wages and hence encourage productivity at enterprise level; a *development fund* to finance enterprise investment projects; and a *reserve fund* providing some protection against risks, particularly against the risk of fluctuating wage increases and the risk of losses associated with unsuccessful investments.

Using the following symbols:

V   = value of sales
C   = costs of materials and transportation

A   = gross value of fixed and working assets engaged
W = annual wages bill
P   = annual taxable profit
a   = wage multiplier
t   = average tax rate assessed against sharing fund profit, calculated on the basis of a progressive marginal tax schedule with respect to Ns/W
Ns = before-tax profit increment for sharing fund
Nd = before-tax increment for development fund
S   = unadjusted after-tax profit increment for sharing fund
D   = unadjusted after-tax profit for development fund
R   = unadjusted after-tax increment to reserve fund

we can determine

1 *annual taxable profit*

$$P = V - C - 0.05A - 1.25W$$

where 0.05 is the tax rate on fixed assets and 0.25 that on wages, and

2 *proportional distribution of profits to the various funds*

$$P = Ns + Nd \qquad (1)$$

$\dfrac{Nd}{Ns} = \dfrac{A}{aW}$ and, as $Ns = P - Nd$, we have

$$Ns = P \left[\frac{aW}{aW + A} \right] \qquad (2)$$

and $Nd = P \left[\dfrac{A}{aW + A} \right]$

It was chiefly at this level of profit distribution that criticism was most common. We have already noted the excessively normative nature of this pattern of distribution, which acted as a brake on any structural modification of the capital–labour relationship and meant that any increase in total profit had an immediate proportional effect on the two funds. The way in which the wages multiplier was handled also seems slightly arbitrary and not always based on fair criteria, and it was a matter of justifying *post factum* an inter-branch distributive norm arising from power relationships rather than of showing the close links between them. In addition, the fact that distribution was regulated annually reduced the chance of any immediate reaction from either the centre or enterprises to changing circumstances.

3 *payment of profit tax*
   S = (1 − t) Ns   (t = tax rate)
   D = (1 − 0.6) Nd (the general linear tax rate was 60%, with,
                     however, variations for some branches, e.g. 45%
                     for agriculture and 70% for trade)
4 *increasing the reserve fund*
   R = 0.1 (S + D) up to the point at which it reaches the combined sum
   of 87% of W and 1.57% of A.

Adjustments to the system of indirect regulation

In this area profit (and hence also wage) regulators were substantially modified, particularly in 1976. It was no longer compulsory to distribute profit proportionally to factors, and the profits tax rate was reduced when a differentiated system of wage control was introduced.

The basis of the 1976 reform was a modification of producer (and hence of relative) prices and an increase in wages tax from 25% to 35%. Assets taxes were also changed, with capital now being taxed at 5% on net and no longer gross value.

The aim of these various measures was to reduce charges on enterprises and encourage a more rational use of factors, especially labour. The reform of relative prices sought a greater reflection of the real costs of factors and hence increased efficiency at enterprise level. Alongside these considerable fiscal changes, however, there was a striking reduction in the role of profits in an attempt to reduce differences between branches and enterprises, which can be seen as a typical macro-economic action taken at the micro-economic level.

A system of progressive taxation of annual profit-sharing was introduced, with a lower profit-sharing bound of 6 days of average wages per employee and an upper one of 36–42 days. In addition, the profits tax rate was cut to 36%, as those in charge of economic policy felt that this would provide further encouragement for enterprises.

With regard to the old norm of distribution, the rigid system of allocating post-tax profit was abandoned, and the following principle adopted. First, 15% of after-tax profit was put into a separate reserve account for enterprise reserves. The enterprise then had to settle its debts to the banks or other creditors, after which it was free to choose how to divide the remainder between the relevant development and investment funds.

Despite the fact that such a choice was implicitly influenced by the wages tax structure, the system introduced in 1976 had the virtue of greater flexibility on the one hand and of increasing the part played by profit on the other. The object of regulating profit had as its primary function paying it into two funds associated with other instruments of economic policy. The wages policy can be described at the macro-economic level, but in reality it was regulated by a number of central and micro-economic parameters. The wage system was also affected by certain constraints arising mainly from social policy and giving rise to a number of measures such as the subsidies and consumer prices policies.

Some wages were regulated by the enterprise's sharing fund, to which, as we have seen, part of its profit was allocated. However, an individual system of taxation was set up to prevent excessive increases in the fund and hence avoid too great a difference between enter-prises. The object of progressive taxation was to make it possible to establish a more or less equal fund in each case. In this area, the system introduced in 1968 provided for a zero rate when the amount of profit allocated to the sharing fund was between 0% and 3% of the wages bill, a 20% rate when it was between 3% and 5%, a 40% rate when it was between 5% and 10%, and a 70% rate when it rose above 10%.

1. The pattern of wage regulation up to the 1968 reform

Wage regulation developed with the system of managing the economy, and the underlying principle behind it followed the pattern of administrative planning, in which, particularly in the early 1950s, wages were largely fixed in terms of the assessment of labour in physical quantities. Since it was coupled with the well-known short-comings of administrative planning, the system had many drawbacks. In particular, it stressed quantity rather than quality, involved a certain degree of waste, made it impossible to introduce new tech-nology and had an adverse effect on the determination of relative income levels in the various social strata.

This early system was abandoned and replaced, from 1957 to 1967, with a different method taking other factors into account – an increase in productivity, equilibrium between the supply of consumer goods and purchasing power, the efficient use of labour and the developing phenomenon of variations in personal incomes within acceptable limits. Enterprises that more than met the objectives set them by central planners could also increase the wages fund. Such developments, however, entailed the risk of inflationary pressure, although in actual fact it was the centre that fixed the size of the fund nationally and then allocated it to branches. The ten-year period saw an increasingly complex system, and the inefficiency of using higher output figures as the sole criterion for fixing wage levels was recognized. Other factors such as increased sales and the part played by profit were therefore also taken into account.

2. Wage regulation 1968–76

In the wages field, the characteristic measure was to regulate the average annual wage rather than the total wages bill, as still happens in the other socialist countries. This was an improvement, especially within a context of decentralized planning, since it got rid of the old practice of fixing wages centrally. It too, however, was not completely satisfactory, and was modified in 1978 to incorporate a partial reintroduction of the overall wages bill as a factor to be taken into consideration.

The purpose of the sharing fund was to increase bonuses rather than to raise wage levels, and a distinction was therefore made between wage levels and wage increases, with the particular aim of avoiding certain abuses that had emerged. Using the sharing fund to pay for increases in the average wage level meant that it was in the enterprise's interest to employ more workers (generally fairly unskilled) or to count those taken on seasonally as full-timers. This produced a drop in the average level of wage per worker, and meant that the level for full-timers could be raised. There were two consequences: a shortage of labour, and a slow increase in its productivity. Between 1968 and 1977, the average increase was 4.6%, but 0.9% and 0.3% in 1968 and 1969 respectively.

Partial changes were introduced, even though the principle of authoritarian profit-sharing was retained. In order to avoid a too rapid increase in bonuses, especially those for managerial grades in enterprises, and to combat practices tending to raise the average wage level in them, the State authorized them to transfer, at the level of the costs of production, a third of the sum needed to pay the additional wages. The effect, however, was to reduce the total profit allocated to the sharing fund and to raise the level of producer prices. A system of regulation taking the overall wages bill into account was also tried out in a further attempt to combat economic over-employment.

External factors were also involved in the wages policy, largely as a result of the inadequacy of the price system and the oligopolistic structure of the productive system. The chief among them were the allocation of direct subsidies and the introduction of a wages growth index not dependent solely on profit, with the state limiting increases in them to 4% per annum. The indicator, $W + P/L$, where W = wages bill, P = profit and L = the number of employees, was used to determine wage increases and used in conjunction with a progressive tax system.

Thus, a 1% increase in the gross income indicator meant that an enterprise could raise the average wage by 0.3%. The sums needed for the increase, however, were taxed at the 50% rate. The enterprise could pass on half the additional wage costs, the other half being met from the sharing fund.

The new system removed the upper limit the State imposed on annual wage increases, but if they went beyond the figures provided by the indicator they were heavily taxed on a progressive scale going up to a maximum of 200% for a 2% rise. The planners do not appear to have found the formula totally satisfactory, however, since they started drawing up plans for new reforms to be introduced in 1976.

Nevertheless, the principle of regulation was modified and the function of the sharing fund was limited to that of financing wage increases and bonuses. This system, which was linked to changes in the way production factors were taxed, encouraged labour-saving investments on the part of enterprises in view of higher labour costs. It also certainly supplied something that had initially been lacking, namely a differentiation of the wages policy. In that area, however, the State, like many sections of the labour force, was very careful to avoid the appearance of excessive differences in pay.

3. The 1976 reforms in wage regulation

The aim of these, which came into force with the fifth plan, was still to achieve both greater economic efficiency and a faster increase in the productivity of labour. In order to ensure a regular rise in wage levels, to keep an equitable wage distribution and to reduce any disproportion, four types of wage regulation were introduced for use in various circumstances. These were the regulation of wage levels and the total wages bill according to the performance of the enterprise, and the *central* regulation of wage levels and the total wages bill.

The principle of an automatic pay rise of between 1.5% and 2% not linked to enterprise performance was also introduced. This exogenous increase was determined annually with regard to the plan for the year. As a means of guaranteeing a wage increase at enterprise level, it arose directly from State social policy.

1 *Regulating wage levels according to enterprise performance*

In part, this type of regulation maintained the status quo. It was based on the wage increase indicator, i.e., on a *per capita* wage plus profit relationship, with an automatic 0.2%–0.4% rise when the indicator went up by 1%. A growth threshold of 6% of the indicator was retained, after which there was progressive taxation, exemption from which fiscalists saw as a means of increasing efficiency. It also provided a way of avoiding excessive differences between enterprises operating under different types of regulation.

2 *Regulating the total wages bill according to enterprise performance*

This was primarily a matter of regulating the disposable wages bill and secondarily of regulating wage levels. In part, increases in the former were the responsibility of the centre, but also depended on a system of comparison reflecting improved performance at enterprise level, based on added value or total production less material costs. The latter were broken down into wage costs, operating results, taxes on wages, charges on capital used, amortization, and other (excluding material) costs. A 1% increase in added value might bring about a rise of between 0.3% and 0.6% in the wage bill.

Alongside this, a combination of the two regulatory systems (wage bill and wage level) with a fixed upper limit to curb excessive wage rises was used.

3 *Regulating wage levels from the centre*

This was a supplementary measure to guarantee progressively increasing employees' purchasing power that was not directly linked to performance. Wage increases were centrally determined, but enterprises were not forbidden to go beyond the authorized level provided they paid progressive taxation. Here, it was the State that authorized rises and determined the annual rate of increase in the average annual wage level.

4 *Regulating the wage bill from the centre*

The wage bill was regulated on the same principle and used as the basis for regulating increases in the average wage. As was also the case when the wages bill was regulated at enterprise level, a maximum (6%) rate of increase was established beyond which an enterprise was liable to progressive taxation.

4. Implementing the various types of wage regulation

The chief aim of the changes was a more effective use of the labour force, and to this end wage increases were linked to productivity. Given the heterogeneous nature of the productive system and the different kinds of market within the socialist framework, however, the regulatory principles were not applied in a standard way.

Regulating the wage bill according to enterprise performance needed to be developed more particularly in sectors the economic activity of which meant that the demand for labour had to be reduced but the productive structure did not call for any substantial changes in the way the factors of production were combined. These were activities in which seasonal labour was employed and which therefore needed specific measures if a repeat of the way enterprises behaved in 1968 and 1969 was to be avoided.

Regulating the level of wages on the other hand was a device more frequently used in dynamic sectors where activity and growth led to the possibility of considering major structural modifications. In such areas, however, the earlier system had tended to discourage enterprise efficiency.

Regulating wages from the centre was important in those sectors where no substantial changes could be envisaged and the State already intervened directly in fixing prices, subsidizing certain activities or allocating inputs centrally. In such circumstances, linking wages to profit was not an appropriate way of achieving either increased efficiency or raising wage levels. Nevertheless, the State kept the sole right of determining which sectors were to be regulated in specific ways, particularly at branch and sector level.

The way the price system has developed over the past 20 years perfectly reflects the ambivalent attitude of those responsible for economic policy to the question of whether prices should be determined administratively or left to the play of market mechanisms. It would seem in fact that they only wanted to see the advantages of both models (the macro-economic coherence created by planning and the micro-economic dynamism created by scarcity prices) and refused to consider their disadvantages (such as opacity on the one hand or the threat to certain aspects of social policy on the other). This lack of decision was harmful and led to such negative results as stabilization measures and continual central price modifications. One of the essential tasks of the price system was to enable enterprises to accumulate part of their profit by making their own decisions about the volume and type of investment they would engage in. Despite the criticism it attracted, a certain number of enterprises were able to achieve relatively high profit rates and to accumulate according to choices made at the micro-economic level. Most, however, were not so successful, largely because of the heterogeneous nature of indirect regulation.

An awareness of these inconsistencies and the impact in the mid-1950s of external economic events, like the oil crisis, international recession and inflation, later led to considerable modifications in the prices and taxation systems and hence in the instruments of regulation. Despite such improvements, however, the system of regulation was to remain normative in nature, particularly where wage and price fixing was concerned.

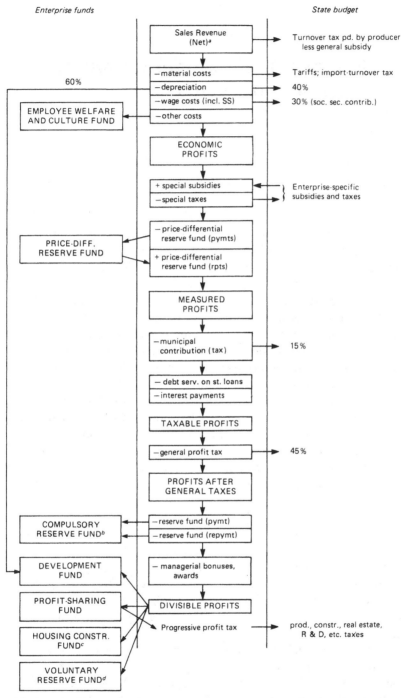

[a] After payment of general turnover taxes that may be levied on the producer and receipt of general subsidies.

[b] Discontinued in 1984. [c] Introduced in 1984. [d] Replaced in 1984 by a profit reserve fund.

The system of enterprise taxation, 1983

5   Macro-economic planning and the behaviour of agents

Once the principle of indirect regulation had been adopted, one of the basic features of the Hungarian reforms was the abandonment of the practice of sub-dividing macro-economic planning and issuing detailed instructions to subordinate authorities. This development is still a characteristic of the Hungarian system, and is unique among Soviet-type economies. Although there is still planning at the micro-, meso- and macro- levels of the economy, it is no longer of a compulsory nature, but forms a coherent frame of reference incorporating the forward planning of enterprises. As has been stressed, the latter acquired a large measure of autonomy with regard to their volume of production, their supplies, and the way they organized their markets.[1]

Macro-economic planning, however, still imposed constraints. Decentralization did not mean the end of bureaucratic control from the centre and certain intermediate bodies. If we bear in mind the inadequacy of the instruments of guidance, this explains why resources (investment credits and funds) were still distributed from the centre and why enterprises not encouraged to act competitively behaved as they did.

As a result of the reforms to the system of management then, there was considerable change in planning methods, but still a number of inconsistencies and conflicts, and a type of bureaucratic control which left increasing scope for activities falling outside the plan proper. There was a more complex approach to planning, which now had room for medium-term projects and the necessary means of achieving aims.

As the character of both the apparatus of production and the system of control became more sophisticated, the view of what planning should achieve and how it should be operated changed. Short-term developments were to be incorporated more from the point of view of economic policy than as a mere section of the five-year plan, which

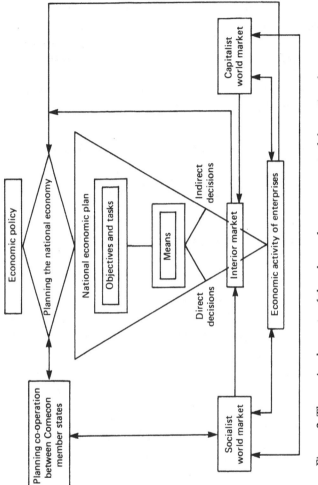

Figure 3 The main elements of the planned management of the national economy

itself was no longer a set of five-year figures expressing the wishes of the centre, but something more open and more easily able to adapt to current developments.

Drawing up and supervising the operation of plans was an ongoing activity. Achieving objectives provided feedback, encouraged reflection, and encouraged planners to think ahead. The interplay of different levels of decision-making and the resultant iterations also made it possible to adjust and fine-tune the plan.

The stages in drawing up the five-year plan

It is possible to distinguish two major phases, conception and elaboration, each covering several points on the time-scale for drawing it up and taking place largely within the National Planning Office. The first is a continuous process of treating data and projecting alternatives, and could be represented diagrammatically by Figure 4.

1. The conceptual stage

This phase can be broken down into several sub-stages. The first is the outline ('technical and economic concepts') plan, based on partial data provided by the execution of the current plan on the one hand and the government's medium-term objectives on the other. The process is started mid-way through the current five-year plan, at which stage the latter is considered sufficiently advanced to provide information about the previous two years. The contents of the annual plan are also known, and these too furnish useful data, since in a sense it is a response to the planning cycle. Thus the National Planning Office analysts have a satisfactory basis for their projections for the next two years. At this stage, they are operating on both a short- and a medium-term basis, with the former (annual planning) covering *reaction* – that is, how economic policy is to make it possible to achieve initial objectives – and the latter future objectives.

The analyses provided at this point give a better insight into the general way the current five-year plan is working, and the projections show what the future alternatives will be in the light of information about the various constraints operating. Demographic factors, for example, might mean that the labour force has to be redistributed amongst branches, or that the rate of replacement investment has to be increased in the branches most directly involved.

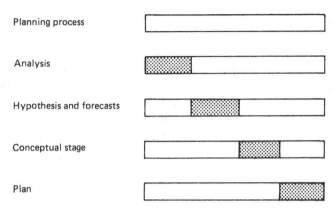

Figure 4 Stages in the five-year plan

At this point, the way in which investment will be distributed amongst branches is still not known. The various constraints operating (capital costs, level of debt, construction delays, and so on) are taken into account, which gives an idea of the volume of investment expenditure, and two alternatives are drawn up. The next stage involves analysing how investment is shared out, first at major and then at various branch levels. Particular note is taken of those branches where excessive discrepancies (between the branch and the investment rate) are observed.

A document summarizing the various analyses carried out by the National Planning Office is then passed on to the political department and the Party leaders form their opinion on the basis of it. Here, the methodology and practice of administrative planning has been reversed. Under the old system, the will of the Party was binding on administrative bodies, whereas now the Planning Office and the Party leaders are engaged in a dialogue which generally leads to a joint analysis.

Once this task has been completed, a second phase begins, and the plan is fleshed out a little. Up-to-date information and the results of calculations based on forecasting models (particularly with regard to investment distribution and the elimination of inter-branch discrepancies and the like) make it possible to define the major directions in which the new plan will move.

The planners' job is becoming more operational in nature. Simulations based on alternative hypotheses about the growth rate are carried out and the various options considered, although in practice the aim is to reduce their scope. It is possible, however, given the elasticity of branches, to use different average rates, especially in areas like construction, where demand exceeds supply.

When the work – which is largely carried out within the National Planning Office – has reached this point, the objectives of the future plan are becoming more coherent, and many of the ideas of economic policy have been enriched by proposals from other functional ministries and draft plans drawn up by the country's 50 biggest enterprises.

The document produced as a result of all the decisions emerging during internal discussion thus makes it possible to specify the major macro-economic balances and the compatible growth rate with regard to rises in the standard of living (the way national income is distributed); the volume of exports and technological progress; regional development; international economic relations (the volume of exports and imports in the two great markets, Comecon and the convertible currency market),[2] and financial regulators and prices. Taking these findings into consideration, having the results of calculations carried out with the help of econometric models and input–output tables, together with the resultant iteration process, are all stages in testing the macro-economic consistency and logic of the plan.

2. Constructing the plan

Discussion with the branch ministries and the largest enterprises and trusts then begins, and the previously horizontal iteration process is now vertical.

The subordinate bodies now examine their plans in the light of the centre's objectives and pass on the data they have, thus making it possible to draw up a branch-by-branch plan. Since the units of production are now directly involved, this stage is rather a long one, involving considerable exchanges of information. As will be seen, each of the parties concerned plays its cards to suit its own interests. In theory, this stage should last about 18 months, but in practice it is a two-year operation.

At the end of it, discussion enters a second phase, in which figures for each branch are established, the details of which are based on more realistic plans. From the start of these calculations to the final stage of this phase an on-going reassessment is in progress based on more recent statistics. Modifications subsequently become more difficult to make, and the planners' task is made even more onerous if there is a decision to introduce general price reform, which means that the whole price structure has to be re-examined.

The draft produced at this stage describes the main objectives of the five-year plan, namely the growth rate of national income; growth in individual branches and the main structural changes in production; major trends in scientific policy and technological development; the volume of investments and their allocation in the case of each main objective; growth of employment, consumption and real income; growth of public expenditure on health, culture, housing and the like; the main trends in international economic relations; developments and modifications in foreign trade.

With regard to ways and means, the following areas are specified:

a description of the objectives, costs and main means of implementing the major development programmes;

decisions on State investment projects;

a description of the objectives of developing enterprises needing
State subsidies, the upper limits of the latter, and of arrangements
for loans;

the volume and main destination of State subsidies for research and
development and technological development;

the principles of the prices policy, particularly with regard to
changes in price levels and relative prices;

the financial policy for maintaining financial equilibrium, and
directives concerning resources and employment in the State
budget;

local finances and in particular State contributions to local development funds;

the principles governing the regulation of State income and the
major directives concerning State subsidies to enterprises;

the main criteria in credit policy, with particular reference to long-
and short-term enterprise commitment and consumer credit;

a description of aims and objectives in raising the standard of living
of the population;

and the regulation of and growth in industrial income, etc.

The plan itself is a document of about 40 pages which emerges from a gestation period of over three years. The fact that the process is spread over such a period should not however blind us to an essential feature of decentralized planning, which incorporates and attempts to synthesize the very divergent behaviour patterns that reflect the particular interests of the various bodies involved in drawing up the plan. Once it has been ratified by parliament, it is no longer merely something of a morally obliging nature, but the chief basis of economic policy. Similarities with French practice are not fortuitous, and decentralized planning in Hungary also has its indicative side. That is why annual plans, which are drawn up on the basis of the results of the preceding year, are much more binding than the indicative five-year plan, as they can be seen as correctives in the development of economic activity. They contain a list of the objectives to be achieved in the relevant year and express in very precise figures both those objectives and the means available for achieving them. In addition, they incorporate the instruments for, or modifications to, indirect regulation.

In this sense, these annual plans can no longer be seen simply as the parts of the five-year plan relevant to a particular single year. Economic policy acquires its own logic, the means of achieving stable growth. What is more, the medium-term options in the plan remain more open, which makes it easier to make more flexible adjustments if there are excessive discrepancies between objectives and execution.

3. Planning at enterprise level

By using indirect regulation instead of the old system of direct orders from the centre and the branch ministries, the NEM radically changed the status of enterprises. Apart from modifying hierarchical relationships, indirect regulation shifted micro-economic aims towards the maximization of profits. Despite the reforms, however, the straitjacket of administrative management and the vertical divisions arising from it were not entirely removed. Under a system of administrative planning, enterprises were subordinate bodies at the bottom of the decision-making pyramid, and units of production were managed at sectorial level. When decentralized planning was introduced, there was a move in the opposite direction. Enterprises were given a different function by linking their activities to central purposes by means of financial and wage regulators. Nevertheless, the mixed nature of the system that grew up as a result of the partial application of indirect regulation perpetuated the tendencies inherent in administrative management and had an adverse effect on the new functional division based on a binary centre–enterprise relationship.

In such a situation, enterprises were still caught up in the meshes of the system of direct and indirect control. Furthermore, the reformers still saw the idea of a harmony between the various micro-, meso- and macro-economic components of the system as an essential element of any system, and in their view micro-economic units should never be in conflict with macro-economic objectives – an opinion frequently reaffirmed by the heads of the National Planning Office and the other functional ministries.

Nevertheless, if we look at the most concrete aspect of the process of drawing up the plan, we can see that it is carried out within the context of administrative planning and more particularly by means of an iterative process linking the centre, the branch ministries and enterprises. The final adjustments are not, of course, made as a result of free negotiations or by a declaration of the preferences of each of the parties involved. The opposite is more nearly the case, since within a hierarchical framework still marked by behaviour patterns dating from the era of imperative planning, what the units of production prefer is necessarily heavily influenced by the fact that for enterprises the optimal situation is one in which they obtain their supplies at the least possible cost and reduce their output. Where that is the case, there is no really unbiased information system, as the units of production deliberately restrict the data they make available in order to maintain their position, and the centre responds by producing rigid plans, which enterprises counter by increasing the total production provided for if exceeding targets is rewarded by a system of bonuses. Here we have one of the origins of the economic cycle of planning.

Where there is administrative planning, planning at enterprise level is directly shaped by instructions emanating from the sectorial ministries which divide the plan up at branch level amongst the various enterprises within a given branch. Planning as such is an integral part of enterprise management, which explains why each enterprise has a planning section and can thus ensure dialogue with sectorial ministries.

Conversely, in decentralized planning decision-making tends to shift towards enterprises, which are free to determine how much they will produce and decide on methods of both supply and the distribution of their production, relying particularly on direct negotiations between units of production. Despite a more relaxed system of instructions as a result of the introduction of indirect regulators however, the crying need of economic policy is still for a more harmonious relationship between the parts and the whole. Striving to achieve it has not completely eradicated the conflicts between macro-, meso- and micro-economic approaches, which still exist even when enterprises are seen as subordinate institutions. Within the various institutions a whole series of conflicts and compromises arising from the variety of functions assumed more or less in isolation is still apparent.

Organizing enterprise planning

It may seem surprising that the micro-economic planning function should subsist in decentralized planning, and autonomy of decision-making and management at enterprise level may seem incompatible with enterprise planning. The fact is, however, that such planning contains two realities. In the first place, the enterprise is where goods and services are created and transformed in a complex and continuous process and must therefore organize its supplies, production and sales on the basis of a logical strategy. If it is to function it has to consider what it will be doing in the future. Secondly, the enterprise is an integral part of socialist planning, and is seen as a subordinate body in the process of directing the branches of the economy. At enterprise level, planning is the implementing, in micro-economic terms, of decisions taken by the centre, and can thus be seen as a sub-section of the functional division of the centrally planned economy.

In decentralized planning, the enterprise or co-operative draws up and adopts its own plan. In theory, its aims must not conflict with those of the national plan, which means that it must achieve those the latter sets it in connection with its own activity. This is the case with enterprises involved in projects directly financed by the State. In other situations, it has to be able to achieve the prescribed objectives by conforming to the system of economic regulation. Outside these limits, it is quite at liberty to define the contents of its own plan.

In both the planning and decision-making fields, however, enterprises are, despite their ostensible autonomy, rather susceptible to suggestions from the branch ministry and the centre. In the sense that the latter intends to control the activity of enterprises by linking them to specific, externally established objectives, the idea of autonomous decision-making at enterprise level is restrictive.

The centre can intervene in various ways. In the investment field, it involves enterprises in grouped investments and can thus involve them more easily in macro-economic projects. This kind of action reduces their autonomy and hence their choice of activities. Yet an enterprise accepting this central influence is guaranteed to have an appropriate volume of activity and regular financing, which means that to some extent it escapes market regulation.

The centre can also intervene through its advisory activities. State bodies help enterprises draw up their plans and are involved in the establishment of inter-enterprise co-operation and co-ordination. The controlling bodies therefore have many functions and provide advice when plans are being drawn up, a continuous flow of information, consultation, aid in establishing inter-enterprise co-operation and co-ordination, and an evaluation of the plans put forward by enterprises.

The consequence of such solicitous help is that it ultimately leads to a perpetuation of the old system of direction based on branches of the economy. All too often the result of a determination to make macro-economic decisions and enterprise planning fit completely together is a failure to see the latter as anything more than a sub-division of the central plan, as has been stressed by the National Planning Office official in charge of enterprise planning:'enterprises should set such targets as would agree with the figures of the computational results of the national plan when added up with the figures of the other enterprises in a given industry' (Balassa, 1977: 54). This leads to results quite opposed to those initially expected and helps to create a certain number of distortions in the working of the plan, amongst which are reduced flexibility and a lack of initiative on the part of enterprises.

The behaviour of the central planning institutions can be attributed to a number of factors. In the first place, there is a certain *de facto* aversion to market mechanisms and a preference for older planning methods. There is also a lack of confidence in the ability of directors to manage their enterprises efficiently. The other side of the coin is that the institutions overestimate the chances of controlling enterprise activities and underestimate the role and function of the plan.

Interference by central bodies in enterprise planning

Both in order to help enterprises plan and to make sure that micro- and macro-economic interests coincide, central bodies intervene in various fields. Initially, when the national plan is being prepared, the Planning Office sends enterprises a series of methodological directives setting out how to start preparing the plan, what it should contain and how it should proceed, and the basic principles to be applied in the relations of the enterprise and the controlling bodies with other enterprises. These first recommendations are supplemented with others from the branch ministries, which are more technical in nature and spell out the main categories and indicators in the enterprise plan, thus perpetuating the administrative type of control branch ministries exercise over enterprises.

The central bodies also ensure that there is a greater amount of information in circulation. The data received by enterprises go beyond what they need for planning and cover various fields such as the general ideas behind the five-year plan, its contents, equilibria and calculations, branch objectives, changes in the system of control, negotiations concerning plans with Comecon, and the like. The desired feedback effect can nevertheless only occur if information circulates rapidly and effectively and really helps units of production and central bodies to make proper use of what it contains. It is not uncommon, however, for the flow to be blocked or for the information to reach its destination late. There are examples of enterprises receiving notification of changes after they have completed and adopted their plans. Nor is it rare for such plans to be called into question when decisions taken within the intra-Comecon framework finally percolate down to enterprises. Here, it might be a question of orders from the centre saying that an enterprise must achieve a given output, to be delivered to Comecon partners and sold at a price for which the enterprise simply is not capable of planning. Or the enterprise might find itself the recipient of semi-finished goods or machines it has not asked for but has received as a result of bilateral Comecon agreements. For their part, enterprises may provide superior bodies with a continuous flow of information but they also hold a certain amount back once there is more bargaining with the centre.

During the various phases of preparing the plan, there are consultations of this kind with the 80 biggest enterprises in the country, a procedure that makes it possible to fine-tune the plan and analyse the interaction between the internal decisions in the enterprise and external factors. The continuity in time means an appropriate structure of exchanges for bargaining between the various parties involved.

The enterprise plan does however run up against a certain number of problems. One reason for this is that it is constructed in a context of information that is necessarily limited, selective and contradictory, given that at enterprise level it cannot be fully assimilated and the theory of choice is therefore incomplete (Loasby, 1976: 5), that the pressure exerted by macro- and meso-economic bodies and the rather biased information they provide usually induce enterprises to prepare plans to meet centrally determined objectives, and that both data from the centre and indications from the market are involved. In such conditions, any considerable change in the economic situation has a direct effect on the way plans are progressing and their relevance.

At the same time, the enterprise plan reflects different functions as far as objectives are concerned, since it seeks to maximize profit and increase factor productivity, expresses market pressures in concrete terms and reflects the macro-economic choices determined by the centre. In other words, it is the point at which macro- and micro-economic objectives become synonymous, and attempting to make the two identical can seem rather artificial if the tensions at work in the planning process are not taken into consideration.

From harmony to tension in planning

Planning has a macro-economic dimension. It is a complex process and the result of many operations carried out at the various echelons of the decision-making system, namely functional and branch ministries and enterprises. It cannot therefore be reduced to a purely mechanical activity, but symbolizes a set of power relationships which in their turn also help both to shape the plan and to regularize the behaviour of the various factors of which the plan is composed.

If this regularity is to be achieved, however, the partial and specialized activities of each of the bodies involved must lead to it and be in harmony with ultimate objectives. The way in which the various institutions concerned with planning are organized and functionally and hierarchically divided are factors at play.

Such an approach nevertheless seems to neglect the conflict relationships within the process. As has rightly been pointed out (Nove, 1980: 82-3), wherever there is a relative shortage of available resources, the divergent interests of the groups involved are more sharply visible. This phenomenon is perhaps not readily apparent where administrative planning is concerned, but it becomes much more obvious within a framework of decentralization.

1. Planning and social redistribution

Planning should be seen as a process of redistributing national income amongst branches, enterprises and households. Thus, despite the functional and hierarchical division of the economy, those agents intervene in the process and make it look like a struggle to acquire part of the social product.

Such phenomena have always been present in centralized planning, although covertly rather than overtly. In decentralized planning, on the other hand, the new relative autonomy of the agents involved has produced behaviour which may not be openly recognized as such but has become increasingly marked by an ever more obvious determination to use bargaining and coalitions to acquire a share of the social product distributed by the plan. The functional and hierarchical division of the planning organizations reflects the split between the two centres of interest.

If we examine the National Planning Office (NPO), we note that it is divided into functional and branch directorates. Its planning section is where these necessarily divergent interests confront each other. Partly dependent on the functional and partly on the branch ministries, the NPO as the institution responsible for drawing up plans is organically linked to the centre. Its director has the rank of vice-president of the Council of Ministers and indeed may be a member of the political bureau or the central committee of the HSWP, which are the highest authorities in the economic and political running of the country. It might therefore seem that the centre directs the NPO but the apparatus has developed its own logic. What happens is that the latter synthesizes divergent interests and expresses them in the options chosen in the plan, which in this sense represents an equilibrium arising from the juxtaposition of the diverging interests at work in the struggle for redistribution. We have already encountered one aspect of bargaining, namely vertical bargaining, and noted in particular the types of relationships appearing at various levels of the hierarchy and the motivation of the different bodies involved.

The same type of behaviour and two-way pressure is apparent at Planning Office level. Its branch directorates espouse the interests of its functional directorates when they try to impose their ideas on branch or enterprise representatives. Conversely, these directorates are usually the real representatives of the branch ministries at the centre, where they tend to put forward their case for increasing the level of growth and sufficient funds to do so quite vigorously.

At first glance, the functional directorates seem to be organized in a more homogeneous way. Here too, however, each of them to some extent puts forward the specific interests of the ministries it represents in the Planning Office.

To that vertical pattern of bargaining has been added a horizontal one. In a situation where there are limits to what is to be allocated, each group tends to argue for the most it can get. That tendency has been increased by the appearance of the large socialist monopolies in the process, all keen to defend their own interests. To the branch and functional directorates fighting for a share of the social product must now be added, it seems, the 80 major enterprises and the representatives of territorial departments participating in preparing the plan.

The trades unions too have a hand in it, and their influence has increased since they stopped being merely a conveyor belt. As representatives of worker bureaucracy, their intervention in decisions concerning social policy will not be insignificant.

It is certain that in a situation of limited allocations and a great number of requests, bargaining is clearly a market strategy. If it is to develop fully, however, it needs to be able to count on support and to enter into more alliances. Planning is now developing its own lobbies. Socialist lobbying is not like the institutionalized lobbying that exists in a market economy. It has not been made official, and is consequently not recognized as such by the parties concerned, but the practice is tending to become more widespread as a means of influencing decisions. In the past, it was based almost exclusively on direct relationships of strength, and even now a monopolist enterprise can negotiate with the centre and get the desired factor allocations. The strategy that is developing is however much more subtle, as it assumes that short-term alliances to achieve particular aims are a possibility. Such alliances are common and can be created or dissolved as circumstances dictate, according to how the overall situation develops or the interests of the parties involved change.

In planning as it is actually carried out, such short-term alliances for one particular aim which can subsequently be dissolved when there are changes in economic policy are not unknown. For example, the decision to invest massively in coal mining was taken in 1974 at the instigation of the National Planning Office and the ministry responsible for heavy industry. When the Hungarian economy was hit by recession in 1976, the attitude of the NPO officials who had initiated the operation changed and the new head dissolved the alliance and favoured a new industrial sector.

Bargaining, which is based on the activities of pressure groups, can change the whole face of certain sectors, particularly when such groups become directly involved. In a specific sector, it is possible to follow a multi form bargaining process involving various partners. The head of a particular enterprise, a pharmaceutical corporation, wanted to increase and diversify its activities. On his suggestion, the branch ministry reorganized activities within his field by ordering the compulsory amalgamation of the enterprise in question and a firm specializing in the production of weedkillers. There was a certain amount of competition between the two undertakings over the question of who would exercise power in the new joint enterprise. Subsequently, an external constraint came into operation. In payment for its oil shipments to Hungary, the USSR asked for certain chemicals with a high added value, and the Hungarian government intervened to ensure that the enterprises in the branch produced the quantities required to ensure that the deal with the USSR could go ahead.

At a different level, this particular amalgamation project was against the interests of the agricultural lobby, who did not want to see it materialize, as its relations with the firm producing weedkillers were good. The agricultural sector was also afraid of having to face up to a stronger industrial partner.

The Ministry of Finance was also against it since, generally speaking, small- and medium-sized firms are competitive in Western markets. It was not happy about creating large groups, which are often poor performers on the hard-currency markets and strong enough to exert sufficient pressure to be able to negotiate with the centre at home. The result was that the Ministry of Finance opposed both the Soviet request, since it would reduce the share of production that could be sold on hard-currency markets, *and* the proposed amalgamation, since it would increase the already considerable strength of monopolies.

When the conflict of interests cannot be resolved at this level, discussions are resumed at the political level, where once again there are differences of opinion taking a different form.

2. Bargaining in the planning process: some theoretical considerations

As has already been suggested, the centralized and hierarchical nature of Soviet-type societies does not mean that the system will be completely hierarchical and bureaucratic. Within it, at various levels, there are internal and personal relations that to some extent make it possible to embark on co-ordinated action and exert pressure, for example. Such societies share out the chances of negotiating rather unequally. Bargaining is the concrete expression of such chances in a system with no other channels for exchanges between social groups.

As a two-way exchange between interest groups, it is common to both East and West. In capitalist societies, however, it is associated with adjustment mechanisms, whereas in socialist societies recourse to it is increased by the monocentric nature of the system, which necessarily entails a high degree of legal regulation of the relations between groups and agents. A 'command' economy is based on a codification of all economic and social activities – indexes, norms, 'nomenclature' and the like. The effect of this hyper-regulation is the need for a bureaucratic economic and institutional apparatus which, at a certain stage, can no longer be controlled by the higher bodies. Once that happens, exchanges between groups at the various echelons of the administrative apparatus can occur, thus allowing people to obtain by direct means what they cannot be sure of obtaining by normal ones, or only after too long a wait. The tendency to bargain is facilitated by the way productive units are organized. In industry, monopolies offer a perfect structure for starting to bargain with the centre.

After economic reforms – that is, in a decentralized system – there is more scope for it than in a centralized one. The new feature, however, apart from the increased scope, is that in the 1970s the old protective devices of programmes and ideology that unified a number of separate lobbies, as diverse as those urging market socialism or administrative socialism, no longer existed. There are now no overall concepts in any sense, only purely partial concepts that ultimately balance each other and shape the economic policy of the moment.

Lobbies, it has been stressed, are not formal, institutionalized configurations. They are informal groupings attached to some major branch of the administration but not identical with it. The agricultural lobby, for instance, is not the Ministry of Agriculture. It may contain people from the Ministry of Finance, the National Planning Office, or the co-operatives coming together to negotiate first with the government and subsequently among themselves. It may be temporary and disappear as the situation changes, or it may be one of the major ones that persist. The main difference between it and Western-type lobbying is the material means used, which are based on the political and economic positions of those involved. Shifts in the balance between various lobbies are explained by the fact that although they exist potentially, they have no permanent programme to argue for, as their opposite numbers in the West would.

A synthesis depends on both the relative strength of the various lobbies and external factors. They all have a hierarchical structure with, at the centre, one person who is director of an institution. The strength of a lobby depends in part on the position its leader holds, inter-lobby coalitions are formed, and some assume a kind of client relationship with a stronger group. The compromise reached is determined partly by relative strengths and partly by the quantity of resources available. Decisions vary according to whether one lobby has more or less investment resources, the favourable or unfavourable balance of payments, market pressures, the foreign and domestic political context, and so on. Although no alliance is formed, the fact that particular interests are evident means that each lobby tries to use its influence to gain its own ends. Thus, heavy industry is clearly important and uses its weight to obtain the investment it needs to expand, and the representatives of sectors working for the Soviet market stress the prime importance of their activity and the need to meet their commitments. Sectors involved in Western markets will use the discussions to obtain the allocations they need if they are to continue to play an important part in those areas. The representatives of the National Bank will stress the country's indebtedness, and the government will encourage the appropriate ministries to ensure that such and such an enterprise produces machines for the Soviet market so that Hungary can get the oil it needs. Conversely, certain enterprises will find that they need to absorb semi-finished Soviet goods and that the government has had to agree to this in order to obtain certain other goods, usually raw materials, in return. From these examples, it can be seen that planning is increasingly guided by a system of co-ordinating the specific interests of the various bodies engaged in bargaining, and that the consequence of this is the line that is in fact followed, even if it has never been explicitly acknowledged.

As a means of allocation, bargaining has developed partly as a result of deficiencies in other systems, i.e. the plan and the market. It provides a way of sharing out a limited supply of goods and resources more or less efficiently. In Soviet-type systems, it seems to be inherent and to tend to replace other types of regulation. Although he sees it as inefficient, one commentator (Johansen, 1979) offers an interesting theoretical interpretation of it.

From a theoretical point of view, the strategy of bargaining can be explained by game theory, which presupposes that the number of agents involved and the fields of action available to each individual or group are known, that the extent to which they are mutually dependent is made clear (since the solution or result achieved in each case generally depends on the actions of all) and that each individual is a conscious subject and also knows that all the others are conscious subjects.

Given these hypotheses, a distinction must be made between *non-co-operative* and *co-operative* games. In the former, each player makes his decisions in terms of the options open to him without collaborating with the others, whereas in the latter the players may communicate and form a coalition before making a decision and taking action. Bargaining belongs to the latter category, and can be described as the range of opportunities for exchanges, communication and coalition-forming defined in game theory. It does not, however, lead to a single result arising from an equilibrium between various relative strengths but rather, it is supposed, from one of a set of possible solutions arrived at through the interplay of various conflicting interests. In that sense, as Johansen points out, 'bargaining is a process by which an outcome is determined in a co-operative game in which no unique point is determined by a sort of coalitional balance of powers' (Johansen, 1979: 501).

However, since bargaining essentially consists of using certain means to acquire what cannot be acquired by following the normal rules, it is by definition non-co-operative, as it necessarily involves conflict between the parties involved. In other words, it is non-co-operative in its aims, since it sets out to achieve an objective that cannot be achieved in the normal way, but co-operative in the sense that in order to attain it there has to be an exchange of information, proposals, threats or promises if the various coalitions necessary for the outcome desired by each agent or group of agents are to be formed. Figure 5 shows the different states of the process and the various options open to participants.

Procedures whereby the parties involved behave according to given rules or as a result of bargaining produce collective decisions. A collective decision is 'a joint decision taken according to well defined rules, which are such that they produce a decision, within a fixed dead-line, even if there is no agreement between the parties involved' (Johansen, 1979: 501). This is quite different from bargaining, for which there are no predetermined rules and which is an arrangement between parties leading to a joint decision. If there is no such agreement, however, they are all free to come to whatever decision they choose, in which case there are other ways – either by means of non-co-operative games or as a result of relative strengths – of coming to a joint decision.

Using such a strategy implies that some objectives, and hence some information, will not be declared. From game theory to the formation of real coalitions is no more than a step, and we are moving into a particular field of group strategies, namely the formation of combines in an economy.

Johansen is of course writing about mixed market economies, that is market economies with a highly developed public sector and large and highly active pressure groups such as industries and trades unions, and reflecting on socialist economies entails moving to a different frame of reference. If all the conditions necessary for the proper functioning of the NEM were met, the strategy would be pointless and the inefficiency of bargaining clear in that case too. In a system which is neither one thing nor the other and uses various methods of control, however, it has its uses. Perhaps its greatest advantage is that it increases the autonomy of institutions, allowing them to negotiate more horizontally than in the past, when the normal way was vertically.

3. Activities not covered by the plan and the spread of the second economy

The desire to produce a plan covering every economic process has always run up against a certain number of problems, the effect of which has been to maintain certain areas in which agents remain autonomous within the framework of planning. Despite constraints arising from wage policies, for instance, workers have always been able to sell their labour freely, even though its selling price is arbitrarily fixed by the central authorities. There are many kinds of activities outside the plan and forming particular markets of 'varying colours' as Katzenelboigen (1978) describes them. Ultimately, however, even the black market is the result of a particular relationship with the planning system, being as it were an antidote to it or an immanent form of adaptation and response to dysfunctions in it. Within limits strictly established by the authorities, such markets are generally tolerated by them and seen as a safety valve for the severe pressures that build up in the first economy, i.e. the State sector.

The development of activities outside the plan is influenced by several factors. The first is the high level of bureaucratization of the productive apparatus, the structure of the seller's market in the economy, where adjustment to demand lacks all flexibility and normally cannot respond continuously or rapidly to it, and the management of shortages arising from the wasted opportunities under administrative management. In real terms, a parallel market develops as soon as the State sector is incapable of meeting the needs of households in such areas as construction, supplies and foodstuffs. The second is the employment situation and wage levels. In Hungary as in the other Eastern European countries, there is a relative shortage of labour, a shortage which must be linked to its relatively low

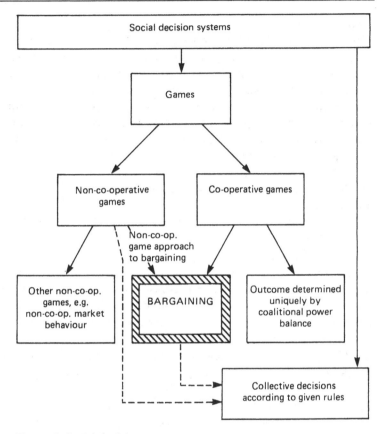

Figure 5 Social decision systems

productivity. In other words, there are considerable reserves of productivity. Politically and socially, however, it seems difficult for the centre to increase productivity without substantial wage rises. Such a step would knock a large hole in the incomes policy and differentials might introduce inequalities in excess of what could be officially tolerated. A further aspect of the shortage of labour has something to do with potential employees who, faced with an inflexible wage level, adjust their productivity to suit it and its purchasing power. The link between productivity and purchasing power is less obvious in Hungary, where there is a continuous and enormous amortization of consumer goods, although there are considerable shortages in other areas such as housing and cars. The combination of low wage levels and expensive durables in limited supply means that a large part of the working population has to resort to second jobs.

The second economy is active in many areas. It has been estimated (Gábor and Galasi, 1981a, and more recently Kornai, 1986, and Chapter 7 of the present work) that several million people are involved, with between 200,000 and 250,000 in small industrial and artisanal undertakings, and five million (over half the population) on small farms and plots, with these undertakings producing as much as would between 750,000 and 800,000 full-time workers. It should be remembered that this work is carried on concurrently with the main employment. The survey carried out by Gábor and Galasi, researchers from the University of Economic Sciences, estimates that retired people and housewives put in 4.5 hours a day and State sector workers at least 3 hours.

Each year 40,000 apartments, equivalent to the output of 120,000 construction workers, are also built during weekends, holidays or periods of sick leave, or when people give up their jobs temporarily. The authors of the survey conclude that every year in agriculture and the building industry the second economy produces the equivalent in hours of work of one million people out of a working population of five million. Such figures in themselves are enough to show how important it is and the effects it can have on the economy. For the sake of social insurance, workers keep their main job. However, the result of their second job is that they are less productive in their first, since it is adjusted to wage levels and they also need to conserve energy to be able to do as much as possible outside. A further consequence is that the shortage of labour in the public sector becomes cumulative, since it is estimated that workers in it spend 10% of their working time in activities other than their main job. Control by means of a wages policy is no longer operative, at least as long as the level of wages offered in the socialist sector is lower than that outside it.

Although the second economy sector is influenced by government, the plan and economic regulators, it is relatively free and has its own rules of behaviour. It is not a private sector in the capitalist sense of the term, for until it was legalized and encouraged by the centre its relation to the official sector was symbiotic (see Chapter 7). A motor mechanic, for instance, employed in a State enterprise in which demand is very high and paid according to the official wage scale, might also work on the black market, dealing with customers directly and carrying out repairs at prices he himself fixes, with some of the costs (spare parts and tools) being met by the enterprise. The same sort of situation applies in the building trade, where the boundary between working for the State and working for private customers is very hard to draw. Agriculture offers the most obvious example, since work on small plots involving machinery is carried out for nothing by State farms or co-operatives, whereas the sale of what the private producer grows is totally uncontrolled. In that sector too some of the costs are borne by the State. In this latter area, the dependence of the non-market sector is very clear. If the government so decided, it could stop or at least reduce the activity of the second economy in agriculture. If it did, however, it would not have the means of putting its policy into practice, for measures of that kind would mean that the socialist agricultural sector would have to be in a position to take over completely from the private sector, whereas in fact they depend on each other. Whilst continuing to aid private enterprise, the government tries to limit it, since it is difficult to regulate it and there is no way of checking the income of producers in these sectors. It has been estimated that in an area totally escaping State control, between 10% and 20% of the national income is involved. Consumers have also come to expect regular supplies from this sector.

In view of the relative scarcity of goods and the dynamic nature of the free sector, there should be scope for unlimited development in the second economy. There are, however, two insurmountable barriers, both connected with the nature of the socialist system. One has to do with public ownership of the means of production, which means that capital and the instruments of production cannot pass into the possession of private individuals. Thus there can be no concentration of the means of production in the hands of individual producers. In reality, it is common to find a way round the prohibition. For example, a co-operative with means of production will make use of the services of a private producer and allow him to use its lorries and plant as he sees fit.

In such a situation, the private sector owes its development to the private activity of an ever more numerous group of people rather than to accumulation. In a certain sense, it is a question of social waste, since the profit brought in by these activities cannot be accumulated and is spent on consumer goods such as privately owned cars and individual houses for the members of the family instead of being ploughed back into the financial circuit. Recent measures have been aimed in particular at attracting capital into official financial channels.

The second barrier is linked to the first, and has to do with the fact that the second economy depends on a socialist sector determined to keep its prerogatives. The logic of private accumulation would bring considerable pressure to bear on the socialist sector and without a doubt strengthen the differentiation process within the bureaucratic system of management.

Nevertheless, the fact that there is an active second economy – quite apart from the function it fulfils – largely helps to feed the economic cycle and, in a sense, to invalidate the projections contained in the plan. This means that the plan is not seen as binding or considered by branch ministries or enterprises to be a realistic expression of the objectives of economic policy.

Since there are a great many heads involved in drawing up the plan, it becomes a co-ordinating device for particular objectives. It is also known that by the end of its first year, exogenous and endogenous constraints will mean that objectives cannot be attained, and so there is a partial modification every year until the last one in the five-year period covered, at which point it will be declared that it has been completed. The truth of the matter however is that there will be no more than a series of rectifications to the objectives initially established, as the central apparatus is generally incapable of predicting fluctuations and changes in internal and external circumstances.

In such a situation the second economy, which is developing within certain limits, acts as a kind of safety valve within the planned system. In part, it helps regulate economic activity by relieving pressure on the first economy, but its role is a wider one, since it is also one of the forms taken by the recovered – and necessary – autonomy of agents. Because of this, it is destined to play a greater part in years to come, as appears to be suggested by the 1981 reforms, which legalized and encouraged secondary activities.

6   Investment choices

With the introduction of a decentralized decision-making process, investment in the New Economic Mechanism (NEM) was a response to requests formulated simultaneously by enterprises and the centre. The demands the two made were reflected in the profit and efficiency indicators with regard to financing on the one hand and output on the other. There was an attempt to use the partial decentralization of investment to combine complementary choices in an optimal way. The institutional structure of the old system of management still heavily influenced the working of the investment system, however, and largely hampered all attempts to achieve the original aims. The emergence of micro-economic interests with varying motivations also brought about a certain number of dysfunctions in investment policy which led to a degree of recentralization of investment decisions.

In the NEM, investment was part of the system of regulation and hence one of the basic components of a way of dynamically combining the micro-economic decisions of the units of production with macro-economic objectives. The choices made at both those levels had particular aims. In the case of those at the macro-economic level vital matters like the growth rate, industrial structure, the gap between the advanced countries and Hungary's productive apparatus, were involved. In that of decisions at the micro-economic level, the importance of development was stressed, at least in theory, and efficiency at this level presupposes that investment needs are established according to criteria which enable optimal use to be made of the factors of production.

In that sense, investment decisions were quite different from those under the old system, where it was fixed centrally and then broken up according to quotas and specific objectives established at branch level. Enterprises received their capital allocations along with the inputs in terms of the targets assigned to them. In such circumstances, the constraint of development – expressed in increased efficiency in the factors of production – was not the prime motive behind the actions of heads of enterprises. Indeed, under the administrative system it was better for enterprises, which were highly influenced by the ministries, to encourage extensive development and increase their productive capacity in order to step up production. The explicit recognition that there were several centres and levels of decision-making did not, however, mean that the process of accumulation was to be made completely autonomous. Indeed, the part played by regulation and particularly by investment financing was such that central functions were still the determining factor, even though decisions were now made at levels closer to that where the investment project was carried out.

There was a multi-dimensional aspect to the decision-making system that was introduced, since several levels were now involved in it. In most cases, initial projects drawn up in the light of one situation were ultimately shifted to another, and investment decisions reflected the relative strength of particular interests. The result was that the centres of decision recognized in the NEM gave rise to a system of or machinery for decision-making that had its own particular features. Trying to determine whether enterprises were now in a position to impose their will on the centre or intermediate bodies shaped the decisions of central planners is a question with no straightforward answer. Any response to it must be sophisticated and qualified enough to take a number of explanatory elements into consideration, for although such bodies might be able to procure the decisions they wanted, the centre was still in a position to make them ensure that its own had priority.

Deciding to invest

Investment is the outstanding indicator of the autonomous activity of an enterprise seeking to use its factors of production in the optimal way. A certain number of conditions have to be met if this is to be achieved. It has to be able to make truly independent decisions about its choice of inputs (plant, technology, raw materials and the like), outputs and marketing strategies. There must also be a homogeneous system of allocating resources, that is, a capital market in which enterprises can both acquire what they need and do so in terms of the credit policy in operation. In a decentralized system of that type, the only area in which the weight of the centre makes itself felt is in macro-economic decisions concerning monetary, credit and stabilization policy, the part to be played by guidance and encouragement, and the like. For market relationships of that kind to develop within the framework of a socialist system, it is certain that a quite different set of conditions would have to be met.

The complex nature of the decision-making process is precisely a result of that kind of duality, and we need to have a clear picture of the respective fields of centre and enterprises and those areas where they intersect.

The dividing line between macro- and micro-economic spheres has always been drawn pragmatically rather than theoretically, although some writers certainly refer to the classical theoretical division formulated by Marx in *Capital*. Huszár and Mandel (1972) for example see investment decisions at enterprise level as forming part of the process of simple reproduction and hence as helping to maintain existing productive capacity and the State, since it creates further productive capacity, as contributing to an extended type of reproduction. They also take pains to make it clear that this is not the whole picture, however, since although there is some theoretical justification for it, the dividing line in the real world is less clear and sometimes hard to draw. The distinction between replacement investment and capacity expanding investment is also to some extent purely a formal one if we remember that the latter, in that it incorporates technical advances, also includes the former. What makes a distinction between the two spheres even more problematic is the fact that the investment funds set aside by enterprises are barely enough to renew obsolete fixed capital and that their old practices always tend to make them increase their productive capacity.

Over a period of time, enterprises played an increasingly large role in investment decisions, as can be seen from tables 6.1 and 6.2.

1. Central investment decisions: bases and criteria

Essentially, two criteria are involved, the first connected with the structure of the system of production and the second more with *ad hoc* concerns. The plan contains provisions for both. Before examining them it would be useful to look at the various types of State investment.

(a) *The main types of central investment* Large investments are the main kind undertaken by the state and include both investments

Table 6.1. *Distribution of investment by decision-making authority in industries*

Years	Government	Enterprises
1970	41.7	58.3
1975	32.0	68.0
1980	36.70	61
1985	31.57	68.47

Source: Statisztikai Evkönyv, various years.

Table 6.2. *Structure by type of investment*

	1970	1975	1980	1985
Major investments	15.4	13.8	30.4	21.5
Group investments	20.4	20.6	7.5	8.5
Other investments	9.1	10.7	0.8	0.8
Total State investments	44.6	45.1	38.7	30.8
Socialist enterprise investments	37.9	42.9	58.3	60.2
Co-operative investments	17.5	11.8	3.0	
Total enterprise investments	55.4	54.9	61.3	60.2
Total investments	100	100	100	100

Source: Statisztikai Evkönyv, various years.

in infrastructures and those too costly to be undertaken by a single enterprise,[1] all of which help to modify the structure of the apparatus of production. They include in particular such projects as the construction of energy and nuclear plants, cement works and refineries. A two-stage approval procedure – either by the planning committee or the government, depending on the importance of the project – is involved. First there is an examination of the overall concept from the point of view of its value, its substitution effect on imports and internal equilibrium, and it is then approved. The next is that of deciding to invest. The planning committee costs the project, looks at ways and means of allotting funds, construction time and profitability indicators.

It then becomes part of the plan, in both its five-year and its annual form, with details of the investment and building and financing schedules. Construction deadlines are often not met, however, and this sets up a snowball effect, increasing the tensions in the invest-ment system when limited resources have to finance both old and new projects.

Investments for specific or 'aim-grouped' purposes differ from those described above, both in what they set out to achieve and in the way in which they are determined. Aim-grouped investment is an integrated procedure in which various enterprises are to be brought together to achieve a particular objective with the help of suitable means of finance. Where a section of a road is to be built, for instance, the project consists of co-ordinating and planning the activities of the enterprises involved, taking into account such matters as increasing productive capacities for bitumen, manufacturing road signs, and estimating the size of the fleet of excavating equipment required.

Such projects are approved by the government. During a five-year period, a programme for each individual group will be authorized. In the case of the building industry, for example, the number of flats to be built is determined, with indications as to how many are to be built by the State, the proportion to be built in towns and in the country in each area, what technology is to be used in what proportion in relationship to the existing stock, the average size of the flats, and so on. At the second stage of the operation, the approval of the various tiers of local government involved also has to be obtained before the project is finally adopted.

With investments by productive group, approval also involves two stages, with the government and then the branch ministries giving their views. This two-stage procedure generally provides considerable opportunities for bargaining.

Other State investments include that part of central investment in enterprises and the socialist 'public sector' such as health and edu-cation. Here, the traditional method is still in operation, with the National Planning Office approving the various projects submitted to it by branch ministries or territorial directorates.

(b) The structural criterion   At the central level, the decision to invest reflects the need to shape structural development in the economy by taking into account both external and internal equilibria and their effect on the system. It follows from an examination of developments in the major aggregates such as the growth and

accumulation rates on the one hand and the specific needs of branches expected to achieve their objectives and thus ensure dynamic growth in the productive apparatus on the other. This means that structural modifications necessarily entail a specific method of allocation for branches if they are to be able to perform what the planners require of them. The latter also take the view that only a macro-economic approach provides the means of both perceiving necessary modifications to structures and implementing an appropriate policy aimed at changing the make-up of capital in the branches once investment has reached its maximum level.

(c) *The criterion of economic policy*   At this level, central investment decisions arise more from a consideration of the measures required by economic policy and are more specifically concerned with ensuring that the investment system works smoothly. This function is therefore an element in the economic process. In this area, however, economic policy measures with regard to investment are remarkable precisely because of current methods of determining accumulation.

From a macro-economic point of view, investment serves various purposes. The function of central decisions with regard to structures has just been considered. Although they *are* central, they belong more to the domain of micro-economic behaviour, particularly when they involve large-scale investment for projects such as building new factories or cement works. In such cases, the centre acts like an enterprise, since it has to meet two requirements, namely providing the best way of financing them and estimating what output can be expected.

In the field of economic policy, central decisions primarily serve to meet the need for a coherent package of investment decisions combining all those taken at both the macro- and the micro-levels. This means that some of them may entail a partial recentralization of the kind that occurred in 1971, when enterprises were able to make their own decisions as a result of the reforms embarked on major investment without having the means to finance it, and again in 1978 to halt the growth in investment and in 1981 to balance foreign trade figures once more.

Controlling the demand for investment and reducing macro-economic tensions are not, however, the sole aim of partial recentralization. It also has to ensure a better allocation of investment, which might at first sight seem rather paradoxical if we consider the macro-economic level of decision-making, which is in fact applied to the micro-economic level. In a situation of that kind, central decisions are actually much more important, contrary to what statistics might lead us to believe.

Bukta (1974: 7) sees central investment as accounting for as much as 70% of the total. He also goes on to say that the remaining 30% can be reduced to 20% if we use the hypothesis that at least 10% of investment is for replacement and not capacity expansion. The economic policy of investment, with its characteristic feature of the primacy of central decisions, was also in his view justified by 'political and economic considerations (the weight of planned infrastructural investments; tasks requiring central interference; actions demanding high concentration of funds, etc.) or by the necessity of solving on the macro-level particular economic conflicts' (1974: 9). More particularly, it is a matter of questions of adjustment, arbitration and stabilization. Adjustment proved necessary in the face of the disequilibrium between the major sectors and at the level of aggregates (growth rate, an increasing investment rate, and so on), arbitration between the various sectors applying for investment, and stabilization in the face of the multiplicity of both central and decentralized decisions.

(d) The various levels of decision-making in the centre   What is known as the centre consists of various functional organizations each with its own role to play at this particular level of the hierarchy of decision. That of the National Planning Office is to construct the plan, to make sure that it is coherent, and to follow and supervise its implementation. The Ministry of Finance is responsible for equilibrium in the budget and the balance of payments; the National Bank for operating the credit policy; and the Prices Office for implementing prices policy, and so on. Each of the various bodies has different concerns, however, and their members do not behave in a single uniform way, as specialists in functional institutions in contact with individual sectors tend to adopt the kind of behaviour usual in such sectors and hence to defend their interests and meet their investment needs.

The functional bodies also have to be aware of macro-economic considerations if they are not to work against their own interests, which means that they are particularly likely to accede to investment requests from enterprises and ministries. On the other hand, leaders and experts, who are concerned solely with major macro-economic equilibria (that is, with the overall proportions of the plan and budget equilibrium) are in quite a different position. There is no advantage for them in increasing the volume of investment, and their prime concern is to rationalize expenditure. They are best placed to ensure that central decisions are in fact rational, since they have no particular axe to grind.

The mere fact that an investment project has been approved is not enough in itself, of course, to guarantee that it is rational and coherent. It is not so much approval that influences the decision to invest as the preparation of the decision and the access to the information on which the project is based. In this area, attempts at the macro-economic level to make sure that investment is efficient will not carry much weight if they do not go hand in hand with an effective constraint.

Decisions at the centre therefore involve various criteria, all of which are appropriate. However rationally the process is carried out it nevertheless reflects a paradox, since although decentralizing enterprises is used as a means of making their decisions more effective, central decisions are used to achieve the aim.

2. Investment decisions at enterprise level

Given the important part played by the centre, enterprises clearly had a reduced margin of freedom in decision-making. What decentralization set out to do was to give them a real degree of autonomy, particularly as regards investment, to help them become the real centres of maximization, but the result was in fact a paradoxical situation reflecting the contradiction brought about by the extension of horizontal mechanisms in relation to the vertical ones perpetuated in the new regulatory system. In other words, the latter still duplicated what the former were intended to do.

Under the old system, micro-economic decisions had to a certain extent been taken into consideration even when central decisions were used to ensure that the same objectives were being sought, and the relative autonomy of enterprises, even if it was not officially recognized, was necessary if their heads were to obtain a regular supply of inputs and to be in a favourable position to negotiate them and their production programmes.

The part played by enterprises in investment decisions seems to justify the opinion of two specialists (Huszár and Mandel, 1973: 32) that there was an explicit distinction between reproduction in the wider sense (capacity expanding investment) and in the narrower sense of replacement investment, with the former being the prerogative of the centre and the latter that of enterprises. The reason for their view seems to be that the freedom of decision of enterprises was caught in a kind of pincer movement by a double system of regulation, with its twin arms of financial regulators and central decisions. Here, the paradox was that although the constraint of maximization was almost entirely imposed by the centre, the behaviour of enterprises seemed to have been dictated by other criteria.

Enterprises were also part of a hierarchical structure, and many of their decisions were a result of that constraint. In this context, their area of autonomy was considerably restricted by sectorial authorities and branch ministries. Even though the latter were formally dissolved in 1968 and finally abolished in 1980, such interventions merely became functional rather than sectorial.

The decisions enterprises took were therefore made within a multi-decisional framework, and here the centre was therefore the rational agency, since it acted within a perspective of maximization, whereas enterprises behaved in such a way as to develop a strategy of which that particular aim formed a part.

(a) *The investment needs and demands of enterprises* Putting forward the idea of the centre as the rational agent in the field of investments involved both questioning and justifying its decisions. Investment demands from enterprises on the other hand correspon-ded, at a certain level, to recognized social needs.[2] What was critical, however, was the lack of connection between the way such needs were expressed at enterprise level and the way enterprises were run. During the period of administrative planning, they normally received investments via the branch ministries. The need for it was assessed using quantitative criteria: what extra output could an enterprise produce if given extra investment? The ways of judging investment efficiency were also based on quite specific norms, and enterprises were encouraged to increase their production not only by injunctions from the centre, but also by their own moral responsibility. They had to meet – and to take steps to meet – social expectations which vaguely reflected 'the will of the people' and party objectives as far as increased production was concerned.

In that situation, it was (and as we shall see still is) up to the enterprise or the next higher echelon in the hierarchy to show that investment was needed if it was to be planned for. For enterprises themselves, this step was vital, since if it was planned for it would be financed by one method or another.

This form of accumulation has deeply affected the enterprise behaviour. The function of investments passed on to them through the branch ministries, which were real centres of decision with regard to industrial policy, was to increase productive capacity. Enterprises, as extensions of the ministries, pursued extensive growth. In their view, that kind of development allowed them to increase their output and hence to strengthen their hand, within the particular system of allocation, when extra resources were being negotiated, thus increasing the demand for investment when the centre was trying to reduce it.

To their way of thinking, optimization was not linked to the maximum output produced by the addition of an extra unit of capital. They saw themselves as obliged to get into a position that would enable them to acquire optimal investment, particularly by means of finance from many sources and largely consisting of preferential credits, free loans or subsidies. This certainly put some distance between them and 'rationality', but ultimately it was a result of the multi-decisional system in operation at the time.

At enterprise level the decision to invest was taken by directors in the light of the interests and potential of the units of production. Micro-economic decisions could nevertheless still be directly or indirectly influenced by the centre, which tried to impose its macro-economic objectives on enterprises to make them comply with its own development plan. To guide the decisions of micro-economic units, it had various instruments at its disposal. These were the general provisions for taxation, affecting the extent of demand and the monetary resources of enterprises, the general regulation of profit, guaranteeing that the postulate of economic efficiency would apply, and the use of administrative provisions prohibiting or reducing certain investments, an example of this being the obligation to cover the costs of importing equipment in advance. An enterprise with sufficient resources of its own to carry out investment was also obliged to notify the central authority, but the documents it filled in to that end took the place of a declaration. The nature of the decision-making system and financing were such that very few enterprises were capable of providing their own finance. There were perhaps a dozen large ones spread over various sectors – aluminium, the extraction of oil and gas and pharmaceuticals – forming an exception to the general rule and the decisions of which, though taken within the framework of current regulators, were seen as autonomous.

There were, however, other sectors in which autonomous investment decisions began to appear, but the expenditure involved was generally well below average. This is reflected in a relatively low investment rate amounting to only 12% to 15% of all enterprise investment. It also represented barely 3% of the value of enterprise fixed capital, whereas over the national productive sphere as a whole the average was 7%. It was therefore not even sufficient to replace obsolete fixed capital.

This contrast seems to justify the distinction Huszár and Mandel make between simple reproduction, about which enterprises made decisions, and reproduction in the wider sense, which was the affair of both enterprises and the centre. It could not be otherwise, given the total amounts of development funds. On average, at the national level, they represented in 1981 6% of the value of the stock of capital. This meant that most enterprises more or less had to seek finance from external sources, despite the fact that in certain sectors there were enterprises apparently capable of providing their own. One reason for the difference was the low scrapping rate for fixed capital (1.4% p.a.) and a high annual rate of increase (6%) for the stock of capital.

(b) The apparent autonomy of enterprises in making investment choices Self-financing, which is an expression of autonomous decision-making, was an exception, and only a tiny proportion of enterprises engaged in it. Several factors were involved here.

In the first place, the situation was the result of a system of regulators which centralized a large part of the resources of enterprises, even if it meant subsequently returning some of them in the form of subsidies, loans or credits at favourable rates. The aim of financial regulation was to unify the behaviour of the various units of production while perpetuating central control.

Table 6.3, which shows various financial indicators, illustrates both the extremely heterogeneous nature of the financial structure of branches and the importance of redistribution by means of subsidies and taxes. Enterprise decisions were usually associated with decisions from the centre or passed on to the branch ministries until they were abolished in 1980.

Several factors influenced enterprise decisions, according to whether the initiative for the investment project came from an enterprise, a ministry or the centre. In each case, the decision was a mixed one, but differed according to its origin. The division between central and decentralized decisions is interesting from a methodological point of view, as it reflects the division of investment as between the two poles.

Table 6.3. *Financial indicators, 1981[a]*

Branch	Structure of capital	Profit rate[b]	Structure of profits	Subsidy/ profit ratio	Tax/profit ratio	Development fund/stock capital ratio	Financing capacity
Mining	8.26	8.63	4.28	0.30	9.27	0.07	29.97
Energy	13.60	1.96	1.60	0.02	5.09	0.	3.74
Metallurgy	10.01	7.55	4.54	1.36	1.26	0.03	22.61
Mechanical	19.17	25.82	29.73	0.15	0.77	0.17	80.40
Construction	7.16	9.06	3.90	0.08	0.50	0.03	47.79
Chemical	15.47	19.53	18.15	0.20	0.60	0.04	39.57
Heavy industry total	73.70	14.05	62.22	0.25	1.45	0.05	35.26
Light industry	11.41	27.66	18.95	0.30	0.47	0.09	98.40
Various industries	1.10	43.91	2.85	0.02	0.30	0.11	57.12
Food industry	1.38	19.27	15.95	0.64	0.57	0.06	53.70
Socialist industry	100	16.65	100	0.32	1.09	0.06	43.02

[a] 1981 is taken as an example. Given the changes in the regulations governing enterprise incomes, it is difficult to present homogeneous data. (Cf. Kornai and Matits (1984)).
[b] Profit/fixed capital.
Source: Calculations based on *Statisztikai Evkönyv*, 1981, Budapest, 1982.

At the level of development policy, however, such an approach may seem both formal and exclusive, since it tends to present any decision falling outside such a classification as an anomaly. But decision-making is not something that can be removed from the system of which it is a part. All decisions are based on a set of elements and factors that to some degree make up information. Decision theory therefore presupposes perfect information. Within the hierarchy, however, the cost of information differs according to the various bodies involved. With regard to investment decisions the centre tends, because it has direct access to information, to proclaim itself to be the agent of rationality and thus to take over some of the recognized functions of micro-economic units. The latter are however in a position to make their own rational decisions in such areas – at least in theory – as although they have information from their own sphere and the markets they operate in, they do not have the necessary means of achieving optimal development.

(i) *The influence of the centre on autonomous decisions.* The influence of the centre on the choices of enterprises is obvious in many ways, since it both makes use of regulatory instruments and draws up its own investment programmes and hence intervenes directly in the process. It decides (and its decision can be seen as the outcome of bargaining) on both major investments and grouped aims. The two types of investment reflect the choice of criteria and also imply co-ordination with the enterprises carrying out the projects, the activities of which are thus guided by central decisions. In that sense, the centrally defined investment policy provides the State with a further means of direct intervention in the way accumulation is to be subject to overall direction. Certain enterprises are in fact keen to have such collaboration, as it means that they will have both resources and outlets, since when an enterprise investment project is in line with one proposed by the centre, the allocations needed to increase capacity will be provided free of charge. In a situation of that type, an enterprise once again comes within the orbit of central decisions, a state of affairs satisfactory to both the centre and the branch ministries in so far as it means that investment is once more monocentric in nature.

(ii) *Seeking the best solution to the problem of financing by enterprises.* The share of enterprise profits paid into the development fund under current regulations is not great enough to permit self-financing, and recourse to external sources is the rule. At the same time, however, the cost of investment, if really borne by enterprises, would be relatively high given both fiscal charges on capital and its relative scarcity. This means that an enterprise contemplating investment, sometimes under pressure from a branch ministry, has to make sure that it has finance from several sources, at least one of which would provide it at no cost, before coming to a final decision. This is much more complicated an undertaking than it might appear, since trying to find external finance influences its whole investment policy. It may receive funds from several sources at the same time, or engage in more than one project simultaneously, 'financing one investment from its own resources while applying for credit for the other, moreover, it may also have an investment project on which it is given a budgetary subsidy. Furthermore, a part of the enterprises carry out investments decided by the state, but may simultaneously invest separately from their own funds, and may obtain in addition either credit or subsidy. True, these are separate decisions but are not independent of each other' (Deák, 1978: 65–66).

(iii) *The part played by macro-economic bodies in investment decisions.* To some extent, such institutions were the vectors of extensive accumulation. Their actions led to a logic producing a policy of over-investment, and ministries functioned as both trusts and enterprises.

As trusts, they helped to create combines in the economy and thus produced a situation in which bargaining became a particular form of allocation, and put themselves forward as partners of the centre in the business of determining and allocating central investment. Their position in the hierarchy meant that they could also claim that in relation to the centre they were enterprises and ask it to consider their own investment projects. On the other hand, in relation to the enterprises in their sector, they were the centre and could impose certain decisions on them.

This two-fold pattern of behaviour did cause certain dysfunctions, which will be examined later. Here, however, the mechanics of the way they conducted themselves in investment decisions needs to be investigated. Seen within the framework of the socialist ownership of the means of production, some contradiction is apparent. As sectorial organizations, they were specialized agencies of the centre and therefore acted as passers-on of central decisions and controllers of the enterprises in their sector. Their part in the hierarchy created by the uniform nature of ownership was that of an intermediary between the centre and the units of production. That kind of functional division however took no account of the organic relationship between officially separate bodies that determined their behaviour.

Within the area of investment in particular, decisions from the ministries worked against rather than towards the achievement of central objectives. Indeed, as one writer has stressed, 'their behaviour in the decision process is motivated not by the efforts of the economy toward equilibrium or by the criterion of efficiency, etc., but by the development needs of the given industry (sector). The various levels of sectoral control (e.g., within manufacturing: the industry, product group, ministry) are always the initiators of expansion of the fields and economic units under their control' (Mandel, 1974: 46). There was also competition between branches for central funds to cover the whole of their investment costs, which in its turn contributed to breakdown of central investment.

At this level the basis for decisions was the desire to increase the economic weight of the branch, however efficient or inefficient the projected investments might prove to be. It was more likely to produce results than attempting to increase efficiency, as extended productive capacity helped to maintain and strengthen the position of branches in central planning, particularly as regards the final destination of the resources it allocated.

If branch ministries behaved in such a way, it was because they could also exert great and possibly decisive influence on the choices made by enterprises. They intervened in negotiations concerning all types of central investment. Getting an investment project involving major works written into the plan was a concrete illustration of the relative power of a sector or branch, since such investment tended to increase its productive capacity, and it was the ministries that brought it to its ultimate execution.[3]

As far as autonomous investment was concerned, the influence of the branch ministries made itself felt in almost every enterprise. Decisions in this field were affected by it when medium-term investment and planning projects they had drawn up were being examined or the performance of their directors evaluated.[4] They also gave an opinion on every request for credits put forward by enterprises, and none could be granted without it. In addition, their representatives were members of the commissions allocating subsidies. Although not in a position to make their decisions alone, they could guide those of the centre and enterprise.

To some degree, they identified with the objectives of those enterprises under their control, especially as far as development projects were concerned, and also helped procure finance for such activities, and were sometimes behind decisions helping to increase the productive capacity of enterprises. In that, however, they had a specific aim, and were all the more likely to support and encourage them if they were not to be subsequently responsible for finding outlets for the extra products resulting from extra capacity. Nor were they involved in the management of units of production.

The situation with regard to investments decided on by large enterprises outside their control was rather different, even if they had access to certain credit facilities. Such enterprises were more exposed to the constraint of profitability, whereas the ministries were not – a fact which largely helped to feed the permanent demand for investment in the various sectors.

The contradictions in such a situation meant that branch ministries could swing decisions their own way and hence protect themselves from criticism by attributing errors or failures to the decision-making system operating at the micro-economic level and counterbalancing unfavourable effects on profits by granting exemptions in individual cases (Mandel, 1974: 47).

It can thus be seen that specific sectorial interests played a large part in investment decisions and also affected the system of making decisions as a whole. Investment decisions were made for various reasons, but were still to a large extent determined by relationships between the centre and enterprises. Ultimately the very varied behaviour patterns of agents at the different levels of the hierarchy were the result of the conflict between, on the one hand, the desire to maintain central control of the bulk of investment and, on the other, the wish to enable subordinate bodies to bring pressure to bear to ensure a suitable distribution of investment resources.

Financing and the attempt to find a norm of investment efficiency

The NEM is based on a certain number of functional relationships between various authorities of a macro-, meso- or micro-economic nature. The autonomy of agents is no more than relative, as some of the features of the centralized system have been retained in the new decentralized one. In particular, the influence of the market is purely relative and felt mainly in the fields of trade and the horizontal circulation of goods and services. However, the centre's prerogatives have been maintained as far as producer and capital goods are concerned.

Although norms for the allocation of capital were introduced, the older ones, of a centralized nature, were still deemed acceptable and

Table 6.4. *State budgets (billions of forints)*

Item	1970	1975	1980	1985
Revenues				
Direct taxes				
Wages taxes and social security				
contributions	25.0	37.4	53.7	161.1
Profits and income taxes	52.0	99.3	102.6	153.3
Production taxes and rents	11.8	25.9	21.9	20.9
Taxes on capital	25.2	25.0	2.4	29.5
Total direct taxes	114.0	187.6	180.6	364.8
Indirect taxes				
Turnover taxes	23.9	30.0	60.9	92.2
Tariffs and import sales taxes	13.1	21.9	22.0	25.2
Differential producers' sales taxes	—	—	71.0	54.0
Total indirect taxes	37.0	51.9	153.9	171.4
Other revenues	20.9	73.8	88.5	57.3
Total revenues	171.9	313.3	423.0	593.5
Expenditure				
Investment	37.4	65.0	69.6	68.8
Price and production support	50.0	103.4	131.8	152.9
Social security	22.2	43.0	77.7	131.5
Health, education, culture	21.2	34.8	56.0	105.2
Defence and internal security	14.8	19.2	27.8	37.7
Other	30.1	50.8	64.6	120.2
Total expenditure	175.7	316.2	427.5	609.3
Budget deficit	−3.8	−3.0	−4.5	−15.8

Note: Dashes indicate years for which there was no such tax category.
Sources: IMF Government Finance Statistical Yearbook (1986) and Hungarian Ministry of Finance.

there was none readily available in connection with investment efficiency. This was partly the result of a failure to enforce proper means of financing investments. Apart from self-financing – which is now the most popular method – investment is currently financed from two sources, the State budget (see Table 6.4) and bank credits.

There has always been a formal distinction between the two (or at least this was the case until 1 January 1987, when the single-bank system broke up) in so far as credit policy concerning the total funds made available to enterprises was linked to planning objectives. The difference between the two ways of financing, however, was connected to conditions for obtaining funds which, as has been seen, were by no means always clear-cut. Given the excessive level of centralization in financial matters, self-financing tended to open doors to other sources of finance rather than to act as a means of limiting enterprise indebtedness.

1. The sources of finance

(a) *The budgetary control of investment expenditure*   Finance for State investments and those proposed by enterprises and incorporated into the five-year plan was provided through the budget. It tended to decrease as a proportion of total finance, falling to 40% or less according to the year. This was the result of a double constraint, since for some years the government had been obliged to adopt a rigorous policy of adjustment, which led to growth in the direct financing of enterprises by increases in their own funds, and an extension of credit policy and the growth of other forms of financing such as the bond market. Mention must also be made of the part played by production subsidies, special subsidies and other types of free loans, which offered indirect ways of arranging financial resources for enterprises.

(b) *Credit policy*   Credit policy was implemented by the Hungarian National Bank. Until the reforms of 1 January 1987 (see Chapter 7) the banking system in Hungary, like that in all the other socialist countries, consisted of a single multi-functional institution, the National Bank, which included all the functions of central, business and deposit banks. Given its nature, it implemented all the recommendations formulated by the government each year in the light of economic circumstances.

Acting as a financial intermediary was what was traditionally required of it.

Credit policy had to serve many purposes. Some of these were to ensure equilibrium, control increases in purchasing power, increase economic efficiency and technical development, implement the investment programmes in the plan, participate in the complicated programme of socialist economic integration within Comecon and to encourage the production and sale of goods potentially saleable on the hard-currency markets in particular. New criteria taking into account international economic developments and the country's indebtedness have recenty been introduced, and consideration is also being given to projects that save foreign currency, rationalize production and reduce the consumption of raw materials and energy.

Investment credits were used to finance enterprise projects and supplement their resources and to swell the investment funds being built up at enterprise level. The National Bank's contribution never amounted to more than the estimated cost of a project, and this was reduced by the total value of any subsidy the enterprise might receive.

Loan conditions were similar to those pertaining in market economies, whereas investment projects had to be part of wider macroeconomic ones. The enterprise had to be in a healthy financial position with a reasonable and viable project and credits had to be repaid from its own funds within the prescribed period. Where machinery was involved, labour-saving projects that also increased productivity were likely to be considered.

There was also a profitability threshold. The Bank's view was that an investment project was viable if it could guarantee an annual profit rate on the sums invested. These were set at: 20% for mechanical engineering and the chemical and building industries; 15% for metallurgy and light industry; and 7% for transport, communications and agriculture. In general, increases in branch efficiency as a result of investment were greater than this, variations between them notwithstanding. Over the past decade, the figures for investments partly financed by investment credits have been 17%, 20% and 18% respectively, and at present the overall average is around 15%.

The interest rates the National Bank offered (until 1 January 1987) varied according to both the loan period and the aims of monetary policy and, more generally, decisions arising from economic policy. Apart from the traditional distinction between medium- and long-term investment, the particular nature of certain investments, such as those for machinery from Western markets, was also taken into account. In itself, the cost of borrowing was not prohibitive for enterprises in a position to acquire finance from various sources, in particular if it came from State subsidies and bank credits. In such cases, the former was a precondition for the latter, which often encouraged enterprises to invest, as subsidies helped to reduce the cost of investment.

The government could also give other subsidies by means of tax concessions, which were an indirect way of providing investment funds. The whole amount was released in the form of an investment credit for the usual period and with the usual stipulations. In practice, there was a certain amount of departure from the rules normally relating to enterprises applying for credit facilities. For short-term or structural reasons, the central Bank might offer particular conditions with regard to interest rates, repayment periods and expected returns on investment. Specific cases in which they might be available included investment aimed at increasing and making more readily available the supply of services to the population (lower interest rates, longer repayment periods, a low profitability rate); those intended to encourage the construction of machinery within the country or to facilitate importing it from Comecon (favourable exchange rates and import substitutions); and those helping reduce shortages in the building industry or develop high-technology equipment, and so on. The National Bank could also make credit facilities for several billion forints available to exporting industries offering projects to increase exports (which generally also helped to increase imports as the GDP increased).

2. The strategy of firms, and multi-source investment financing

As we have seen, financial regulation provided for the allocation of resources at two levels. The first was within the enterprise, by means of various funds (development, wages and, to a lesser extent, reserve) and the second between enterprises and the government, where funds were released according to a system of allocation unfavourable to them as a result of the over-centralization of profits. The consequence of this was that their cash flow was relatively low in relation to fixed assets and reflected their great dependence on external sources of finance. The position they were in illustrates the contradictions and in particular the overlapping present in the system of financing. The inadequacy of the regulatory system is clear; its only function was to reflect central decisions and in particular its determination to make sure that it had sufficient means of controlling the behaviour of enterprises. The resulting paradoxical state of affairs arose from the fact that it was the centre that assumed the function of acting as the agent of rationality in micro-economic matters, whereas enterprises, given the rigidity of the institutional system and the pattern of activity developing at the level of intermediate and subordinate bodies, had no inducement to behave rationally or make the best use of the factors of production. Here, in fact, their best move was to seek finance from several different sources and hence reduce its cost.

The reason there were so many sources is that it was impossible to have a dual system based on two principles, that is with major investment financed by the State by budgetary means alone and that at enterprise level financed partly from their own resources and partly from bank credits. Since, however, there is a high degree of correlation between methods of financing and investment decisions, any major deviation between them will inevitably give rise to tensions within the investment system. Nevertheless, the fact that there were many mutually complementary sources of finance and means of repayment meant that enterprises had the opportunity to use a combination of various possibilities.

(a) The many different ways of financing enterprise investment
Originally, the various sources of investment finance served quite specific purposes, with central funds earmarked for centrally determined projects and enterprise development funds used essentially for those determined at the micro-economic level. Subsidies were allocated according to certain planning objectives, with a tripartite committee consisting of representatives of the National Planning Office, the Investment Bank (a specialized branch of the Hungarian National Bank) and the branch ministries deciding which enterprises would receive them.

The way in which subsidies were allocated could vary. They might come directly from the centre, or be a form of price support or, more generally since 1976, take the form of tax concessions, with the centre reducing the rate on certain assets. In that situation, an enterprise might ask for investment credit and receive it in the form of funds released by the lower tax rate, with the State taking its due through different channels.

With regard to investments decided upon by the State, there were two types of finance, budget allocations and State loans. The first provided direct finance via the State budget, which enterprises were not required to repay if they decided to proceed with the investment; the second were repayable from pre-tax and pre-amortization profits. It has been estimated that enterprises provided between 6% and 8% of the cost of central investment. This might seem strange, but in the view of those responsible for such projects it was quite reasonable, since enterprises had investment funds which otherwise would not be used, and increased capacity normally goes hand in hand with the replacement of obsolete fixed assets, which meant that enterprises were contributing to central investments rather than replacement investments.

Investment credits from the National Bank had to be repaid from the enterprises' development fund but here, as will be shown in greater detail later, there were interactions that could wipe out the benefits of this type of finance. It is also important to work out the extent to which the various possible types were used in the investment enterprises engaged in and the connections between them.

(b) The various methods of financing used

(i) *Investment credits*. The initial aim of the reform of the system of allocating investments was to link it to the needs of enterprises by means of the indicators (profits, development funds, payments to amortization funds and the like) provided by the units of production. The attempt to create a more homogeneous system was also to lead to increased emphasis on one particular source, investment credits. Before the new round of reforms implemented in the early 1980s more than a quarter of investment costs were supported by credits from the National Bank, or more precisely its subsidiary the State Investment Bank. Two-fifths of enterprises used these and they contributed two-thirds of the costs of investment at enterprise level. They are not, however, the only financial resources available to enterprises wishing to invest, as there are also subsidies, State loans and so on.

A former director of the State Investment Bank draws from this a conclusion that casts a great deal of light on the way in which investment financing is carried out:

> It turns out that a great part of *enterprises can raise credits for some investment project because another one is financed from state subsidy, or state loan, perhaps budgetary allocation.* But these are never independent of one another, it is precisely one of the investment that provides favourable opportunities for another one! Moreover, it is by now quite common that they cannot be distinguished even to this extent, but subsidy and credit are simultaneously used for financing the same investment. A possible interpretation of this intertwining is that an enterprise would not be creditworthy without subsidy for as big an investment project as it intends to carry out ... *It is the subsidy that makes it creditworthy.* (Deák, 1978: 69–70)

More generally, it has been estimated that half the total investment credits go to enterprises also receiving State subsidies and a third to investments chiefly supported by allocations from the State budget.

(ii) *The part played by subsidies in investment.* There are several reasons for the wider part played by subsidies, the chief of which has to do with the objectives contained and defined in the central plan. They are also means of dealing with the insolvency some enterprises suffer from or, to be more exact, the inability of some of them to mobilize the resources they need to meet some of their financial obligations in the framework of central investment. This also explains the larger number of central objectives, which is a reflection of the recentralization of decision-making. It seems to those operating at the macro-economic level that it is there and there only that such objectives can be formulated. In that kind of situation, allocating subsidies becomes an important activity, even if the total sum involved is lower than that of investment credits. It has been estimated that such subsidies have been awarded to over two-fifths of the enterprises accounting for almost two-thirds of all enterprise investment.

Nor are these subsidies necessarily tied to enterprise development plans aimed at rationalizing the productive process or increasing production. They are usually granted to particular enterprises or trusts, which are therefore sure to receive a subsidy before they have even submitted a project. In certain branches like mechanical engineering, seven out of the twelve branch objectives were assigned to specific enterprises, and in the food industry, most of the sixteen specified objectives were taken over by a single trust which therefore benefited from almost all the subsidies.

Multi-source financing is thus a characteristic feature of the behaviour of Hungarian enterprises. There are several reasons for it, the chief of which is the fact that they do not have sufficient funds to carry out their own projects, and the second most important is that State interests are involved in enterprise decisions, particularly when they take part in attaining planning objectives, which generally consist of major investment projects. Resorting to credit to obtain finance may be widespread, but it does not provide enough to carry out major investments. In particular, it raises the question of insolvency, since enterprises are tied to repayment periods. In the case of some, it introduces a constraint that has absolutely nothing to do with the way they behave in relation to public funds. All this explains the reason for the State policy of subsidies. It is not based on a single criterion, but dictated by a number of reasons: an enterprise or sector with an activity that, often because of the price system, is not profitable enough but which merits development (e.g., mining, transport and communications); the achievement of certain objectives producing greater benefits for the economy than they would at enterprise level (e.g., energy-saving plant, labour-saving investments, setting up enterprises outside the capital, etc.); planning provisions which mean that certain sectors need greater investment than they can provide for themselves, when the credit is limited by the ability of the enterprise to repay within given time-limits; or enterprises receiving subsidies because they cannot carry out on their own the investments to increase capacity or to modernize their premises (e.g., Ganz-Mavag, the Danube oil industry, Hungarian Aluminium and the like). In general, if an enterprise can justify the adoption of its project as meriting a subsidy, it can embark on the necessary investment with very little of its own money and not much credit, a chance very few refuse to take. The latitude enterprises have in submitting investment projects to the centre and asking for financial help raised a further question not so far considered, that of assessing the efficiency of investments.

(iii) *Assessing efficiency in investment decisions.* In both economic theory and applied economics the way investment is financed and whether it is efficient are two aspects of the same problem, and it is hard to imagine them being considered separately. In view of what has been said of practice in Hungary, however, it does seem that efficiency has been a secondary consideration and financing the chief concern of those seeking capital allocations. Investment for invest-ment's sake has been carried out on a large scale and intensified by the heterogeneous nature of the system of financing it. Yet the variety of sources of finance could in itself be evidence that investments are efficiently made, as it might lead one to suppose that enterprises are engaged in increasingly severe competition for the necessary funds, which in its turn would lead to a desire to make sure that investment *was* as efficient as possible. The fact of the matter, however, is that there are so many sources not because there is competition between them, but because they are complementary and have different methods of allocation and repayment. This even tends to operate against competitiveness, since there are occasions when they encroach on each other's territory and hence reduce efficiency and encourage enterprises to pursue policies of over-investment, a trend which is in fact strengthened by their widely differing ways of conducting their business.

Since it is the source of central decisions concerning both the ends and the means of regulation, the State is presumed to be the rational force working towards more efficient investment. However, the ministries also develop their own kind of rationality, but one which is not immediately concerned with efficiency, since what they really want is extended productive capacities in their own branches. The real object of enterprises is the best kind of multi-source finance enabling them to fund their own investments with external and if possible *State* aid, and drastically reducing the financial constraints they would be under in the normal way. Thus efficiency is not always a prime concern of investors.

In reality, however, there are various calculations that make it possible to establish a norm of efficiency, even if that norm is not as constraining as it used to be. Under the old planning system, when all investment was centrally determined, there was a Code of Investment which fixed upper limits for investments within sectors. These could vary from sector to sector, but all projects had to be individually specified and describe exactly both their objectives (such as increased capacity) and their likely economic effects (type of product, intermediary consumption, the technology required, their time span and so on). The Code also used indexes to provide ways of calculating how efficient the investment was likely to be. The Gn index offers a useful example:

$$Gn = \frac{S}{\gamma P + R}$$

where S = income from annual production in the factory built with investment aid

P = the total cost of the investment, i.e. all the initial costs involved in building the new unit of production

R = the fixed costs incurred in production, i.e. maintenance costs of the new investment

γ = the interest rate on the capital loaned

Once the NEM came into operation, this formula was abandoned, but this did not mean that no attention was paid to efficiency in the new scheme for allocating investment finance. The norms were less strict, but that was because the reformers thought that the financial constraints on enterprises were enough to make them take its benefits into consideration. From this point of view, the old system of norms was justified, as when funds were allocated from the centre it had to be borne in mind that they were not repayable immediately. This did not mean, however, that investment efficiency was really a criterion in the excessively macro-economic approach reflected in the indicator.

As against this, the introduction of something like a capital market, even though it was in fact no more than a multi-functional bank, was to lead to a more rational approach to investment policy and in particular to greater efficiency.

The investment projects decided on by the centre, and particularly those involving major works, entailed painstaking preparation and were based on appraisal of the investment required, with the calculations used in it being very like those in the old system. The G index was replaced by the new D index, as shown below.

$$D = \frac{\overset{15}{\underset{1}{S}} (Y_i - I_i) R^i}{\overset{n}{\underset{1}{S}} K_i R^i - VR^{15}}$$

where Y_i = net income (i.e. value added) generated by the project in year i

I_i = additional capital costs in year i (to maintain or replace worn-out capital)

R = discount factor, $1/(1 + r)$, the discount rate, r, being usually 12%

n = construction period of project (years)

K_i = capital outlays in year i

V = residual value of the capital equipment after 15 years

As Hare has pointed out (Hare, 1981: 98) this equation requires very little adjustment to express it in the usual net present value (NPV) form. In general, however, reference to this norm of calculation is no more than formal, even in those cases (i.e. major investment projects) where it is most often used. For others, simpler indexes (e.g. repayment periods) are used.

Despite the reforms, however, the planners have still a fondness for the old ways of calculating, working out the increase in output and capacity that an investment will produce in terms of physical quantities. In addition, a prerequisite for using the norm for calculating investment efficiency is a homogeneous price system more closely linked to world prices. In Hungary, however, it is still both too domestic and too heterogeneous, even though it has been largely based on world prices since 1980 (see Chapter 7).

A further factor, this time of a qualitative nature, is involved in efficiency appraisal: indicators like the degree of technical progress, energy or labour saving, or the reduced use of foreign currency resulting from an investment are now more evident than imports, particularly from Western markets.

The period of repayment is also taken into account, from two points of view. The first is that of the annual return on an investment, or the relationship between net income and capital invested. This provides only a partial explanation of profitability, since it is only relevant when the activity of a new unit of production is being considered, and it is harder to establish an analysis if the aim of the investment has been to increase the capacity of an enterprise by additional machinery differing only from existing machinery in that its level of productivity is higher. The second is that of the time taken to complete the project, which appears to be longer in Hungary than in developed socialist countries such as Czechoslovakia or the GDR and the West.

The mixed system of allocation is not a real constraint on enterprises, and the older methods offer certain advantages in that investment funds were centrally allocated and generally involved no repayment commitment. This partly accounts for the constant demand for investment from enterprises, the normal strategy of which is to seek priority planning recognition of their project. Only then is any efficiency assessment undertaken.

In such a situation, where several sources of finance with different provisions regarding repayment are involved, it is not easy to say how efficient an investment is, particularly since many of those determined individually by enterprises are not subject to this kind of analysis by their proposers. Appraisal is therefore a difficult matter.

The imperfect and inflexible price system means that the State has to grant investment funds to enterprises in the form of production or price subsidies, when they are in fact also paying tax on production. In addition, there is a whole range of financial measures in existence, and treatment of this kind is not conducive to increased efficiency. Indeed, efficiency is a purely relative concept to the extent that, on the one hand, there are enterprises which try to apply rigorous management principles and, on the other, there are those which only continue to exist because they are subsidized. It is hard to judge the two by any kind of common yardstick. Hence, perhaps, the rather disenchanted observations of the former director of the State Investment Bank:

> Because of the shortcomings of the price system the complicated interlocking of the financial resources, and the overlapping levels of decision-making, it is by now impossible – as far as I can see – to perceive what is and what is not efficient. This is why despite the

best intentions and guidance economic efficiency is pushed more and
more to the background. (Deák, 1978: 74)

Economic efficiency has been measured in terms of the types of
investment enterprises engage in, using the following indicators: the
share of net income (with subsidies deducted from total net income);
share of the total income from exports; share of total fixed capital;
proportion of total investment; net income per unit of capital (i.e., a
measurement of efficiency); cost for a unit of income from exports
(considered as an indicator of the profitability of exports). Exclusively
self-financing enterprises produce over a third of the total net income
and account for about a quarter of exports. As against this, the
contribution of industrial enterprises under these two headings is very
low, with small- and medium-sized firms doing best in that sector.

Those enterprises using their own funds and credits to invest are the
most efficient economically at both branch and national level. Their
contribution to both exports and net income is very high, and their
creation of gross fixed capital is considered to be the greatest of all the
various groups. Those using their own funds, credits and subsidies
perform in much the same way, but as they need more capital and
hence more investment their profitability is much lower. Their wage
costs are almost twice as high as those in the first group and – although
this is not taken into account here – the enterprises in them use up
twice as many State subsidies. Nevertheless, they enjoy rapid growth
and an accumulation rate of around 14% of the value of fixed capital.
The final group of enterprises, those carrying out State investment
projects, also enjoys a high accumulation rate and plays an important
part with regard to fixed assets and total investment. Their profitability, however, is low.

Dysfunctions in the investment system

The origin of malfunctions in the investment system is to be
found in periods before the introduction of the NEM, as Bauer (1978,
1981) and Kornai (1980) have shown. At the present moment, the
juxtaposition of the various forms of regulation shows up the
inconsistencies in the system more clearly. There are several causes – a
disequilibrium between jobs and available resources, the ways in
which investment projects are drawn up and approved, and the lack
of clear criteria for measuring both efficiency and real financial
constraint.

In the first place the government is permanently torn between two conflicting objectives at the macro-economic level, trying both to maintain equilibrium between jobs and resources and to provide finance for investments included in the plan and requested by almost insolvent enterprises[5] whose appetite for public funds is increased by the sectorial authorities. The second factor is technical, relating to the time span involved in meeting the objectives set out in the plan. This is not directly related to the financial aspect of the question but it is a permanent feature of the planning system. It is, however, indirectly linked to it to the extent that any failure to meet deadlines entails increased costs, which then generally amount to between 15% and 25% more than was originally envisaged. This is due to a number of causes, including the shortcomings of the price system and a lack of proper planning. At the planning stage, the nature, scope and even the technology of the investment capacity can be modified. In all three cases this generally increases costs, extends schedules and causes stockpiling. A comparison of the time taken to carry out projects shows that in Hungary it is 1.5 times as long as in the GDR or Czechoslovakia and between 2 and 2.5 times as long as in the Western countries. On average, 46 months are required, and major investments take 6 to 7 years. Finally, there is the lack of precise criteria for assessing efficiency and profitability clearly and unambiguously. There are too many different kinds of exemptions for there to be any clear-cut way of proceeding under the present system.

In such circumstances, enterprises are aware that the State is likely to give them subsidies and are always ready to ask for funds to develop at any cost. In order to be sure of getting them, they therefore tend deliberately to underestimate investment costs to ensure that their project is included in the plan. It then has the blessings of the law, and will have to be carried out, however long it may take.

The State considers the proposal. With regard to finance, subsidies are sometimes used to start a project which will be financed by credits in the following year. In negotiations of this type, the case of those requesting funds is based exclusively on technical arguments and an approach relying on the physical quantities involved in the return on the investment. This is because the central bodies cannot revise projects submitted to them for inclusion in the plan. In theory, if both sides respected the principles involved, such revision would only need to be a matter of pure form, as happens in Western economies, for example, when national banks revise their credit via immediate access to data concerning company accounts. In the Hungarian context, however, where the job is first and foremost to get adequate finance irrespective of whether or not the project will stand up to critical scrutiny, such cumulative procedures are to be expected. The fact of the matter is that the bodies ensuring State control, such as the Planning Office, the National Bank or the Ministry of Finance, are not in a position to carry out checks – often because of a lack of time, but mainly because most investment projects have a built-in uncertainty as far as efficiency is concerned. What needs revising is the overall policy.

From this point of view, a number of options ranging from maintaining the status quo to introducing a virtual capital market to provide greater stimulation can all be envisaged. In the Hungary of the 1970s and 1980s, a number of reforms were aimed at rationalizing the behaviour of enterprises and making the macro-economic decisions being taken in an unfavourable economic environment more coherent. Various types of encouragement were found acceptable. Amongst them were drawing up specific targets and providing the appropriate finance, particularly when it was a matter of providing credit facilities for exporting industries, which could compete for them with other undertakings, paying greater attention to the technology available when preparing projects for obtaining credits, and contractually obliging suppliers and investors to keep to schedule, thus reducing the time span of manufacturing and the number of investments not completed. When the contract was not met, investors were progressively taxed on the total investment and according to the extent to which deadlines were not met, and those carrying out the work were paid only for that part of it actually completed.

In themselves however such measures were not a lasting solution to investment dysfunctions. Others, forming an integral part of a wider reform of the mechanism of indirect regulation, were approved and introduced in stages during the eighties. The adjustment policies implemented by the government also led, *inter alia*, to a significant drop in the level of investment.

7 Adaptations of the decentralized model

An analysis of the performance of the Hungarian economy over the past ten years could easily, although perhaps unexpectedly, lead to the conclusion that there is little, if anything, to choose between market socialism and administered economy. It is true that countries like the GDR or Czechoslovakia, where the leadership has shown a certain reluctance to engage in Hungarian-type reforms, have achieved much more in terms of growth in the GDP, increased trade and personal incomes. For their part, the Hungarian leaders had to make a choice between maintaining the status quo and so running the risk of allowing the economic situation to get worse, and pursuing further reforms in the knowledge that they could call into question the principles preventing any development. Choosing the latter alternative also went hand in hand with the introduction of a policy of structural adjustment based on two facts: the increasingly important part played by external constraints with regard to what the Hungarian economy could achieve and the resources at its disposal, and the incomplete nature of economic reform and the need to modify the planning system. To their way of thinking, a combination of structural reform and institutional adjustment should make it possible to finish the job started in 1968 and set the economy on the noble road to growth. After the high degree of recentralization during the 1970s the 1980s therefore saw two waves of reforms (1979–82 and 1984–7), with an intervening liquidity crisis between 1982 and 1984, which helped to bring about a radical change in the nature of planning and modified institutions.

Several areas were affected by the various measures introduced at this period (Hare, 1986: 10): from 1979 a system of competitive prices, with subsequent adjustment, was introduced; three branch ministries were combined and an Industry Ministry was set up; the functional ministries were given greater importance and the control functions of certain party organizations with regard to the economy were re-defined; major enterprises and trusts were split up (also from 1979); the setting up of new economic units (small enterprises and co-operatives, economic working groups and the like) was encouraged; the banking system was reformed; a bond market was developed; and enterprise management was reformed.

The fall-off in growth

After a period in which growth rose by between 4% and 5% a year, it began to fall off slowly following the first oil crisis, and poor performance accompanied by the appearance of lasting macro-economic disequilibrium became features of the situation (see Table 7.1). Growth rates remained low and Hungarian exports to the West declined, as trading terms with both the capitalist and Comecon markets worsened. The increase in the prices of raw materials, shrinking Western markets and the ever more severe competition in them did nothing to help Hungary acquire a larger share of them. Imports were also highly elastic, which helped to aggravate the country's trading deficit. In such a recessionary situation, the need for external finance and the consequent increase in indebtedness also made it harder to use national income for other purposes. Disequilibria of this type affected domestic prices, and the inflation rate was soon running at over 7%.

As Balassa (1985) points out, the beginning of the 1980s saw Hungary faced with a two-fold constraint. The country had to reduce its internal debt (public finance deficits and subsidies) by freeing resources by a more efficient use of national income to increase exports and introduce drastic measures to reduce domestic demand (particularly from enterprises). It also needed to maintain the purchasing power of the population. One of the constant features of government policy since 1956 had been a more or less automatic increase in such purchasing power without any immediate link to increased productivity, and it was only late in the day that efforts were made to use adjustment policies to limit its growth.

The structural adjustment policies that were implemented only partly achieved what they set out to do. Attempts to rationalize investments made it possible to limit expenditure – with a very low accumulation rate – but did not increase the productivity of capital, which fell both at the overall and industrial levels.

The crisis induced the Hungarian leaders to modify industrial

Table 7.1. *Macro-economic indicators (annual % charges)*

	1976/80	1981/85	1981	1982	1983	1984	1985
Net material product	2.8	2.3–2.8	2.5	2.6	0.3	2.5	−1.0
Labour productivity[a]	3.7	2.2	2.6	3.6	0.2	3.6	1.0
Capital productivity[b]	−3.1	−2.8	−2.7	−1.5	−4.2	−1.4	−3.4
Gross investment	2.2	−4.0	4.3	−1.6	−3.4	−3.0	−3.2
Foreign trade turnover	n.a.	n.a.	0.5	−1.0	−2.3	−3.3	−3.4
Industrial output growth	3.4	2.1	2.4	2.5	1.2	3.2	1.0
Industrial labour productivity[c]	5.0	3.7	5.0	4.9	3.4	3.5	1.6
Industrial capital productivity[d]	n.a.	n.a.	−1.9	−2.3	−4.2	−2.2	n.a.
Real income per head	1.8	1.4–1.6	2.9	0.9	1.1	1.1	1.0–1.5
Consumer prices	6.3	6.8	4.6	6.9	7.3	8.3	7.3
Indebtedness[e]	8.0	7.5	7.0	7.3	7.5	7.2	7.7

n.a.: not available

[a] Net material product per employee in the material sphere.
[b] Net material product per fixed assets in the material sphere.
[c] Ratio of industrial growth output per employee.
[d] Ratio of industrial growth output to fixed assets.
[e] In billions of US$.

Source: United Nations, Economic Commission for Europe: *Economic Survey of Europe, 1985–1986.*

Table 7.2. *Structure of Hungarian industry (in % of total industrial production)*

	1960	1980	1984
Electrical and thermal energy	4.2	5.8	5.9
Fuels	9.8	7.6	6.6
Iron and steel (including extraction)	10.1	6.3	5.2
Non-ferrous metals (including extraction)	3.3	3.3	3.1
Mechanical engineering and metalworking	25.1	30.0	30.9
Chemical industry	4.4	13.2	14.6
Building materials	2.8	2.0	1.8
Wood and woodworking	3.0	3.0	3.0
Textiles	10.9	6.8	6.0
Foodstuffs	18.8	14.7	14.9
Various	5.0	7.3	8.0

Source: Courrier des pays de l'Est, Documentation française, August–September, October 1986: 54.

priorities and abandon the major central programmes such as the development of the petrochemical, aluminium and car industries, data processing and the use of light structures in building. Production from these was intended for the socialist countries within the framework of specialization programmes or, as in the case of data processing, as a substitute for imports, and in addition the branches in question could not help but affect others in their turn. Worsening trade terms and the need to acquire hard currencies meant that the government had to take stock of its priorities to encourage the production of higher value added goods in the mechanical engineering sector of light industry (buses, machine tools, precision apparatus, communication plant etc.). This belated reversal of policy did not, however, help to bring about any appreciable change in the structure of the Hungarian economy (Table 7.2).

Hungarian industry was also, according to the heads of the country's Chamber of Commerce, lagging behind in equipment, products and organizational techniques (Economist Intelligence Unit, 1986). According to figures in Courrier des Pays de l'Est (1986, no. 10), plant was used for only 52% of working time, products had been introduced 15.7 years previously on average, and 14% of manufactures were under three years old in 1984 compared with 17% in 1980. In an unfavourable context and faced with what was still a very high

Table 7.3. *Foreign trade by groups of countries and products (in current prices)*

	Exports		Imports	
	1980	1985	1980	1985
Total (billions of forints)	281.0	424.6	299.0	410.1
of which (in %)				
Socialist countries	55.1	58.6	51.1	54.4
Comecon countries	51.5	—	47.8	—
Western countries	33.9	30.8	39.4	38.5
Third World countries	11.0	10.6	9.5	7.1
Convertible currency zone	57.0	52.5	54.5	53.0
Total (in %)	100	100	100	100
Energy, fuels	4.1	4.6	14.8	20.8
Raw materials, semi-finished	31.2	30.2	49.2	44.8
Machinery, equipment, means of transport	26.2	28.8	19.3	16.8
Industrial consumer goods	16.1	15.1	8.3	10.4
Agriculture and foodstuffs	22.4	21.3	8.4	7.2

Sources: Külkereskedelmi statisztikai evkönyv (Foreign Trade Handbook) 1982. *Statisztikai havi közlemenyek* (Statistical Monthly Bulletin) (9) 1986.

level of indebtedness, Hungarian enterprises still continued to make fairly unprofitable products, and the country had to undertake a further modification of its productive structure in the three sectors defined in the complex Comecon programme of December 1985: electronics, biotechnology, and the food and agriculture industry.

Opening up to the exterior, without which decentralization could not succeed, received setbacks during the 1970s and 1980s, despite a remarkable increase in the share of exports (from a quarter in 1965 to between 40% and 50% in the early 1980s) in national production. During the 1970s, however, Hungary suffered from a double disequilibrium in its trading with Eastern and Western partners and saw a considerable deterioration in its trading terms, especially in the rouble zone (a decline of 20% between 1970 and 1981) where the situation was worse than in the convertible currency zone (a decline of 19%; 50% with the Third World and 6% with Western countries). Chronologically, the decline was asymmetrical as far as the West was concerned, with the most difficult period for stabilization and subsequent improvement occurring after the first oil crisis. With regard to the rouble zone on the other hand, the situation worsened later, after the revision of the system of fixing intra-Comecon prices in 1974.

With regard to zones, the greater part of Hungarian exports (55% to 62% between 1976 and 1985) went to the socialist countries, and imports from them increased from 50% to 54%. Conversely, the share of trade with the West did not increase appreciably, especially if the increase in trade with the developing countries is taken into account. If, however, the gap between the volume of trade and methods of payment is borne in mind, the considerable share of intra-Comecon trading in strong currencies (between 20% and 25%) becomes apparent. This enabled Hungary to cover the deficit in its trade with the West and the developing countries (see Table 7.3).

What was chiefly involved was a matter of paying for non-quota deliveries in addition to the quantities provided for in bilateral agreements in foreign currencies. At present, that source of income is threatened by several factors. The first is the Soviet Union's determination to call in debts incurred by its partners in the early 1980s. Since socialist countries have severe liquidity problems, they have been unable to meet their trading obligations with the USSR (Lavigne, 1984). The second is the changed method of fixing prices within Comecon, and the third the Soviet Union's demand that its partners redirect hard goods exports towards it as part of bilateral agreements. This has been the position since the 1985 Comecon summit, when a complex specialization programme was approved.

The breakdown by products varies from one exchange zone to another and highlights Hungary's dependence with regard to both high value added products like machinery and industrial consumer goods, despite a considerable reduction in imports of the former as a result of austerity measures to re-establish equilibrium and bring the level of indebtedness down, and raw materials, particularly from Western and Third World markets as a result of falling supplies from the Eastern bloc. The high figures under this heading clearly indicate the high proportion of investments in basic industries such as metallurgy and chemicals.

In its exports to the West and the Third World countries, Hungary has only been able to establish a marginal comparative advantage in the form of a slight increase in the share of machinery and spare parts. The protectionist measures adopted by the EEC have tended to reduce that of agricultural products. (see Table 7.4).

Given the current high level of indebtedness and the importance of modernization programmes and the adjustment policy, increased

Table 7.4. *Market shares of Hungarian exports (in %)*

	1975	1980	1983	1985
In total OECD imports				
Total	0.21	0.20	0.19	0.19
Industrial articles	0.21	0.23	0.18	0.16
Chemical products	0.23	0.30	0.29	0.33
Material intensive commodities	0.23	0.25	0.22	0.19
Machine, equipment	0.09	0.12	0.08	0.07
Manufactured commodities art	0.49	0.43	0.33	0.25
In CMEA exports to the OECD				
Total	7.1	6.7	6.0	7.1
Industrial articles	11.7	13.2	12.7	13.1
Chemical products	9.8	10.5	11.0	13.0
Material intensive commodities	10.9	11.7	9.9	10.4
Machine, equipment	7.7	12.0	13.6	14.2

Source: Hungarian Business Herald, 1988/1.

trade with a new and lasting equilibrium must remain high-priority aims in the current reforms.

Reforming the instruments of guidance

The aim of the Hungarian government's successive waves of reform has been to make the system of indirect regulation more efficient by including measures of an institutional nature seeking to widen the framework in which the economic mechanism operates. The attempt to find a more effective price system, however, has taken place within a relatively limited field, and the prevailing approach is still based on a stimulated market within which the centre tries to predetermine price structure in accordance with a certain number of objectives. The object of institutional reform on the other hand is to loosen the constraints imposed by meso- and macro-economic authorities and, by breaking up enterprises, to stimulate competition between firms.

1. Reforming the price system

In January 1980 a system of competitive prices covering some 60% of industrial activities representing about 35% of national production was introduced. The 1968 reforms had had little appreciable effect on price structure and formation since their basic principle still reflected primary domestic costs plus an average profit rate. Their main aim had been to increase the share of free prices and those allowed to range between fixed maxima and minima at the expense of fixed prices. The 1980 reforms, however, meant that domestic price movement and structure responded directly to the influence of world (i.e. market economy) prices. The current competitive system is therefore still administered (by the Office of Prices and Materials), although now on the basis of actual export prices rather than on the 'costs plus' principle.

In concrete terms, pilot enterprises exporting at least 5% of their production to Western hard-currency markets cannot apply to the rest of their output on the domestic market a rate of profit higher than that achieved in convertible currency sales, whatever the level of supply and demand on home or Comecon markets may be. In the case of a certain number of enterprises, the new principle applies either indirectly or not at all. In the latter situation (mainly in agriculture, transport, building and consumer-linked services) the old 'costs plus' domestic price system is still operative. There is also a third ('proportional') category of prices linked to both competitive and domestic prices. Those enterprises subject to it include the effect of world prices in their calculations. The latitude this allows them usually means increased control by the authorities responsible for determining prices.

The final category is that of 'imported prices'. This is chiefly used in connection with raw materials, energy products and the transportation of energy, and ensures that such products can be used in Hungary at their marginal cost. With this in mind, there has been an attempt to standardize the price of raw materials, particularly in the case of those from Comecon countries. Such prices are literally cancelled and replaced by world prices. The products are then delivered to Hungarian users at Western prices. Thus a firm using energy from the USSR has to pay the 'world price' for it, although the planned price is lower.

The purpose of introducing such a system was to bring deflationary pressure to bear on the Hungarian economy and – in a quite artificial way – to apply the level of prices in the world market to domestic industrial production.

Since, however, there is no competition as regards exports, the whole exercise is a simulation of what would happen if there were. It can be seen as a second-best solution reflecting a compromise between

Table 7.5. *The three centres of price formation (in %)*

| | Price types | | | |
Sectors	Competitive	Proportional	Cost-plus	Total
Industry	65	15	20	100
Construction			100	100
Agriculture		100		100
Transport/communications		100		
Others		30	70	100
Total	35	35	30	100

Source: Csikós-Nagy, 1983: 54.

the forces of protectionism and those favouring a greater opening up of the system (see Table 7.5). In that sense, it is not inappropriate to make certain observations, even though the system is aligned on world prices. The first of these observations is that the 1980 price system is in no way a real free-price system in which enterprises themselves freely fix their own prices according to market indications. What really happens is that a large number of strictly defined and continually checked central regulations specify the profit norms to be applied by industry. The second is that it does not open up the economy to direct pressure from the world market but is simply a substitute for a missing factor, namely competition in the imports field. The third is that it has led to a limitation of the function of prices because of the increase in central regulation necessary to make such a hybrid system work. Nor, as can be seen in the budget, has it meant a complete end to subsidies. Its very complexity has made it necessary to increase central control in order to prevent enterprises seeking unwarranted profits by, for example, paying too much attention to the domestic and neglecting the hard-currency market.

This means that implementing the system has had several consequences. Enterprises have become more dependent, and in more complicated ways, on the centre. Bargaining in planning and financial matters has acquired a new dimension, that of horse-trading about the regulations (and how they are applied) governing the formation of prices. One of the basic principles of the 1980 modifications was the introduction of a single normative rule, the application of which would, amongst other things, reduce the area of subsidies and tax exemptions. Before it was applied, however, it had to be individually negotiated with enterprises, which meant that it encouraged the evils it was meant to remedy.

Given the heterogeneous nature of both the price system and the negotiations between the centre and enterprises, it proved impossible to reduce the part played by the State budget in the redistribution of enterprise incomes, a process which still in one way or another drains off 75% of the revenues of Hungarian enterprises.

Competitive prices represent 35%, proportional prices a further 35% and cost (or 'costs plus') prices 30% of the value of production. The first mainly consist of prices in the industrial sector (65%), where proportional and cost prices account for 15% and 20% respectively. In the other sectors, either proportional prices predominate (as in agriculture and transport) or cost prices are the norm (as in the building industry). Alongside this system of price formation, there is a second distinction – that between *administered* and *free* prices – to be taken into consideration. Bearing in mind costs, the authorities can decide whether prices are to vary freely or are to remain fixed. In industry, 52% of prices come into the first category, as compared with 71% before the 1980 reforms. The figures for production as a whole are 67% and 57% respectively. The sectors with fixed prices are either protected or come under the heading of services.

In the field of consumer prices, the distribution of prices by their mode of formation is even more complicated. There are four methods of determining prices: fixed prices; prices with a minimum; administratively limited prices; and free prices. Fixed prices (energy prices, books, services) are determined by the centre in the light of social objectives (such as general living standards) plus transport and culture and these account for only 8% of consumer prices. Prices with a maximum (or 'ceiling') also apply to only a proportion of such services, the theory being that beyond a certain limit market equilibrium is broken. Administratively limited prices – which have in-built maxima and minima – are used in cases in which prices would otherwise be erratic, as with fruit and vegetables, for example. Free prices, 55% of the total, are subject only to supply and demand.

In determining the prices of certain basic products, preference is given either to the prices of imports from capitalist countries (reference to world prices) or to actual export prices to Western markets (competitive prices). The aim here is at one and the same time to internalize the movement of world prices, particularly as regards resources and raw materials, to encourage Hungarian producers to use their factors of production more efficiently and in particular to take international competition into account, and to pass on to consumers the weight of both internal and external constraints, particularly by means of increases in consumer prices and reduced subsidies. In all cases, however, price movements are closely watched by the centre.

The two chief criteria involved in the lower prices for consumer goods are market and social considerations. The aim of the Hungarian price policy is to produce greater clarity, even though the country is to a large extent in a pseudo-market situation, with the centre encouraging, from a macro-economic point of view, ideal market conditions. This means that there is, as we have just seen, a matrix of consumer prices which incorporates the prices of imported consumer products. These are subject to the general regulations governing prices and fixed according to a particular method (a reflection of world prices, domestic determination, or indeed subsidized prices). The move from wholesale to retail prices is subject to the same rules as those applying to Hungarian products (wholesaler's and retailer's mark-up, transport costs and the like) and there is no difference between price formation for goods imported from the West or the East, apart from the fact that the former include customs duties as a cost.

There are still one or two exceptions, however. In the case of imported luxury goods, the conversion rate is applied to the import price (including customs duties) and there are no subsidies. Examples of this are goods sold in the Pierre Cardin boutique in Budapest, alcohol, cigarettes and the like. Such imported goods can still be sold in specialist shops in convertible currencies, as is the case with alcohol, cigarettes, perfumes, silk goods etc.). Consumer goods such as ready-made clothing, children's games and materials are imported subject to customs duties, but subsidized for reasons of social policy. They come under the 'fixed price' category.

The new price regulators put into operation on 1 January 1984 cover price formation and production in certain sectors of the processing industry. The machinery for drawing up producer prices, based on export prices, is much simpler and more flexible than in the past. In the processing industries' sector, where there was already an equilibrium between supply and demand and enterprises could compete in foreign markets, adapting producer to world market prices was not a matter of rules and regulations about price formation but of agreements between suppliers and customers.

In the system introduced in 1980, prices for fuels and raw materials were based on import prices in convertible currencies. For processing industries producing for export, a system of prices adjusted to exports was brought into use. The average profitability of the enterprise was fixed in accordance with the profitability of exports and variations in enterprise price levels adjusted in the light of those obtaining for export prices. Thus, as a result of the introduction of a price system based on exports, a system of simulated competition prices was instituted. It incorporated a two-fold limitation based on both the profitability of exports and the export price level. There was a conflict between the importance of this as a stimulant for increasing exports and the efficiency of exports, a situation that it was hoped could be resolved by limited measures. As it was important to stress the need to encourage the volume of exports, it seemed necessary to abolish the profitability limitation. In other words, the connection between the formation of export and domestic market prices was broken. The measures, which were introduced from 1 January 1984, were implemented in three stages, as follows. Initially, the formation of industrial prices on the domestic market was based on export prices and invariably entailed a double limitation. The limitation of profitability then lapsed. Adjusting to world market prices was not carried out according to the rules hitherto in force but within a framework of agreements between suppliers and purchasers. That too was a kind of limitation, since the producer prices of manufactured goods cannot normally be higher than the actual or potential price of the imported product. At the third level, enterprises no longer acted according to the normative rules of the simulated competition price system. Their price policy depended on market requirements alone.

It is now thought that the type of development of the system of producer prices described above is impossible without radical changes in the methods of calculating them and in the financial system. However, certain changes are already being made in the system of accounting, particularly with regard to amortization, where enterprises are allowed to determine their own policy. The government is also seeking to increase budgetary constraint not only by maintaining the centralization of some of the income from enterprises by such measures as a reduction in the sums allotted to investments from 13% to 10%, but also by virtue of the power the centre now has to suspend its share of financing investment projects when the enterprises involved are not profitable. This reduction has made it possible to set up an *intervention fund* to help branches affected by the structural crisis. In addition enterprises can, in order to increase liquidity and working capital, set up a profits fund into which they can pay what they like once they have met their tax commitments. In particular, they can sign bonds for a sum not exceeding 30% of this reserve fund.

To sum up, the aims of the new price regulation and the financial measures introduced in early 1984 are:

to remove obstacles to competition and the free formation of prices where that is already possible;

to stop enterprises opting out of competition by massive reductions in subsidies and various exemptions;

to bring market relationships more fully into the open at the domestic level in particular by increasing budgetary restraint (through reduced payments) and financial constraint (through profitability); and

to introduce a single rule of conduct by abolishing individual measures.

2. Other aspects of reforms in indirect regulation

Concurrent with the reform of the price system there was a series of reforms affecting the way the exchange rate was determined, providing wider rights to trade abroad and regulating the income of enterprises and economic agents.

The rigidity of the price system and the major part played in it by subsidies, which have both been discussed already, were counter-productive with regard to the behaviour of enterprises. The 'costs plus' type of price structure favoured the domestic market to the detriment of exports, where the structure was quite the opposite, and prices were lower than production costs as a result both of the gap between domestic and world prices and of subsidies at home.

The protectionist exchange policy, seen as a defence against the effects of world inflation, merely made the defects in the system of export prices worse. As well as offering financial inducements in the form of tax remission, monetary inducements in the form of credit facilities and a lower rate of customs duty in conformity with GATT recommendations, the government moved towards an active exchange policy.

Between July 1979 and October 1981 there was gradual progress towards a single exchange rate of 34 forints to the dollar. To this end the commercial rate (which was too high, specifically as a hedge against the effects of inflation at home) and the tourist rate (which was rather too low, as it was based in part on subsidized domestic prices) were combined. Since then, the forint has been successively revalued and devalued, the first as a way of protecting the country from the influence of world price levels and contagious inflation, the second as a way of implementing an active exchange policy.

The exchange rate is adjusted every Tuesday, and it is expected that it will eventually be done daily, although there may well be some problems, since the departments involved will need to be reorganized to some extent. Exchange specialists take into consideration a basket of currencies corresponding to Hungarian export markets, which is modified annually to take account of changes in trade. The weighting of the various currencies (US dollar, Deutschmark, Swiss and French francs, pound sterling, Italian lira, Swedish crown, Austrian schilling and Dutch guilder) is not published. Any currency representing more than 1% of Hungarian exports must be included in the basket.

Parity is adjusted whenever there is a variation of 0.5% or more, and the National Bank is empowered to adjust the exchange rate, or in other words to revalue or devalue the forint, within a 1% limit. Within a limit of 1% to 3%, this can be done by agreement between the president of the Bank, the Minister of Finance, the president of the Planning Office, the Minister of Foreign Trade and the president of the Prices and Materials Office. Beyond 3%, or below it if there is no agreement between the representatives of those institutions, any change in the average parity level of the forint is decided by the government. It should be noted that at the present moment the possible convertibility of the forint is a purely academic question, given both current financial restrictions and the low level of real market relationships with Hungary.

During the 1970s the government made a series of mistakes when faced with the early stages of world inflation. In a bid to protect themselves against the effect of world prices when the forint was overpriced, they regulated prices by using prices of the costs plus profits type, which internalized inflation cumulatively with a combination of expensive imports, a high exchange rate and proportional profits. To avoid such pressure, they were led to subsidize imports in an attempt to bring down the excessive level of profits, which resulted in both internalized inflation and the complete distortion of the price system, and hence, the 1980 reforms. The remedy since then has been an active exchange-rate policy coupled with an extension of the right to trade abroad to industrial enterprises and agricultural co-operatives, in a bid to increase their exports. Alongside the established import–export authorities, specialized bodies can now act as intermediaries by widening their range of services or entering into association with exporting enterprises.

In addition to dealing with the commercial aspects of trade, the reformers also envisaged the possibility of creating joint enterprises with Western partners in an attempt to speed up the process of structural adaptation and technology transfer. For the host country, such an arrangement also offered a way out of having to finance all its fixed assets, especially as legislation on such matters was becoming more liberal with regard to participation beyond the 51% level. It should be pointed out, however, that as a result of financial and salary restrictions and the like, this type of enterprise had little managerial or organizational impact on Hungarian industry (Richet, 1986b).

A further series of measures related to incomes policy and intended to link directly wage levels and productivity was also very important. It marked a break with one of the basic principles of economic policy in that area, namely that wages should be more or less automatically increased by means of central regulators, a principle fully in keeping with the spirit of semi-administrative regulation. Full employment and the high level of social benefits enjoyed by workers were also not very conducive to increased productivity.[1] The methods of wage regulation resulting from such a normative system meant that wages in profitable enterprises were scarcely higher than those in unprofitable ones.

The government therefore abolished the progressive annual increases guaranteed by the wages fund and introduced tax inducements for enterprises increasing their wages fund by cutting wages costs or the use of materials. In such cases, the annual wage increase was higher (6%) and the progressive tax on the wages fund lower. Currently, the wages policy depends on the results achieved by an enterprise. The regulations now in force admit of bigger differentials, and enterprises have to try to reduce production costs, particularly by using labour more efficiently. The right to dismiss workers has been re-established, and measures to protect wage-earners mean that those affected will have an income for at least six months (Balassa, 1986). Few enterprises avail themselves of the possibility, however, and those which collapse are few in number and usually small undertakings or co-operatives.

At enterprise level, the machinery of bargaining about wages has shifted. Industrial democracy – worker representation and the expression of their interests – goes hand in hand with the developments of new bargaining strategies. Here, therefore, the search for greater rationality is sometimes countered by alternative strategies (Koltay, 1986).

3. Decentralization and monetarization: the reform of the banking system

Although the 1968 reforms (Kornai and Richet, 1986) made provision for extensive decentralization in enterprise management, in particular by means of the instruments of indirect regulation (prices and the tax system) banking was relatively unaffected and kept most of its functions (issuing money, distributing credit and budget funding arising from planning objectives, foreign currency transactions). The anomaly can be explained in several ways. It could be suggested that the banking system had acquired such a strong monopoly that it managed to escape the zeal of the reformers, as other monopolies like the branch ministries and the large socialist trusts did for a time. The situation affected the working of the decentralized system by watering down certain principles of it and weakening the instruments of indirect guidance. A better explanation, however, is perhaps that the centre needed a watchdog to keep an eye on the behaviour of enterprises and the working of the decentralized market, with a centralized financial system providing alternative ways of perpetuating administrative centralization once the units of production were more autonomous.

(a) *Financial constraint and the behaviour of firms*   To a greater extent in centrally planned than in market economies, the nature of the banking system offers an opportunity of effectively measuring the real extent of decentralization. Several writers have shown the impact of the way a banking system is organized on the way the market works and the dynamism of enterprises. Zysman (1983) and Eliasson (1984), for example, have shown that in Western economies the types of institutional patterns gave rise to particular kinds of organizations and financial structures, such as the market banking system in the USA and the UK, a joint State–industry system as in Japan, a State system as in France and Italy, or a State–industry–unions system as in Sweden. The financial power of banking firms is also a crucial factor. Cable (1985) has shown the many kinds of involvement – going beyond that of acting as financial intermediaries or establishing credit policy – of banks that organize bond markets, concentrate voting rights and have seats on company management boards. All these

activities are ways of influencing enterprises and shaping their decisions. This reminder of the facts of life in the West serves a purpose,
since it makes it possible to highlight the characteristic features and
the limits of the reform currently being carried out in Hungary.

In centrally planned economies monetary and financial functions
are the concern of a single-bank system (Lavigne, 1979). Here, one
organization and its specialized departments and subdivisions are
responsible for both issuing and circulating money by making planned
credits available to the appropriate enterprises. It also centralizes, in
accounts they have opened with it, a proportion of their resources, the
remainder being centralized by the tax system.[2] In such a situation,
money has a passive role, being issued by the socialist sector as a
means of achieving planned objectives and with funds available to
enterprises only when they present the authorization of their administrative supervisory body to go ahead with their investment. Circulation and accumulation are therefore strictly controlled. Nevertheless,
there are certain anomalies, particularly in the consumer sector, which
is made up of individuals able to spend their money as they like, or in
the free economy (Gabor, 1986; Galasi, 1984). It can also be said that
although the central bank has kept its prerogatives, economic
decentralization has helped to stimulate circulation to some extent via
enterprises and their transactions and wages policy. Nor should it be
forgotten that before the present reforms deficits in public spending
were financed by issuing money.

Making greater use of instruments of indirect guidance in recent
years (1979–82), on the one hand, and monetary and financial
centralization, on the other, have had mutually contradictory effects in
that each has produced a different kind of behaviour in agents. For its
part, the partial monetarization of the economy has given enterprises
the chance of making more autonomous decisions, but has not been
able to change their attitude towards the centre (Antal, 1986). This fact
has allowed Kornai (1980) to apply and show the pertinence of his
concept of soft budgetary constraint by demonstrating that enterprises, even in the presence of prices and money, adjust their
behaviour by incorporating other objectives than monetary
constraint. Given the more or less paternalistic nature of the centre –
which flows from the confusion between ownership and control in a
socialist economy – the instruments of guidance, and primarily
money, are not operated with full vigour. The result is that firms
behave in a way made possible by a combination of several sets of
circumstances. To cite a few: most enterprises determine their own

Table 7.6. *Enterprise profitability before and after redistribution (in %)*

Type of enterprise	Before	After
Loss-making enterprises[a]	14	1
Fairly unprofitable enterprises[b]	22	76
Averagely profitable enterprises[c]	40	18
Highly profitable enterprises[d]	24	5
	100	100

[a] $<-2\%$ profitability   [c] $+6\%$ to $+20\%$
[b] -2% to $+6\%$ [d] $>+20\%$

Source: J. Kornai and A. Matits, 'Adok és támogatasok. Allami Vállalatok nyereségének ujrafelosztása' ('Taxes and subsidies. Profit redistribution in state enterprises'), in *Heti Vilaggazdasag* (World Economy Weekly) 18 September 1986.

prices rather than have them imposed on them and can pass on their increased costs to the purchaser; the tax system is lax, and enterprises can influence the wording of its regulations and obtain certain concessions; they can receive free State finance in the form of contributions, payments or various non-repayable subsidies; credit is easy in that amounts and repayment periods do not depend on the enterprise's ability to meet them.

All these factors have a number of consequences. Survival, growth and price adjustments in the face of soft budgetary constraints do not depend on the level of macro-economic constraints. In addition, the aim of such behaviour on the part of enterprises is, *inter alia*, to reduce uncertainty and to protect themselves by laying great emphasis on routine ways of doing things.[3] Given the size of inter-enterprise redistribution laid down in the plan and achieved by financial centralization, this objective cannot necessarily be achieved. As against this, the consequences mentioned do explain why there is a virtually insatiable demand for inputs, which does not depend on either their cost or the expected current income of enterprises.

If the differing structures of enterprises, such as the number of people employed and the volume of sales, are taken into account, the way in which they are affected by budgetary constraints can be seen to be rather asymmetrical. Such constraints are generally not as rigorous in the case of industries serving the major aims of economic policy or for large enterprises, and the asymmetry is also apparent with regard to profitability, as the level of profits falls as the size of the concern increases.

What we have therefore is a combination of soft budgetary constraint and a high level of inter-enterprise redistribution having a considerable effect on enterprise performance by creating a significant difference between their pre- and post-redistribution profitability (see Table 7.6).

(b) The objectives of banking reforms: towards rigorous budgetary constraints The general reform of the banking system that came into effect on 1 January 1987 completed the long process of adapting the economic mechanism. It was part of the continuation of the 'second wave' of 1979–84 (Csaba, 1986) that saw wider decentralization, modified instruments of regulation, a less concentrated productive apparatus and the creation and development of small enterprises and independent work collectives.

Coping with external constraints – reducing indebtedness and an active exchange policy (Salgo, 1986; Richet, 1985a) – and the need for structural adjustment led the reformers to stress the desirability of adapting the banking system to the reforms in the other sectors of the economy. Looking beyond a decompartmentalization of the existing system, they saw the possible emergence of a kind of capital market with the chance to issue bonds and engage in cross-participation and the possibility of control by banks. So far, only the monetary side of things – credit and financial broking – has been affected by current reforms, although there has already been a bond market for some years, with exchangeable securities issued by large enterprises and government departments.

Current reforms have led to the setting up of a two-tier banking system, with a separation of the functions of issuing (the Central Bank) and credit (commercial banks), a state of affairs that had already existed *de facto* with the Hungarian National Bank since 1985. At present, there are seven types of banking establishments organized in four distinct types of legal forms (see Table 7.7).

Alongside the issuing HNB and the five new commercial banks, which are all share companies with State capital and more recently capital from financial institutions, there is the system of people's banks controlled by the State and the people (co-operative banks). For the present, the commercial banks are not allowed to take deposits from the population at large, and their first task is to finance ownership. One of the State banks, the Public Development Institute, finances

Table 7.7. *The new banking system in Hungary, January 1988*

Type of establishment	Legal form	Capital in millions of forints
Central Bank		
Hungarian National Bank (NHB)	LLC[a]	10,000
Commercial banks		
Hungarian Creditbank, Ltd	LLC	8,983
Commercial and Creditbank, Ltd	LLC	7,600
Budapest Bank, Ltd	LLC	5,332
Hungarian Foreign Trade Bank, Ltd	LLC	4,374
General Banking and Trust Co., Ltd	LLC	1,000
Banks for the general public		
National Saving Bank	State bank	1,300
Savings Cooperatives	260 co-operatives	40,651
Central Corporation of Banking Companies	State bank	1,000
Development financial institutions		
State Development Institute	State institute	
Specialized financial institutions		
Industrial Development Bank, Ltd	Share company	3,200
General Bank for Venture Financing, Ltd	LLC	2,200.5
Interbank	Share company	2,175.5
Agrobank	Share company	1,500
Investment	Share company	1,233
Innovation bank for construction industry	LLC	1,126
Mezöbank	Share company	1,166
Industrial bank	Share company	1,060.7
Komsumbank	Share company	850
Bank for small ventures	Subsidiary of National Saving Bank	673
Innofinance	Subsidiary of HNB	500
Merkantil	Subsidiary of the Commercial and Credit Bank, Ltd	500
Bank for Investment and Transactions	Subsidiary of Hungarian Credit Bank, Ltd	250
Banks with foreign participation		
Central-European International Bank, Ltd	LLC[b]	US$43.071
Citibank Budapest, Ltd	LLC[c]	1,000
Unicbank, Rt	n.s.	1,000

Table 7.7 *continued*

Type of establishment	Legal form	Capital in millions of forints
Hungarian Banks abroad		
Hungarian International Bank Limited, London	LLC	£10,000
Central Bank of Exchange and Credit, Ltd, Vienna	LLC Öst.sch	200,000

[a] LLC: limited liability company

[b] shareholders: National Bank of Hungary, 34%, Banca Commerciale Italiana, 11%, Bayerische Vereinsbank, 11%, Creditanstalt Bankverein, 11%, Long-Term Credit Bank of Japan, 11%, Société Générale, 11%, Taiyo Kobe Bank, 11%.

[c] shareholders: The Citibank N.A. New York, 80%, Central Bank of Exchange and Credit Ltd., 20%

Source: *Héti Vilaggazdasasag*, 20 September 1986 and *Banking system in Hungary 1988*, National Bank of Hungary, 1988.

central planning investment, the number and size of which are decreasing as financing by means of bank credit increases.

There are also a dozen or so small banks or financial institutions specializing in clearly defined fields such as foreign trade or risk capital. Their commitments are limited, but there is a higher risk in such activities and they are allowed to amortize at a faster rate. Their funds come from a limited number of shareholders.

Joint banks in association with Western establishments have also appeared on the scene. The first to do so, the *Central European International Bank* (CIB), was created in 1979. Although the major shareholder (34%) is the HNB, there are six others, all from outside the socialist bloc, with 11% each.[4] The emergence of the CIB marks the first time that the capital of a joint East/West undertaking was mostly controlled by foreigners. As an 'off-shore' bank, however, it is not part of the Hungarian banking system as such, and can carry out numerous commercial operations throughout the world, trade with all Hungarian enterprises in convertible currencies, and is not subject to national banking regulations. The second of this type of undertaking, Citibank in Budapest, was set up in 1984. Unlike the CIB, it has acquired the right to operate partially in forints on the Hungarian domestic market. In three areas, however, its activities are limited: it cannot conduct insurance business in Hungary; give credit to Hungarian citizens or accept their deposits; or engage in trading in transferable roubles.

The main functions of the Central Bank are to regulate money, to ensure bank refinancing and to issue Central Bank money, working on the open market.

The commercial banks operate within banking regulations laid down by the government through the Finance Ministry, intervening directly and assuming the risks in enterprise financing. They are not restricted to a single branch, but cover the whole of the economy apart from the population at large. For a transitional period, their 'customers' have been allocated to particular banks by administrative means in order to accustom both enterprises and banks to the new system, to spread risks equitably and to avoid, from the very earliest days, an excessive disequilibrium. At a later stage, free competition was to be the only factor determining customer distribution, and the public was to be able to use the banking market for deposits and credit.

The banking reforms, which are part and parcel of the *sui generis* process of adapting the Hungarian management and industrial system, are also a kind of resting point in it. A monetarized economy, created by monetary and credit policies, is expected to help to make indirect regulation more efficient and to be the main tool for making the degree of constraint on the economy really effective by encouraging enterprises to mobilize their resources dynamically. Perhaps only for the time being, however, the greater part played by monetary relationships in a socialist economy means that little attention is being paid to a number of particularly difficult problems. Should the forint be totally or partly convertible? Should foreign capital be allowed direct access to the domestic market? What sort of link should there be between an active monetary policy and transferable rouble trading with other socialist countries? What financial strategy should enterprises and commercial banks adopt, other than that of financing operations? What is the possibility of a virtual capital market in Hungary? Although such questions have still not been openly addressed, they will soon arise if the reforms of the banking system prove successful.

The search for a socialist entrepreneurship

The abandonment of the rigid forms of control and the transmission of orders that has marked recent years has given socialist

Table 7.8. *Size of enterprise and profitability (1980)*

Value of capital plus annual wage bill (million forint)	Number of economic units	Average profitability (%)	Share in the net output of industry (%)
10.1–15.0	69	26.1	
15.1–30.0	232	21.3	
30.1–50.0	183	20.5	
50.1–100.0	219	19.7	
100.1–150.0	75	16.1	
150.1–300.0	121	16.6	
300.1–500.0	72	13.4	
500.1–700.0	61	11.1	
700.1–1300.0	144	9.9	19.1
1300.1 and more	131	6.9	59.2

Source: Kornai, 1983: 236.

enterprises a fairly sharp rise in status. The widening of the field of action, the legalization and the support of small units of production also raises the question of entrepreneurship in an administered economy. The decentralization of the banking system completes the institutional reforms and aims to strengthen financial constraints on enterprises.

1. Breaking up large enterprises and the new form of management

The concentration of the productive apparatus fits in well with the well-known socialist principle that 'big is beautiful'. A combination of theoretical and practical reasons – the aim of socializing the forces of production and the needs of administrative management – led to enterprise concentration. The tighter the centre's control, the greater the certainty that it will be in charge of growth. That does not mean, however, that there is any correlation between the extent to which enterprises are controlled and greater productivity or efficiency or, *a fortiori*, with profitability. Indeed, the bigger an enterprise gets, the less profitable it is. Finance Ministry figures show that profits decrease regularly as capital stock increases and that although enterprises in the last two bands from the capital stock point of view have the lowest profit rates, they account for 78.3% of total net product (see Table 7.8).

Table 7.9. *Organization structure of the economy*

	1970		1975		1980		1985	
	1	2	1	2	1	2	1	2
State industrial enterprises	812	1491	779	1515	699	1392	974	1294
Industrial co-operatives	821	238	793	239	661	222	956	200

1. Number of organizations.
2. Average number of persons employed (thousands).
Source: Statisztikai Evkönyv, various years.

In those sectors of the economy with the greatest number of monopolies (such as the extractive, food and distribution industries) more than a dozen trusts are being abolished since there is no economic need to maintain them. Similarly, a certain number of State sector enterprises are being broken up to create more manageable units of production, some of which will have the right to trade abroad (i.e., to make contracts directly with foreign undertakings) and to create competition between State enterprises on the domestic market.

Despite such measures, the government has continued to encourage fairly unprofitable large enterprises by granting them funds for investment. Thus, over the period from 1982 to 1984, the 73 largest enterprises, with an average profit rate of 5.4%, financed 37% of their investments with State funds (Balassa, 1986: 28). Their rate of investment was higher than that of the second group (average profit rate 7.2%) which received 17% of their investment from State funds. As for small- and medium-sized enterprises, where the average profit rate was 8.1%, they received only 9.5% of their investments from that source. The 73 largest enterprises had a higher investment rate than the two other groups put together.

At the same time, the system of appointing managers has been changed, except in the case of major-State enterprises. In the past, they were appointed by higher bodies – the branch ministries – but are now directly elected by the employees of the enterprise. Apart from a desire to separate two functions – ownership and management – this move in the direction of self-management involved several other factors. One was that it was based on procedures introduced into agricultural co-operatives in the early 1960s and was partly responsible for their success. Another is that it is a compromise between the old system of nomination by ministries and the inherent logic of deconcentration, which involves the control and setting up of industrial groupings. Finally, it made it possible to keep an indirect form of central control by means of non-economic channels, through unions and political channels by means of the mass intervention of Communist Party organizations.

Although such reforms are positive in nature, they nevertheless raise the possibility of setting up, in a socialist economy, industrial groupings and of developing an industrial strategy. Amongst other things, this would imply setting up holdings in which not only State interests but also those of the group could be represented, and hence an extension of the capital market.

Keravi (1981), Kopatsy (1981) (and see also Molnar, 1983), reflecting on the aim of a more efficient allocation of resources, see several ways of achieving this, in particular the possibility of enterprises issuing bonds or shares to an investment holding company. Enterprises could be responsible to a ministry itself responsible for controlling the State sector and with the power to start up or close down enterprises. Each enterprise would have a supervisory board and a management committee appointed in equal proportions by the government and shareholders. The job of the Finance Ministry would be to determine the level of dividends and to avoid excessive differences in income between enterprises. The project attempts to settle the thorny question of financial control in a socialist economy but ignores some much less obvious points, in particular that of the possibility of enterprises accepting the acquisition by upstream or downstream branches to make up real industrial groupings. Although it might want to break the link, industrial organization is still too closely modelled on the branch ministry system.

A further aspect of the reforms is the possibility of bankrupting unprofitable enterprises. In this connection observers have pointed out that it is still a dead letter, since most of those involved are major undertakings. Currently, in fact, it is mainly small enterprises or co-operatives that are at risk, although since the early 1980s more than 10 large firms alone have accounted for 80% of accumulated losses.

The purpose of the whole range of measures has been to make enterprises play a more dynamic role by making them less passive and giving them greater opportunities to engage in tactical games – i.e. bargaining – on the one hand, and develop their horizontal links between firms – i.e. sectorialization – which has hitherto been controlled by the division into branches, on the other. The reorganization of the financial market has been the means of putting this policy into practice.

Enterprises will be able to keep a larger share of their profits either for their own use in investment and reserve funds, as loans at interest to other firms, or as a means of acquiring shares in them. That possibility is not restricted to enterprises, and financial institutions can also make use of it. The Foreign Trade Bank, a subsidiary of the HNB, for example, has at its disposal credit facilities to be used for mergers or to set up mixed enterprises, and the State Investment Bank has also extended its activities to include such operations. It is expected to act as an industrial partner in several projects.

Various organizations and institutions now have the chance of issuing bonds to finance industrial activities. Buying bonds can help in various ways both to group financial resources and to finance investment. In order to finance their activities and to increase the monetarization of the economy, banks and financial institutions as well as State sector enterprises and co-operatives can issue bonds, a right also granted to local authorities to help them finance their equipment projects. All sectors of the economy, and no longer only those producing public services, can now offer bonds to the public (see Table 7.10)

The January 1987 reforms of the banking system complete these measures.

2. Integrating the second economy

In Soviet-type economies, there have always been informal legal or illegal activities which have been either tolerated or condemned. By concentrating on the weak points of bureaucratic systems and supplying goods that the first economy cannot produce in sufficient quantities or quickly enough, the second economy reduces shortages, particularly with regard to consumer goods, building and services. It also indicates the extent of dysfunctions in its official counterpart and reveals the existence, at the margins of the official system, of an entrepreneurial stratum capable of dealing or producing in difficult conditions.

Like investment, its activity is cyclical and its growth or decline reflects the degree of shortage and the measures taken by the political authorities to curtail (where there is relative tolerance) or prevent too great a difference in incomes once shortages are no longer so severe. That cycle, which has always been a feature of planned economies,

Table 7.10. *The availability of bonds, May 1986*

	Total nominal value (billion forints)	Yields (%)	Relative size (%)
Available to private citizens	4.5	7.0–13.0	2.0[a]
Available to firms and institutions	2.0	7.0–15.0	9.7[b]

[a] Total nominal value: stock of household deposits in saving banks.
[b] Total nominal value: stock of outstanding bank investment credit.
Source: Kornai, 1986: 1712.

took a different turn in the Hungary of the early 1980s (Gabor, 1982) when the second economy was officially recognized and encouraged by the government.

Although it is hard to provide a precise outline of it, given the lack of statistical data, the high rate of tax evasion in a country with no income tax until a progressive tax system was introduced on 1 January, 1988 and the fact that most transactions are not recorded, current studies have succeeded in describing the size of the sector and assessing its contribution to the production of certain services (Table 7.11).

3. The emergence of new forms of enterprises

In order to expand and link auxiliary activities and, more generally, small units of production, from 1982 onwards the Hungarian government extended the opportunity of setting up different types of enterprise to virtually every area. It was intended that their activities, whether autonomous or complementary to that of major undertakings, should increase the supply of goods and services and make the economy as a whole more flexible. These measures affected both the State and co-operative socialist sectors and the second economy.

In the socialist sector, enterprises have had the right to set up joint ventures since 1977. These independent legal entities are governed by profit and loss and receive no government aid (Richet, 1986b). Two or more enterprises can set up *associations* in order to achieve shared objectives. Such associations cannot, however, make autonomous decisions or use the profits they may make. Since 1982, enterprises

Table 7.11. *Size of the second economy*

	First economy (State-owned firms and co-operatives) (%)	Second economy (formal and informal private sector) (%)
Distribution of total active time in 1984[a]	67	33
Contribution of social sectors to residential construction in 1984[b]	44.5	55.5
Contribution of social sectors to repair and maintenance services in 1983	13	87

[a] Excluding time spent on household work and transport.
[b] Measured by the number of new dwellings.
Source: Kornai, 1986: 1707.

have been able to create one or more subsidiaries, and some scores of new undertakings have come into being, providing a legally recognized means of creating inter-branch liaison and configurations based on a group strategy. It has also been possible to set up small specialized industrial and agricultural co-operatives to carry out specific tasks, and the regulations governing small industrial and service enterprises have been made more flexible with regard both to their field of activity and to the size of their tied-up capital in the form of means of production, transport etc., which was previously strictly limited.

The most important innovation has been the creation of *enterprise work collectives*, or *enterprise economic working groups*. These are workers' collectives of between 2 and 20 people employed by an enterprise, who contract with it to do jobs outside their working hours that otherwise would not get done for reasons of cost or shortage of labour. Management provides the equipment and materials and decides to set up the collective, but workers join it on a voluntary basis. In non-agricultural co-operatives, similar groups (called industrial and co-operative special groups) have been set up on the same contractual basis (see Table 7.12).

The extent to which this system is used or how successful it has proved to be are not clear, as the figures show. Here, one cannot

Table 7.12. *New economic units, 1982–4*

		1982	1983	1984
Small enterprises:	number	23	204	285
	employment	2,226	19,322	30,048
Small co-operatives:	number	145	255	368
	employment	6,014	9,853	16,087
Industrial and service groups:	number	477	1,243	2,253
	employment	n.a.	41,396	78,734
Enterprise economic working groups:	number	2,775	9,192	17,337
	employment	29,331	98,006	196,014
Individual economic working groups:	number	2,341	4,741	7,397
	employment	11,145	23,667	42,516

Source: Statisztikai Evkönyv, 1984.

properly speak of entrepreneurship, since up to a point it is a question of the legal recognition of a *de facto* situation in which related activities are carried out alongside the main task. This type of organization is also rather akin to a primitive wage-earning class and reflects the inability (or reluctance) to introduce a homogeneous wages system and policy lest it lead to the loss of control of an open labour market. It does, however, mean that enterprises can keep their most skilled workers, who otherwise might be tempted by the second economy.

Individual economic working groups, which bring together workers in groups which are independent of enterprises or co-operatives, are of greater interest, since they are more like the models of small-scale enterprises encountered in Western economies and are, in fact, private undertakings. They are self-organizing, seek their own markets and accept risk, and offer their services to the public or to other enterprises or collectives. Members can work full-time for them or have a second job. They show greater initiative, which explains why, despite the great increase in the number of enterprises and workers employed, they do better statistically than enterprise collectives with greater protection and less risk. The government hires out such groups or makes them available on contract hire to private persons or groups such as restaurants and laundries.

Introducing such a system has undeniably had beneficial effects. The growth of the idea of risk has encouraged initiative amongst the (still admittedly small) entrepreneurial sections of the population. Shortages are reduced as supply increases, productivity is higher and there are fewer tensions on the labour market. There has been an indirect effect on large enterprises wishing to keep their most highly skilled workers, who are tempted to offer their services to or operate in the second economy. There have, however, been corresponding drawbacks, such as the appearance of clear social inequalities which are difficult to tolerate and the growth of a dual structure, a phenomenon not without consequences for the values of the system and references to socialist morality.

Such considerations aside, however, the private sector is rapidly discovering its own limits, which are restricted because of the difficulty of breaking into the input and output markets. There is also the question of the growth strategy of small firms, both internally and externally. Finance, labour management, economies of scale and type of specialization are all limiting factors arising from two problems. The first of these is confidence, since as the political and economic cycle moves on it is quite possible that the role of the private sector will be restricted either by regulations or tax disincentives. The second is one of mentality. Since small entrepreneurs or operators are narrow specialists with one technical skill and little wider know-how, they are tempted to make a quick profit and then to stop work and rely on the social benefits provided by the official sector. The result of this is a series of phenomena already visible in the second economy. The services offered are worse, and speculative behaviour is leading to unproductive savings of no benefit to official channels or the effort to produce tangible goods. It is for such reasons that the government and the party have not addressed the central question of the reform of property rights within the socialist sector, where entrepreneurship needs to be able to develop.

4. Tailoring the reforms or extending their scope?

Like the debate preceding the implementation of the NEM in 1968,[5] the measures aimed at stabilizing the economic cycle and introducing new reforms gave rise in the early 1980s to major discussions involving economists, researchers, practitioners, top civil servants and politicians, which have been exhaustively listed in Kovács (1984). These were more sophisticated and the level of argument was higher, and a number of hitherto taboo questions such as the introduction of a virtual capital market, the redistribution of the rights of ownership or the withdrawal of the Party from economic activities were raised. Although there was general agreement on the

need for reforms, their scope was limited by the need of the authorities
to maintain the existing social situation, and there were consequently
differences of opinion with regard to both the desirable scope and rate
of reform and the objectives it should seek to achieve. It is none the
less undeniable, as the political and economic cycle (successive phases
of decentralization and recentralization going hand-in-hand with the
economic cycle proper) has shown, that there has been strong opposition to any decentralization or thorough-going reform of the
institutional system. Looking back to the earlier situation and the old
ways of doing things, what Bauer calls the 'restorationist' element
sought to improve methods of organization in order to strengthen
discipline, fight waste and the bureaucracy and contain problems.
Their aims were limited, and they sought to achieve external equilibrium and maintain living standards at the cost of other disequilibria
or costly decisions such as import substitution and keeping declining
sectors going.

At the other end of the spectrum, more radical projects emerged.
Examples of these were the spread of small enterprises in a Walrasian-
type competitive system, a self-managing market socialism involving
real decentralization, and micro-economic efficiency and worker
control at enterprise level with no central intervention. The majority of
the reformers found themselves on the middle ground. To their way of
thinking, the system could only be improved by an overall reform that
managed to achieve the major objectives of trading equilibrium in the
short term. Doing so was not, however, to mean reducing the part
played by market mechanisms or hampering new growth. Nyers and
Tardos (1982) have shown clearly that the new policy in Hungary had
to have three interdependent but not necessarily immediately obviously compatible aims: the consolidation of the position of foreign
trade; the preservation of political stability and confidence (which
depended on the first aim); and preparation for new growth (which
depended on both the first and the second).

Restrictions on investment and imports (the first aim) hampered
new growth, which by stressing micro-economic efficiency also
worked against the preservation of political stability and confidence.
This meant that the Hungarian leadership was faced with the choice of
either keeping economic change to a minimum and hence perhaps
risking less from a social point of view in the short term but more in the
long term, or speeding up economic change and perhaps risking more
in the short term while being able to count on more structured growth
in the longer term. There was nothing new about this, and that kind of

choice had arisen in more or less the same form, albeit in different circumstances, in 1956, 1964, 1978 and 1984. The authorities had usually met the situation by deciding on the relative importance of the three aims.

Conclusion
The limits of decentralization

In many respects, planning in Hungary is moving further and further away from the traditional Soviet model still dominant in most other Soviet-type economies (STEs). Explicit reference to the virtues of the market has become a major theme in official speeches, even though there is constant mention of the various forms of central control. What Bauer (1982) calls the economic elite had adopted a more sophisticated and complex *modus operandi* combining elements of central and market control with the constraints of social expectation, which increase in importance as the occasional difficulty the first two have in attaining their objectives becomes apparent.

Plan versus market

For theoretical, practical and political reasons, centrally managed STEs set up a system of quantitative planning. At the theoretical level, it was a matter of setting up a non-market economy based on some of the principles of the Gotha Programme and setting out to define in advance all the needs of society and to find the appropriate means of meeting them. In practice centralization was unavoidable given the situation of chronic shortages of capital goods, skilled labour and infrastructure in which STEs developed. It also seemed to be the appropriate way of achieving the often over-ambitious objectives the planners set themselves. Its political dimension cannot be ignored, since the way the economy was organized – as a 'command economy' – involved the same pyramid structure of political organization, which meant that the various echelons of the productive system could be controlled politically.

The importance of the political apparatus and the part it played in the economy cannot be over-emphasized, since in a socialist system the economy is fundamentally the result of politics. The Party is a particular system with a plurality of functions which both plays an informal part and personifies them all. It intervenes simultaneously in the political, economic and trade union fields, it plays an informal role through the central economic organizations, branch ministries and enterprises and hence in the bargaining relationships growing up between and within such bodies, and its various functions are all personified and represented by people of the same ilk, which means that there are more opportunities for extending control, ensuring that information circulates, and co-opting each other.

The rationality of quantitative planning, or planning in kind, is obviously measured in terms of a different yardstick from that used in market economies. It sets the highest store on administrative management and the central allocation of resources without reference to micro-economic calculations, and its logic therefore necessarily entails an increasing waste of resources as the gap between the complexity of the productive system and the archaic form of management widens. The latter may be modified by the introduction of value indexes and normative prices but this does not fundamentally change the behaviour of the various authorities – the centre, the branch ministries and enterprises – involved in planning, which are an additional element in the panoply of means of control. This means that disequilibrium is not a temporary state of affairs but an organic reflection of the dysfunctions of the system. The appearance of this method of allocating resources can be explained by a number of factors, the chief of which is the combination of a hyper-concentrated apparatus of production and oppressive administrative control. The reduced role allotted to demand and the corresponding detailed central allocation of resources create a sellers' market within which production finds its own outlet. A highly concentrated state industry and the dovetailing of ownership and management thus give rise to a strongly paternalistic attitude on the part of the State towards enterprises which, since they do not address themselves directly to the markets for capital, inputs and outputs are not subject to real budgetary constraints. Hence their wastefulness, low productivity and lack of innovation or dynamism.

Plan and market

The partial opening up of the centralized model has made it possible to rationalize to some extent, in particular by introducing new forms of macro-economic guidance, some decentralization of the system of production, and ways of letting market mechanisms play a bigger part. The market, which represents a break in the pyramid-shaped structure of the economy, is still under close scrutiny, which limits its role as an agent of stimulation and decentralization. In fact – and this is one of the first limits to such reforms – central prerogatives with regard to the regulation of income, price formation, the allocation of resources and the control of foreign trade have been maintained.

It is clear that the addition of a new form of regulation and the persistence of an industrial structure going back to the period of administrative planning have given rise to a new type of dysfunction and to some extent reduced the reform movement to a kind of no-win game. The impetus given to enterprises by the new methods of regulation has often been thwarted by some directors of such units, whilst others have tried to play by the new rules. Such schizophrenic behaviour has not been peculiar to enterprises alone, and has been passed on to the upper echelons of management, notably in the branch ministries and certain functional ministries. In other words, market mechanisms have been added to administrative management but have not replaced it, which has meant that regulation is even more mixed in nature. In Hungary – and this is one of the merits of the reforms – this juxtaposition has made it possible to reduce the dysfunctions arising from an administrative-type model (i.e. crises like those occurring in Poland) by introducing greater flexibility and providing scope for the development of secondary forms of resource allocation through the informal economy. Shortages, however, have persisted, shifting towards other sectors, particularly the areas of capital goods, advanced technology and the like, and have been reflected in increased imports from Western countries. The intro-duction of the new forms of macro-economic guidance has also had effects both on procedures for establishing plans and on the redistri-bution of powers within the central bureaucracy. Here, administrative procedures have been replaced with a type of parametric regulation based mainly on prices and tax structures. Planning may now be more functional than administrative but that does not mean that market mechanisms have been incorporated to any great extent. Indeed, any step in that direction soon encounters its first hurdle – the prerogatives of the centre.

The most characteristic feature of this phase has been the change in the way in which the centre intervenes. It can be said that economic reforms in the STEs reflect a process of reorganization, namely that involving a redistribution of powers in the central bureaucracy, i.e. the

State and Party apparatus – without affecting the hard core of the system. Thus there has been a shift of competence away from political power towards managers, yet the new division of labour within the governing class has never led to any questioning of the way in which society is organized or power distributed within it. It is in this respect that the multi-functional nature of a Party capable of combining various types of interventions needs to be taken into consideration. The centre has thus both to decentralize the economy by partly redistributing power – the management of large units of production and the activities of the second economy – and to co-ordinate and control these processes. There is, however, one limit beyond which decentralization cannot go: the socio-political system must be perpetuated, and the need to maintain the prerogatives of the centre explains why the market must be held on a tight rein and broken up into segments. In doing so, the centre is manifesting its ability to handle both macro-economic variables and the old administrative instruments and increasing its intervention in the economy. It is in this framework that it is possible to describe the features of the Hungarian model and analyse the alternatives it faces.

Neither plan nor market

Although not anarchic, the current system of regulation is different from one based on either the plan or market mechanisms, and in this sense it is no longer fully appropriate to talk of an STE in connection with the country's economy. Planning in kind and by objectives is a thing of the past. While the plan is being drawn up, enterprises and the centre may refer to data in physical terms, but they are never grossed. Enterprises are no longer allocated physical factors and have to obtain them through the five-year plan, which is now more like a medium-term projection than a detailed quantitative statement of objectives to be achieved. Thus the organic and proportional development of branches is no longer, since the dismembering of administrative planning, a central objective in a situation in which enterprises themselves adapt to the changing conditions of production and competition.

Yet market mechanisms have not entirely replaced planning and are still weakened by the intervention of the centre. It is thus a question of a market regulated from the centre and not of an automatic mechanism ensuring that the units of production function without central control. If we except the mercantile sphere in the field of goods and services, it is more proper to talk of market forms for several reasons. In the first place, the monopolistic nature of the productive apparatus makes it difficult to operate a system of scarcity prices, also, because there are no market relationships in the other sectors (this is particularly true of producer goods) and because of the way in which wages policy is regulated, there are in-built limits to the effects of market forces. Despite its often very realistic attitude, the economic elite is relatively distrustful of a market that gets bigger as one goes down the bureaucratic pyramid. Resisting its influence means preserving the stability of the system, ensuring that it works in a regular way, and maintaining the social consensus.

It is here that we see the intervention of the third type of mechanism – a particular method of allocating resources called social expectations. In STEs, it is inseparable from planning, and it forms the natural complement to systems of injunction. It is all the more important because the other mechanisms – the plan and the market – have partially failed. An ideological stimulus created by the centre, it is passed on through political and union channels to micro-economic units, and although it is typical of the administrative planning phase it has survived efforts to decentralize and introduce indirect regulation.

In decentralized planning then the centre can make use of several variables in order to achieve its aims. In such conditions, State enterprises are regulated on the basis of many criteria, with profit playing a relatively limited role compared with other objectives like the total exports to Comecon or the absorption of Comecon imports, higher productivity, a supply of cheap consumer goods or a reduction in numbers of workers. Traditional bargaining between the centre and enterprises is less important and a new and much more tolerant type of co-operation is taking shape around the new objectives. This complex mode of central intervention in enterprises still gives sense to the notion of state paternalism and weakens the budget constraint: budgetary (and hence monetary) constraint is now one of several variables the state has at its disposal.

As the theoreticians have shown in their studies of cycles in market economics, such cycles occur and develop for both political and economic reasons. The concept of social expectations has such a role to play in socialist economies and produces cumulative effects. Social expectations are both an expression of the political and economic will of the Party and a means of ensuring a consensus in favour of its objectives. There can be no denying their political and economic importance, as their function is to homogenize society by avoiding political, social or economic divisions.

Two examples will show how the mechanism is vital to enterprises. After the break-up of administrative planning with its central allocation of resources, enterprises now have to assume some of the former functions of the centre. Each enterprise, for instance, has to avoid any shortage of stocks and make sure that it has regular supplies. This obligation, coupled with a chronic shortage of certain goods and raw materials, absorbs a great deal of the enterprise's energy, with the result that other functions suffer and other types of disequilibrium are produced. The financial crisis and the country's high level of indebtedness led the Hungarian leadership to apply restrictive policies with regard to general living standards and, more particularly, to reduce the volume of imports from Western countries. With regard to the latter, not only the central institutions but also social organizations at enterprise level (unions, the Party, women's councils, Communist youth organizations etc.) all brought pressure to bear on directors of enterprises to implement the measure. Thus the decision at both micro- and macro-economic levels to reduce imports was not the result of an *economic* choice, taking into account such factors as the import elasticity coefficient in relation to the GDP, but of a *political* one. The consequences of such decisions on enterprises highly dependent on imports can easily be imagined.

A new form of regulation and 'bureaucratic know-how'

Changes in forms of regulation can be explained by several factors, both external – constraints from outside sources affecting a small country very dependent on foreign trade – and internal. The latter include both the need to adapt to the increasingly complex nature of management and the obligation to keep what Bauer calls consensus government in a changing environment. That concept reflects one of the features of STEs, where the aim of the mode of central intervention is always to ensure an organic link between the various macro-, meso- and micro-economic authorities as a means of unifying society, an idea reflected in what Morin (1984) calls the need to contain the totalitarian complex. The essence of STEs lies in fact in united and cohesive social activities, which means that the monistic approach and procedures involved in producing them can only limit any decentralization and *a fortiori* any chances of controlling social activities by means of a real market mechanism.

Currently, the Hungarian model is characterized by the fact that behind the appearance of decentralization there remains the unitary vision of society even though in qualitative terms the *modus operandi* of the centre has been modified, chiefly by the introduction of more sophisticated instruments of management. On the one hand, there are no longer any such things as administrative planning or traditional bureaucratic control. On the other, the market mechanisms introduced in the various reforms since 1968 have been segmented and the function of money relativized as a result of several factors. These include the limited function of prices, where movement is controlled both by formal limits and informal pressure on enterprises, a drastic limitation of labour supply and demand and hence of the price of labour, and a very rigid investment system in which enterprises cannot, given the hybrid nature of the price system and subsidy policies, ensure sufficient income on the market and therefore come more easily under central control. These various factors mean that in practice enterprises are still controlled by the visible hand of the State, even though the old direct methods are no longer used. Central control is now a matter of selective financial policies, informal pressures and the like. In the field of investment or foreign trade, these forms of control may be very selective, but they are laxer as far as the volume or choice of type of production or innovation are concerned at enterprise level.

In a modern economy, how is it possible to avoid using both traditional administrative procedures such as planning injunctions, central allocation and market mechanisms? For certain theoreticians, and Bauer in particular, the centre's attitude reflects a simplistic view of the economic relationships characteristic of primitive societies and an archaic understanding of the way a collectivist economy functions. In this respect, the process of enterprise concentration preceding the 1968 reforms is illuminating. That quasi-monopolization of the socialist economy (up to recent times, Hungary had the most concentrated economy of any industrialized nation) was part and parcel of a coherent overall effort on the part of the Hungarian leadership. The point of creating large monopolies was to unite the micro- and macro-economic levels without allowing a go-it-alone mentality to develop in the minds of those responsible for micro-economic units. Indeed, the aim was to make them work together by directly informing them of the needs of the economy as a whole and persuading them to pursue national objectives. Thus the monopolization of the economy perpetuated the large units of production and enabled a small group, the economic elite, associated with the Party, the state apparatus and the managerial staff of large undertakings, to control the working of the economy without the pressure of market forces, of public opinion, or of possible parliamentary control.

That controlling but uncontrolled group resists the market by sectionalizing it and makes its sometimes questionable decisions on the basis of its interests and its micro-economic approach. Over the past decade, for example, it has embarked on costly investment programmes increasing autarky at Comecon level (particularly in the chemical industry, computers, and agricultural and nuclear equipment), combined generally competitive agricultural and industrial co-operatives with much less viable State enterprises, and developed expensive technology appropriate to bureaucratic methods of management and organization in agriculture, house building, services and the like. The area of influence of the market has also been restricted at the ideological level by means of will-of-the-people slogans stressing national interest, conscious reconstruction and the minimal part to be played by the market.

Status quo or market socialism: what is at stake in the current debate

In themselves, economic will and the incantatory power of slogans are not enough to solve the numerous problems or cure the dysfunctions the Hungarian economy has to face. 'Bureaucratic know-how' seems to be running out and now needs to be replaced by major reforms if both general living standards and a dynamic economy are to be maintained. Major steps to secure those aims have already been taken with regard to institutions (the final abolition of the branch ministries and more important functional ministries) to organization (the dissolution of certain trusts and large monopolies and an increase in the number of medium-sized enterprises) and to the market (the recognition of the role of the second economy, the semi-privatization of State assets, the encouragement of small private enterprises and agricultural and industrial co-operatives). The current debate among economists is directly connected with the issue of the overall reform of the system of managing and regulating the economy.

The liberal wing advocates an extension of market mechanisms as a necessary replacement for the power of a bureaucratic elite. In their view, the end of controls and interventions of various kinds can only be achieved if an aggressive policy of encouraging growth is put in their place. Such a policy would be based on a thorough-going reform of incomes policy and an end to the system of wage regulation as a means of encouraging productivity; a rigorous separation between the functions of ownership and management in State enterprises aimed at both stimulating real competition between them and putting an end to state paternalism; the creation of a quasi-capital market enabling enterprises to be financed on non-discretionary criteria (as happens at the moment) and hence of a multi-form financial circuit and financial organizations controlled by an authority other than the centre; the development of small enterprises with the means of financing themselves; and the encouragement of trade with hard-currency markets to enable the country to obtain the technology it needs in order to develop.

What the reformers are implicitly, although perhaps not explicitly, asking for is the disengagement of State and Party from economic affairs and the introduction, within a framework of socialist relationships, of a real economic mechanism. Such ideas are currently more or less condemned by the advocates of economic elite, who see them as providing a recipe for a return to capitalism. Their attitude to such proposals also reflects the government's immediate preoccupations and ideological and political reluctance to introduce further reforms. They are in favour of a piecemeal approach and fearful of the consequences of implementing the kind of programme the reformers suggest. Indeed, such a programme, since it questions State paternalism – the 'two-speed' economy and wage regulation from the centre – might well end the social and political consensus that has grown up in the country since the 1956 period by precipitating an economic crisis.

The debate, which was initially of an economic nature, reflects a deeper concern, that of picturing the future of the socialist economy by renewing the political and ideological framework that gave birth to it. It is about reflecting on the changes needed in a system which has on several occasions showed a deep reluctance to change, despite successive attempts at reform.

Notes

2 The centralization and decentralization of the socialist economy

1 Of the many definitions of the concept of a system, the one preferred here is Kornai's: 'The system constitutes a set of interrelated elements functioning according to definite behavioural regularities. The structure of the system can be described by defining the constituent elements, the behavioural regularities in the operation of the individual elements and the connections existing between the elements' (Kornai, 1970: 301).

2 'In the marxist classics, future society is seen as a system in which everything will be obvious. The aims of the people will be obvious, and the resources to be transformed into the products the people want will be available. It is quite clear that Marx and Engels projected future society by analogy with the nineteenth-century factory, which for them – and not the market mechanism – was the organizational model' (Katzenelboigen, 1978: 123). On the theory of socialism in Marx, see Richet, 1978a.

3 As Nove points out (1980: 40, and 1983) no action is possible in any system without information, motivations and means.

4 In the view of the present writer, it is not so much the refutations of Lange (1936) that – temporarily – invalidate the objections formulated by von Hayek and von Mises (1939) to the impossibility of economic calculation in socialism as the massive use of extra-economic means in Russia in the 1930s. Cf. Lavoie, 1985.

5 Attachment to this idea also provided, at the time of the reforms in particular, a kind of safety-net for the reformers, which sometimes stopped them raising and answering questions, such as those of the extension of the rights of property, the forms of control of industrial enterprises and the like.

6 'The inevitable rise of a state bureaucratic ethos is reflected in revolutionary Marxism itself: once it has got rid of spontaneistic ideologies of the anarchist or anarcho-syndicalist type, revolutionary marxism, as the post-revolutionary utopia, simply provides a generalized etatism. In its programmatic vision, all economic units, and the state itself, are to be organized within a single gigantic collective enterprise whose structure will correspond to that of the state' (Konrad and Szelenyi, 1979: 133).

190

7 There would seem to be several good reasons for choosing self-management. Before the 1948 break, the Yugoslav economy was organized on the same model as that prevailing in the USSR; the same was true of the political structure. At the time of the break, moreover, the country's technological needs were very considerable, and the level of debt to the USSR very high. The introduction of self-management was the political means of ensuring popular support at a time when the Yugoslav leadership was totally reorienting its political alliances and sources of supply, with Western countries in particular.

3 Opening up the centralized model

1 Kornai (1959). The theses in this book were discussed among economists in 1956 and the work was published in Hungary in 1975.
2 Kornai (1986) shows that it is a matter of a recurring phenomenon. In present-day discussion of the reforms under way, there are sharp differences of opinion between radical and 'naive' reformers and 'Galbraith-type socialists' (to use Kornai's phrase).
3 See T. Liska, an 'econoclastic' theorist, who originated many suggestions, in particular the concept of personal social property.
4 Comisso (1986) shows that recently the decentralization of power in Hungary has made it possible to avoid economic failures, whereas in Poland protests against authority and bargaining with wide social groups (workers, peasants, intellectuals, the Church and so on) has not provided a means of controlling the economy. In Hungary, conflicts or bargaining take place within a restricted area and within the ruling elite (Party, ministries, factory boards).
5 The idea of reform was not a new one. Before and just after 1956, the idea of considerable changes in the management system had been envisaged (Antal, 1981).
6 'Its [the party's] way of protecting itself and developing is a monopoly of decision making from which the rest of society is excluded, a monopoly which might help to renew not only the apparatus as such, but also the individuals within it. There might be a conflict between the conditions determining the reproduction of the apparatus and the preservation of individual posts. It is at that moment that the apparatus becomes identically a subject and an object in which on the one hand it is a historical subject in so far as it monopolizes all political decisions and the direction and control of all the essential activities of society, and on the other it is an object in relation to itself, given the many possibilities that exist within it for removing oneself from its control' (Rittersporn, 1978: 15).

4 The instruments of indirect guidance

1 The convertible forint is the value of the domestic forint deriving from the sale of export goods and the foreign currencies used to pay for imports as calculated at the official average exchange rate by the Hungarian National Bank.

2 At a rate of 5% on fixed and circulating capital and 25% on the wage bill, comprising 17% of contributions to social security plus a supplementary tax of 8% on the wages bill. (These rates have been modified on several occasions.)

3 A fact deplored by some industrialists, since direct vertical relationships would ensure greater efficiency. Some heads of enterprises did in fact initiate moves in that direction with, it is true, the support of the centre. Since the 1981 reforms, that type of action has been partly authorized (see Chapter 7).

5 Macro-economic planning and the behaviour of agents

1 In the projected reforms of Soviet planning proposed by Mr Gorbachev, provision is made for abandoning the practice of breaking up the plan and allowing enterprises to fix their own objectives along Hungarian lines.

2 It should be pointed out that within Comecon a significant proportion of trade (often outside quotas) is conducted in strong currencies. Some estimates put this as high as 20%.

6 Investment choices

1 Chiefly because of legislation forbidding enterprises to set up consortia in order to achieve such objectives themselves (until 1981).

2 There might be several reasons for needing investment, as Botos's survey of a number of enterprises indicates. The sample he gives includes some 15 enterprises in various branches. The question asked was connected with reasons for investing during the period of the fifth five-year plan (1976–80).

Reasons for investing	No. of enterprises
1. Increasing capacity	12
2. Rationalization	5
3. Improving quality of products	10
4. Launching new products	9
5. Technological innovation and new manufacturing methods	1
6. Research and development	1
7. Improving working conditions and infrastructure	10
8. Anti-pollution measures	4

It is striking that 12 responses indicated increasing production capacity and only 5 rationalization. The responses in the sample reflect a preference for increased capacity rather than increased efficiency. One explanation of this is the pressure of the social system on the productive system to maintain extensive growth even if it ultimately runs up against the relative shortage of labour.

3 On this, see Kornai and Matits (1984).

4 It should be borne in mind that ministries nominated and dismissed the first three directors of an enterprise, with the branch ministry assessing

their achievement periodically. This task now falls to the Ministry of Industry.

5 Their insolvency was not necessarily their own fault, since it was largely due to an excessively centralized financial system in which few funds were available.

7 Adaptations of the decentralized model

1 The notion of a shortage of labour so often mentioned in socialist countries is not really appropriate, since it does not clearly bring out the fact that unemployment is sometimes due to the under-utilization of the labour force. What prevents increased labour productivity is the institutional system (Dezsenyi-Guellette, 1986).

2 Household financing is carried out through the savings banks (OTP).

3 This is not peculiar to enterprises in a socialist economy (see Hay and Morris, 1979: Chapter 8).

4 Banca Commerciale Italiana, Bayerische Vereinsbank, Creditanstalt-Bankverein, Société Générale, Long Term Credit Bank of Japan, Taiyo Kobe Bank.

5 The first great debate on the economic mechanism in fact took place, as Szamuely shows, between 1954 and 1957, interrupted by the violent events of 1956. It contained the germ of the ideas that were to lead to the introduction of the NEM 11 years later.

Bibliography

Andreff, W. (1976) *Les variations du degré de centralisation dans les pays de l'Est européen*, Paris, Université Paris I.

Antal, L. (1981) 'Historical development of the Hungarian system of economic control and management', *Acta Oeconomica*, 27 (3–4), 251–66.

(1986) 'Développements avec quelques digressions. Le mécanisme économique hongrois dans les années 70', in J. Kornai and X. Richet (eds.) (1986).

Archambault, E. and X. Greffe (eds.) (1984) *Les économies non officielles*, Paris, Editions La Découverte.

Asselain, J. C. (1981) *Plan et profit en économie socialiste*, Paris, Presses de la Fondation nationale des sciences politiques.

Balassa, A. (1977) 'Achievements and lessons from the medium-term planning in the Hungarian enterprises', *Acta Oeconomica*, 11 (1), 53–68.

Balassa, B. (1959) *The Hungarian Experience in Economic Planning. A theoretical and empirical study*, New Haven, Yale University Press.

(1985) 'Reforming the economic mechanism', in B. Balassa, *Change and Challenge in the World Economy*, London, Macmillan.

(1986) 'Next steps in the Hungarian economic reform', *Tenth Hungarian–US economic round table*, 1–5 December, Budapest, mimeo, 33 pp.

Bauer, T. (1978) 'Investment cycles in planned economies', *Acta Oeconomica*, 21 (3) 243–70.

(1981) *Tervgazdásag, beruházas, ciclusok (Central Planning, Investment, Cycles)*, Budapest, Közgazdasagi és Jogi Könyv-Kiado.

(1982) 'The Hungarian alternative to Soviet-type planning', Institute of Economics, Budapest, mimeo, 23 pp.

Benassy, J. P., R. Boyer and R. M. Gelpi (1979) 'Régulation des économies, capitalisme et inflation', *Revue économique*, 30 (3).

Berend, I. T. and G. Ránki (1985) *The Hungarian Economy in the Twentieth Century*, New York, St Martin's Press.

Boissieu, Ch. de (1978) *Principes de politique économique*, Paris, Economica.

Bornstein, M. (1981) 'L'évaluation d'une réforme économique dans une économie planifiée est-européenne. Un exemple: La Hongrie', *Revue d'études comparatives Est–Ouest*, 12 (1), 5–26.

(1985) *Comparative Economic Systems. Models and Cases*, Homewood, Illinois, Richard D. Irwin Inc.

Bródy, A. (1970) *Proportions, Prices and Planning*, Budapest, Akadémia Kia.

Brown, A. A. and J. Licari (1976) 'Hungary: movement towards the visible hand', in E. Neubeger and W. Duffy (eds.) (1976).

Brus, W. (1968) *Problèmes généraux du fonctionnement de l'économie socialiste*, Paris, Maspéro.

(1973) *The Economics and Politics of Socialism*, London, Routledge and Kegan Paul.

(1979) 'The Eastern European reforms: what happened to them?', *Soviet Studies*, 31 (2), 257–67.

(1986) 'Institutional change within a planned economy' in M. C. Kaser (ed.) 1986.

Bukta, L. (1974) 'Investment decisions in the decentralized sphere', *Eastern European Economics*, Fall, 3–23.

Cable, J. (1985) 'The Bank–Industry relationship in West Germany: performance and policy aspects', in J. Schwalbach (ed.) (1985).

Comisso, E. (1986) 'State structures, political processes and the collective choice in CMEA states', in E. Comisso and L. D'Andrea Tyson (eds.) (1986).

Comisso, E. and L. D'Andrea Tyson (eds.) (1986) *Power, Purpose and Collective Choice. Economic strategy in socialist states*, Ithaca, NY, Cornell University Press.

Comisso, E. and P. Marer (1986) 'The economics and politics of reform in Hungary', in E. Comisso and L. D'Andrea Tyson (eds.) (1986).

Csaba, L. (1986) 'Le processus de réforme hongrois et son évolution possible en 1985–1987', *Revue d'études comparatives Est–Ouest*, 17 (3), 7–22.

Csikós-Nagy, B. (1971) 'The new Hungarian price system', in I. Friss (ed.) (1971).

(1978) 'Contribution to the theory of price mechanism', *Penzugyi szemle*, 69, 572–92.

(1980) *A magyar ár 1979–80 (The Reorganization of Prices in Hungary, 1979–1980)*, Budapest, Közgazdasági és Jogi Köniv Kiado.

(1983) *A magyar árpolitika (The Hungarian Price Policy)*, Budapest, Közgazdasági és Köniv Kiadó.

Deák, A. (1978) 'Enterprise investment decision and economic efficiency in Hungary', *Acta Oeconomica*, 20 (1–2), 63–82.

Deszenyi-Guellette, A. (1986) 'Du chômage déguisé au chomage réel: le cas hongrois', *Revue d'études comparatives Est–Ouest*, 17 (4), 93–108.

Duchêne, G. (1980) 'L'officiel et le parallèle dans l'économie soviétique', *Libre*, 7, 150–88.

(1984) 'Economie parallèle et déséquilibre dans les économies de type soviétique', in X. Richet (ed.) (1984).

Economist Intelligence Unit, London (1986) *Country Report, Hungary*, 2, 10–11.

Frey, B. (1978) *Modern Political Economy*, Oxford, Martin Robertson.

Friss, I. (1971) *Reform of the Economic Mechanism in Hungary*, Budapest, Akademia Kiado.

Gabor, I. R. (1986) 'L'économie seconde (auxiliaire)', in J. Kornai and X. Richet (eds.) (1986).

Gábor, I. R. and P. Galasi (1981a) *A második gazdasag (The Second Economy)*, Budapest, Közgazdasagi és Jogi Köniv Kiado.

Galasi, P. (1984) 'L'économie non-officielle hongroise', in E. Archambault and X. Greffe (eds.) (1984).

Ganczer, S. (1976) 'Price calculations and the analysis of proportions within the national economy', *Acta Oeconomica*, 1 (1), 55–68.

Granick, D. (1976) *Enterprise Guidance in Eastern Europe*, Princeton, Princeton University Press.

Hare, P. (1976) 'Industrial prices in Hungary', *Soviet Studies*, 28 (2), 189–206; 28 (3), 362–90.

  (1981) 'The investment system in Hungary', in P. Hare, H. Radice and N. Swain (eds.) (1981).

  (1986) 'Hungary: internal economic development', *The Economies of Eastern Europe and their Foreign Economic Relations*, NATO Colloquium, Brussels, mimeo, 32 pp.

Hare, P., H. Radice and N. Swain (eds.) (1981) *Hungary: a decade of economic reform*, London, George Allen and Unwin.

Hay, D. and D. Morris (1979) *Industrial Economics. Theory and evidence*, Oxford, Oxford University Press.

Hayek, F. (ed.) (1939) *L'économie dirigée en régime collectiviste*, Paris, Librairie Médicis.

Hegedüs, A. (1976) *Socialism and Bureaucracy*, London, Allison and Busby.

Horchler, G. (1974) 'La réforme des prix en Hongrie', *Revue de l'Est* 5 (1).

Huszár, T. and M. Mandel (1973) 'The investment decision-making system in Hungary', *Eastern European Economics*, 11 (3), 3–26.

Jacquemin, A. (ed.) (1984) *European Industry: public policy and corporate strategy*, Oxford, Clarendon.

Jacquemin, A. and B. Remich (eds.) (1988) *La coopération entre les entreprises. Entreprises conjointes, stratégies industrielles et pouvoirs publics*, Brussels, De Boeck-Wesmael.

Janossy, F. (1970) 'The origins of contradictions in our economy and the path to their solution', *East European Economics*, 8 (4) 357–90.

Johansen, L. (1979) 'The bargaining society and the inefficiency of bargaining', *Kyklos*, 32 (3), 497–521.

Kaser, M. C. (ed.) (1986) *The Economic History of Communist Eastern Europe*, III, Oxford, Oxford University Press.

Katzenelboigen, A. (1978) 'Quelques commentaires sur les mécanismes verticaux dans l'économie soviétique', *Revue d'études comparatives Est–Ouest*, 9 (4) 7–20.

Kende, P. (1983) 'Qu'est-ce que le kadarisme?', *Interventions*, 3.

Kenedi, J. (1982) *Faites-le vous mêmes. L'économie parallèle en Hongrie*, Paris, François Maspéro.

Keravi, B. (1981) 'A forrasok aramlasa és a vagyonjog strukturaja' (The flow of resource and the structure of property rights), *Figyelö*, 45.

Knight, P. (1984) *Economic decision-making structures and processes in Hungary. The dilemmas of decentralization*, Washington DC, The World Bank.

Koltay, J. (1986) 'Réforme économique et démocratie industrielle en Hongrie', *Revue d'études comparatives Est–Ouest*, 17 (2), 41–52.

Konrad, G. and I. Szelenyi (1979) *La marche au pouvoir des intellectuels*, Paris, Le Seuil.

Kopetsy, S. (ed.) (1981) 'A Vallalatok szérépé a holding ban' (The role of holding companies), *Figyelö*, 44.

Kornai, J. (1959) *Overcentralization in Economic Administration*, Oxford, Oxford University Press.

(1970) 'Economic systems theory and general equilibrium theory', *Acta Oeconomica*, 6 (4), 297–318.

(1971) *Anti-Equilibrium*, Amsterdam, North Holland.

(1975) *Mathematical planning of structural decision*, Budapest, Akadémia Kiado.

(1980) *Economics of Shortage*, Amsterdam, North Holland.

(1983) 'Comments on the present state and the prospects of the Hungarian economic reform', *Journal of Comparative Economics*, 8 (3), 225–52.

(1984) 'Bureaucratic and market co-ordination', *Osteuropa Wirtschaft*, 29 (4), 306–19.

(1986) 'The Hungarian reform process', *Journal of Economic Literature*, 24 (4), 1687–737.

Kornai, J. and T. Liptak (1965) 'Two-level planning', *Econometrica*, 33, 141–69.

Kornai, J. and A. Matits (1984) 'Softness of the budget constraint. Analysis relying on the data of firms', *Acta Oeconomica*, 32 (3–4), 223–49.

Kornai, J. and X. Richet (1986) *La Voie hongroise. Analyses et experimentation*, Paris, Calmann Levy.

Kovács, J. M. (1984) 'A reformalku sürüjeben. Nyilvanos vita a reformarol' ('Bargaining about reform; public debate about reform') *Valoság*, 3, 30–55.

Láki, M. (1982) 'Liquidation and merger in the Hungarian industry', *Acta Oeconomica*, 18 (1–2), 87–108.

Laky, T. (1984) 'Small enterprises in Hungary. Myth and reality', *Acta Oeconomica*, 32 (1–2), 39–63.

Lange, O. (1936) 'On the economic theory of socialism', *Review of Economic Studies*, 4 (1–2), 53–71; 123–42.

Laurencin, J. P. (1976) *Le système des prix préférentiels dans la planification soviétique*, Grenoble, Université de Grenoble. II.

Lavigne, M. (1977) 'L'oligopole dans la planification', *Economies et sociétés*, serie G, 11 (6–9), 991–1042.

(1979) *Les économies socialistes soviétiques et européennes*, Paris, Armand Colin.

(1984) 'Les politiques d'adaptation des pays socialistes européens à la crise: le rôle du COMECON', in X. Richet (ed.).

Lavigne, M. (ed.) (1978) *Economie politique de la planification en système socialiste*, Paris, Econom.

Lavigne, M. and W. Andreff (1985) *La réalité socialiste. Crise, adaptation, progrès*, Paris, Economica.

Lavoie, D. (1985) *Rivalry and Central Planning: the socialist calculation debate reconsidered*, Cambridge, Cambridge University Press.

Loasby, B. J. (1976) *Choice, Complexity and Ignorance*, Cambridge, Cambridge University Press.

Mandel, M. (1974) 'Interest aspects in the determination of development targets', *Eastern European Economics*, 13 (2), 38–54.

Marer, P. (1986) 'Economic reform in Hungary: from central planning to regulated market', in *Slow Growth in the 1980s*, Washington DC, Joint Committee of Congress, USGPO.

Marrese, M. (1981) 'The evolution of wage regulation in Hungary', in P. Hare, H. Radice and N. Swain (eds.) (1981).

Molnar, P. (1983) 'Emissions d'obligations', *Heti Világgazdaság*, 9 April 1983.

Morin, E. (1983) *De la nature de l'URSS. Complexe totalitaire et nouvel empire*, Paris, Fayard.

Neuberger, E. and W. Duffy (1976) *Comparative Economic Systems: a decision-making approach*, Boston, Allyn and Bacon.

Nove, A. (1980) *Marxist Economic and the Economics of Feasible Socialism*, University of Glasgow, mimeo, 83 pp.

(1983) *The Economics of Feasible Socialism*, London, George Allen and Unwin.

Nyers, R. and M. Tardos (1978) 'Enterprises in Hungary before and after the economic reform', *Acta Oeconomica*, 20 (1–2), 21–44.

Polányi, K. (1983) *La grande transformation*, Paris, Gallimard.

Péter, G. (1956) *A gazdaságossag és jövedelmezöség jelenttösage a tergazdalkodásban (The Importance of Economic Efficiency and Profitability in the Planned Economy)*, Budapest, Közgazdasági és Jogi Könyv Kiado.

Richet, X. (1978a) 'Théorie du socialisme chez Marx', *Cahiers du CEREL*, Université de Lille, 45 pp.

(1978b) 'Processus de planification et de régulation en économie socialiste', in M. Lavigne (ed.) (1978).

(1980) *Régulation dans la planification décentralisée. Un essai sur le NME hongrois*, Nanterre, Université de Parix X, Nanterre.

(1985a) 'Politiques d'ajustement et réformes institutionnelles en Hongrie', in M. Lavigne and W. Andreff (eds.) (1985).

(1985b) 'Les expériences contrastées de développement agricole en URSS, Pologne et Hongrie', *Problèmes économiques* (1952), 26–32.

(1986a) 'Réformes et non-réformes en Europe de l'Est', *Analyses de la SEDEIS*, 51, 16–22.

(1986b) 'Entreprises conjointes et coopération Est–Ouest: un commentaire', in A. Jacquemin and B. Remiche (eds.) (1988).

(ed.) (1984) *Crises à l'Est?*, Lyon, Presses Universitaires de Lyon.

Rittersporn, G. (1978) 'Nouveaux tsars et aspirants mandarins', *L'Anti-mythe*, 22.

Salgó, I. (1986) 'Ouverture, coopération et monétarisation du commerce extérieur', *Revue d'études comparatives Est–Ouest*, 17 (2), 55–64.

Schwalbach, J. (1985) *Industry, Structure and Performance*, Berlin, Edition Sigma.

Sóos, K. A. (1986) 'Politique de stabilisation et croissance économique', *Revue d'études comparatives Est–Ouest*, 17 (2), 1–24.

Statisztikai Evkönyv (Statistical Yearbook), Hungarian Central Statistical Office, various years.

Swain, N. (1985) *Collective Farms Which Work?*, Cambridge, Cambridge University Press.

Szamuely, L. (1982) 'The first wave of the economic mechanism debate and the 1968 reform in Hungary (1954–1957), *Acta Oeconomica*, 29 (1–2), 43–67.

(1984) 'The second wave of the economic mechanism debate and the 1968 reform in Hungary', *Acta Oeconomica*, 33 (1–2) 43–67.

Zaleski, E. (1984) *La planification stalinienne. Croissance et fluctuations économiques en URSS, 1939–1952*, Paris, Economica.

Zysman, J. (1983) *Governments, Markets and Growth. Financial systems and the politics of industrial change*, Ithaca, NY, Cornell University Press.

Index

accountable autonomy ('khozraschet'),
32–3
adjustment policies, 150, 154–5
aggressive co-ordination, 19, 20
agriculture: co-operatives, 7, 46, 172, 176,
188; pre-war, 37, 38; prices, 72, 73, 75,
76, 80; production, 35; productivity, 1;
reforms, xi, 8, 9, 34, 39, 45–6; and the
second economy, 116, 117; State farms,
62
aim-grouped investment, 123
amortization: and prices, 71, 72, 75, 76,
80, 160
Andreff, W., 33
annual planning, 44, 51, 98, 102
Antal, L., 3, 165
assets taxes, 88
authoritarian profit-sharing, 90

Balassa, A., 105
Balassa, B., 42, 150, 163, 172
banking system: credit policy, 136–8;
nationalization of, 38; and reform, 7,
11, 150, 164–70; State Investment
Bank, 140, 145, 174; see also National
Bank
bankruptcy, 173
bargaining: and investment, 131, 132;
and the planning process, 108, 109–14,
115, 182; and reform, 3, 157, 163, 185;
in a socialist economy, 18
Barone, E., 24, 25
Bauer, T., 146, 179, 181, 186, 187
Benassy, J. P., 17
Berend, I. T., 8, 35, 48
black market, see second economy
Boissieu, Ch. de, 16
bond market, 167, 175; development of,
150, 161, 164
bonus funds, 75
Boyer, R., 17
branch ministries: and centralized

planning, 27, 42, 53–4, 182; and
decentralization, 22, 31, 172; and
enterprise planning, 104, 105; and
industry, 36; and investment, 123, 124,
127, 128, 129, 139, 143; and planning,
107, 108; and recentralization, 46,
55–61; and prices, 75; and the five-year
plan, 100, 103; and reform, 6, 11, 51,
54–5, 56, 57, 58, 59–60, 149, 188; and
the second economy, 118; setting up
of, 39
Brody, A., 49, 71
Brown, A. A., 37
Brus, W., 15, 28, 29–30, 50
budgets, state, 135–6, 139
building industry: and investment, 123;
and the price system, 73; and the
second economy, 116–17
Bukta, L., 125
bureaucracy: and centralized planning,
21, 50; and co-ordination, 18, 19; and
decentralization, 13, 96, 183–4; and
heads of enterprises, 63–4; and reform,
188; see also branch ministries;
functional ministries

Cable, J., 164
capacity expanding investment, 121, 126
capitalist societies: and bargaining,
110–11; and Marxist theory, 25–6
centralized planning, 6; and agent
behaviour, 107; and decentralized
planning,184–6; and economic
reforms, 183–4; and enterprise
planning, 104–5, 105–7; and
investment, 121–6, 144; and the
market, 181–2; model of, 2–3, 15–33,
34–64; and wage regulation, 91, 92, 93
Chamber of Commerce (Hungarian), 6,
152
CIB (Central European International
Bank), 168, 169

201

Soviet and East European Studies

The following series titles are now out of print: